MEITEI FAMILY IN FLUX

MEITEI FAMILY IN FLUX
An Empirical Study

NINGOMBAM BASANTA

AKANSHA PUBLISHING HOUSE
NEW DELHI

AKANSHA PUBLISHING HOUSE
4649-B/21, Ansari Road
Darya Ganj, New Delhi - 110 002
Email: ektabooks@yahoo.com
Ph. : 23263193 / 9811582579

Meitei Family in Flux: An Empirical Study

First Published 2010

Reprint 2026

ISBN 978-81-8370-195-2

PRINTED IN INDIA

Published by Akansha Publishing House, New Delhi and Printed at Mehra Offset Press, Delhi.

Contents

Part II

Preface

This book is an outcome of the project report submitted to Indira Gandhi National Center for the Arts (IGNCA), New Delhi on the topic - Meitei Family - a process of transformation from traditional to modernity". The scholar accomplished the research project in two phases. In the first phase only two chapters are discussed which are Myth associated with the evolution of Meitei family and Traditional house and the deities associated with it. In the second phase six chapters are discussed which are Marriage and Rituals, Traditional family education and institution, Wits Test. Terms of address within the kinship and outside, Belief, Practices and Superstitions and Rites of passage. Chapter 1 traces in brief the history of Meitei identity. Behind the history of evolution of Meitei identity it also discusses the myth associated with the birth of the Meiteis. It also discusses at length on the background of the' Yumnaks' (lineages) or in other words, the circumstances on the naming of the lineages. The study reveals that the traditional Yumnaks are around 432. But at present the figure is much more than this. This chapter also makes an attempt to find out the circumstances which led to the increase in the number of 'Yumnaks'. In the last part of this chapter a discussion is made on the traditional social division of labour in the Meitei Society. In this we find that the palace was the hub of State administration. As conditioned by the subsistence nature of the economy where money economy was out of question, the assignment of a particular trade, job or duty to a particular'

Yumnak' was the only way to run the State administration. Chapter -2 exclusively discusses the traditional 'Meitei Yumjao' (a house of four or five rooms). Such a traditional 'Yumjao' stood on a large homestead of around 3 to 4 'Paris' of land (where a Pari is equal to two and half acres). The traditional homestead was a planned one, where the large area was surrounded by a trench and followed by a 'Leipan' (earthen wall). A traditional *Yumjao* is surrounded by a number of outhouses, viz. *Mamang Sanggoi, Awang Sanggoi, Fou-Kei,* etc. Then comes to the study on the mode of arrangement of rooms and their respective names. Included here is also the secluded places for the household deities like Sanamahi, *Leimarel* and *Emoinu,* etc. This chapter also studies the architecture of Meitei Yumjao along with the philosophy and beliefs embodied in it. Chapter 3 Discusses the various stages involved in the engagement form of marriage which is considered as the most noble and prestigious form of marriage. It is found out from the study that engagement form of marriage perform a number of rituals at its different stages till the final marriage ceremony. In a superficial observation the traditional Meitei society is seemed to be bound by exogamous clan marriage system, but a closer examination has revealed us that the Meiteis followed a very intricate marriage laws. Chapter - 4 works to assemble the traditional family education, which again is traditional in its form and content. The parents and elderly persons are always in the look out to train their children as regard to discipline, art of maintaining a house, etc. at any opportune moment and place. Chapter 5 discusses the various forms of wits test as found scattered in the society. Chapter 6 is a collection of terms of address within the kinship and outside it. The nature of terms of address reflects the close blood relationship in the kinship and relationship established due to marriage. Chapter 7 is also a collection of different beliefs, practices and superstitions which are found scattered in everyday life of the Meiteis. Chapter 8 discusses the various rituals and ceremonies performed since birth of a person till death with the exception of marriage.

The study is heavily relied on manuscripts. But there are areas which need to consult the local scholars, priestess and priest and craftsmen etc. So, a significant amount of information is collected orally from different persons engaged in different occupations. Consequently a large part of the topic is corroborated by the findings from such oral interviews. For an easy and vivid explanation of the rituals and ceremonies a number of photographs are included at appropriate places. In order to make the study a near perfect one the research consults some secondary sources also.

NINGOMBAM BASANTA

Acknowledgements

I owe a great deal of thanks to IGNCA, New Delhi for financial support for this work.

I express my sincere thanks to A. Thoiba, N. Khelchandra, N. Manijao, Ng. Kullachandra, N. Ibochouba, S. Nilbir, Kh. Thambalngou, Ksh. Boro Singh, Mutua Bahadur, M. Norendra, Mangi Ningomba, Y. Budhichandra and to R.K. Chittaranjan for typing the report. My thanks also goes to M.P. Misra of Akansha Publishing House, New Delhi, for his kindly agreeing to publish this work.

NINGOMBAM BASANTA

Introduction

Manipur which lies on the easternmost frontier of India is bounded on the north by a series of hills called Nagaland; on the north-east, east and south by Myanmar (Burma); on the south-west by Mizoram; on the west and north-west by Assam. The territory of present Manipur lies between 23°50'N and 25°30'N Latitude and 93°10'E and 94°30'E Longitude. The total area of Manipur is 22,327 sq. km. Out of this 20,089 sq km is covered by the hilly tracts and 2238 sq km by the valley. This valley is surrounded in all directions by the hills. What we generally call the valley is in reality is a plateau, its height above the sea-level varies at different places but may be taken to be about 2,600 feet. The elevation has a great influence on the climate and consequently to culture. The ranges of hills are higher on the north and gradually diminish in height as it reach the southern part of Manipur. The valley itself slopes down gradually towards the south. That is why all important rivers of Manipur flow from the north to the south and this is also the reason why all lakes are situated in the southern part of the valley. In the past lakes were plenty in the valley, the biggest being the Loktak lake in the Bishnupur district. Even in the heart of Imphal there were lakes like Lamphel pat, Akam pat, Porom pat, Sanggai pat and Takyel pat.

It will not be a wonder that there were routes connecting Manipur valley with Surma valley. There were at least three routes connecting the two valleys. The northernmost of them connected Banskandi near Silchar with the place now called Jaipur in the Manipur valley. The middle one connected Banskandi with Bishnupur in the Manipur valley and the southernmost route connected the western bend of the Barak river with Torbung, a village in the southern-western part of the Manipur valley. There were one or two routes connecting the Brahmaputra valley with the Manipur valley. But they were more difficult. Likewise, there were a number of routes connecting Manipur valley with what is now called upper Myanmar (Burma). It was through these routes that people both from East and West of Manipur migrated and settled in the valley. These people acted as carrier of cultures from West and East to Manipur. Later on these people helped in the development of Meitei family in its present form. Certainly, the technology and skill they accompanied had its impact on Meitei society.

The soil of Manipur is fertile. The rainfall from the monsoon is plenty. The rich soil, the plenty rainfall and the sufficient sunshine combined to give rich crops. The main cereal was, as it is now, rice. Various kinds of vegetables grew. Bamboo, which helped in shaping the material culture of Manipur also grew abundantly. Since the valley is about 2600 feet above the sea-level, the climate is cool. The hills are still higher and therefore colder than the valley. May is the hottest month. In June, July and August, there is monsoon downpour. Though there is monsoon downpour the windspeed is not high as it is in other monsoon fed places.

The people inhabiting the hilly tracts of Manipur belong to two main ethnic groups, namely: the Naga group and the Chin-Kuki group. Altogether there are 29 different recognized tribes in Manipur. They are: Anal, Aimol, Angami, Chiru, Chothe, Gangte, Hmar, Kabui, Kacha Naga, Koirao, Koireng, Kom, Lamgang, Mao, Maram, Maring, Mizo, Monsang, Moyon, Paite, Purum, Ralte, Sema, Simte, Salte, Tangkhul, Thadou, Waiphei and Zou.

The location of the place which is at the meeting point of two great culture of two great races, its routes opening to the East and West, its pleasant climate, a fertile valley with plenty of lakes, its small population, its neighbouring with numerous hill tribes, its rich vegetation; all these had its direct or indirect impact in shaping the present Meitei family.

This small valley is the abode of as many as nine *Salais* (clans); besides there were some smaller Salais. The unification of Salais began as early as during the reign of King Nongda Lairel Pakhangba (33-154 A.D.). And the task was accomplished during the reign of Kling Charairongba (1697-1709 A.D.). Thus out of the fusion of the Salais a new identity named "Meitei" emerged in the history of Manipur. A myth on the creation of Salais says that all Salais are produced from the different organs of "Kuru Mee". Later on the breaking up of "Kuru Mee" by itself came the different *Sageis* (*Yumnaks*). There are around four hundred and thirty two (432) Sageis (Yumnaks) for the traditional seven Salais. But in due course of history people from East and West migrated and settled in Manipur valley. Meitei society had its potential to accommodate these people and they were admitted to Meitei society either by creating new *Yumnaks* or by admitting to any of the original Yumnaks. Migration from the East was mostly from upper Myanmar (Burma) and they were few in number. However, migration from the West was in great number and they included Brahmans and Muslims from mainland India. But majority of them were from the adjoining territories of Manipur, viz., Takhel (Tripura), Cachar, Tekhao (Assam), etc. The movement of these people had its influence in the development of present Meitei family.

Each of the Meitei *Yumnaks* has a background in its meaning, especially the traditional (around) 432 Yumnaks. The naming was based on the profession, habit, nature, post, occupation, etc. of the progenitor. Among the original

Yumnaks there was a tradition of social division of labour by assigning certain duty of the State to a particular Yumnak.

In the past a big *Engkhol* (homestead) of 3 to 4 acres was the home of a family and these big homesteads settled successively till the far-flung areas. However, after the World War II such homesteads began to disappear. In such a big homestead, besides the *Yumjao* (the main dwelling house), there were many outhouses, viz., Mamang Sanggoi. Makha Sanggoi, Awang Sanggoi, Shingkei, Foukei, etc. Generally there were three types of houses, viz., five-roomed house (Yumjao ka Manga) for general people, seven-roomed house for noble man and nine-roomed house for the King. The architecture of Meitei Yumjao is enveloped by an aura of beliefs where the hoomdang (the lower roof support) is the representation of ribs of human beings, the hearth is that of navel and U-ras that of flesh, etc.

The building materials were limited in number. They were tree, bamboo, thatch, reed, nails, etc. And the tools and implements were also limited as well as traditional; *hakmei*, *shingjang* (axe), *horai* (saw), *thangjou* (dagger), *paija*, etc. were the implements and tools used in building traditional houses.

Coming to the architectural aspect of a Meitei Yumjao there are parts known as Urep, Khangel, Loikhang, Khongtenba, Hoomdang, U-ra, etc. Some rules were also followed in erecting the pillars in which the first one to be erected was Urep (the main pillar). It is found that the building materials for the nine-roomed house for the king were strictly selective. Only a few selective trees and bamboos were allowed to include in the building of such a house. Again the places where these materials were to be collected were also strictly particular.

In a traditional house there were three secluded places for the three principal deities, viz., Lainingthou Sanamahi (the supreme household deity), Leimarel and Funga-Lairu (the place of Emoinu). And they were prayed daily in the evening. However, there were also other minor deities in the other areas of the house.

But in a modern Meitei house the above architecture and mode of arrangement of rooms are hardly followed. As a result of such changes their attitude to the household deities are also changed. In such a modern house the place for 'Leimarel' and 'Phunga-Lairu' are almost missing. However, a room for the "Sanamahi" is always reserved with utmost care.

A number of marriage forms are practised by the Meiteis. Among them the engagement form of marriage is regarded as the most noble and prestigious form of marriage. This engagement form of marriage involve a long process with various rituals and ceremonies at different stages. There are stages like 'Yathang Thaba', 'Waroipot', 'Heijingpot', 'Bor Barton' and finally marriage ceremony. Still there is a ritual named 'Phiruk Nungshang Hangba' which is held on the fifth day after marriage ceremony. Again the marriage laws among the Meiteis are various and very intricate. At the first glance one will find exogamous clan marriage system, but a closer examination reveal a very intricate marriage laws. The laws are, viz.:

1. E-Tinnaba or Pudinnaba,
2. Pen Tinnaba,
3. Sairuk Tinnaba,
4. Leinung Pentinnaba,
5. Pi-tinnaba, and
6. Pellol Tinnaba.

Family education of the past imparted to children by parents and elderly persons is traditional in its form and content. It was mainly on the teaching of discipline 'Thakshi Khasi', the art of maintaining a house and some vocational education, etc. The code of 'Emoinu' is basically the art of maintaining a house. Fungga, the hearth is the centre of teaching moral and social education to children with its warmth and delight environment. The only institution found so far is 'Shinnaipham Kaba'. But this place is limited for girl children, boys have no place in this institution. Basically 'Shinnaipham'; is workpalce but in due course of vocational training the social education was inserted at opportune moments. The terms of address of the Meiteis reflect a close blood relationship in the kinship and this continues in the relation developed after marriage. The use of the sound 'E' as prefix in addressing someone indicating the relationship is a clear testimony of this. However, with the gradual contact with the west there is a visible change in the terms of address. Again the royal families follow a different way of terms of address. And this includes the way of addressing to members of royal families by its subject people.

The Meiteis perform a number of practices in their daily life which are mostly based on certain beliefs and superstitions. Beliefs and superstitions are still widespread among the Meiteis. However, due to the influence of modern scientific education the beliefs and superstitions are gradually loosing its ground. In the midst of these various practices there are few which has their merit in society mainly in the form of maintaining discipline in utilizing their home products, in maintaining personal discipline, etc.

The Meiteis perform a number of rituals and ceremonies from birth till death. And this include 'Epan' (birth ceremony), 'Yumshengba' (another simple ritual on the twelfth day after birth of the baby), Chak-umba, Na-Hutpa, Luhongba (marriage) and 'Lanna Thouram' (cremation and death ceremony), etc. 'Epan' is basically a prayer asking health, wealth and long life to deity 'Pitai Khomtaibi'. 'Yumshengba' is a simple ritual of sacreding the house which is considered desecrated with the birth of the baby. At present cremation is the only form of disposal of death. According to literature 'Cheitharol Kumbaba' it came into force since A.D. 1724 during the reign of Maharaja Garibniwaj (A.D. 1709-1748). Before this secondary burial is the predominant form of disposal of death. According to literature 'Shakok Lamlen' other forms like in the air, in fire, in water were also prevalent along with burial. The cremation is found to be executed on the basis of a belief system, and the crux of the belief is - soul is immortal, only the body is mortal. And the belief continues that the soul transmigrate to another living object after departing the mortal body. *Firoy* - the death anniversary is also executed on the basis of this belief in transmigration of soul.

History

The emergence of Meitei identity is rooted in history and it is evolutionary in nature. The name 'Meitei' appeared on the scene of history only when the different *Salais* (clans) were unified into one and transformed into a new political entity. There were nine Salais, e.g. Mangang (Ningthoucha), Luwang, Khuman, Angom, Moirang, Khaba, Nganba, Sarang and Leisangthem. Besides these there were also smaller Salais inhabiting in different places of Manipur valley and they were Haorok Konthou, Hairem Khunjan, Thanga Kambong, Urok Ushay and Selloi Langmai, etc. The clans maintained a definite area of their own. However, at this point of time it is difficult to determine precisely the boundaries of these principalities. But their probable sites can be located.

1. The Ningthouja Salai settled mostly on the western bank of Imphal river and both banks of Nambul river. Its eastern limit was Imphal river and in the west it extended upto Lamphel Pat (Lake) and Langjing hillock. It was bounded in the south by northern limit of the Khuman principality and in the north by Chingmeirong hill. Its capital was at Kangla.
2. To the east and north-east of Ningthouja principality there was the Angom Salai. Modern Pukhao and Chalou were in Angom principality.
3. The territory lying between Langjing hill and Koubru hill was the home of Luwang Salai.

4. The Khumans maintained a comparatively larger area. The important lakes like Ekop and Pumlen were in this principality. Its capital was at Thoubal but later on shifted to Mayang Imphal. The principality was bounded on the west by the Loktak lake; on the south by independent villages of some peoples like the Heirem Khunjans, on the east by villages of hill-tribes; and on the north by Ningthouja and Angom principalities.
5. Moirang principality was bounded on the north-east by Loktak lake; on the east by the Imphal river; on the south by hill villages; on the west also by hill villages; on the north by Luwang and Ningthouja principalities. The capital was at Moirang. The boundaries of the remaining four Salais, e.g. Sarang, Leishangthem, Khaba and Nganba are more difficult to trace; because they were first to be attacked by Nongda the Lairen Pakhangba under his policy of annexing his adjoining principalities.

Though each of the Salais had an independent principality of its own a person belonging to a particular Salai could move to the area of another Salai and settled there provided he accepted the allegiance of the principality in which he domiciled. The task for the unification of the Salais began since the reign of Nongda Lairen Pakhangba (A.D. 33-153) with the annexation of Sarang, Leishangthem, Khaba and Nganba to his reigning Kingdom. However, the task remained discontinued for many centuries only to be revived during the reign of king Sameirang (A.D. 518-568). From the time of king Sameirang, the Ningthoujas embarked on the policy of conquering and absorbing the principalities one by one. This was an arduous long struggle which took many centuries. King Sameirang defeated and killed the prince of Angom and realized tribute from them. However, this was the beginning of the protracted conflicts between the two clans which ultimately led to the absorption of the Angom principality in the Ningthouja kingdom. But one point be clearly understood. Although tributes were realized from the Angom principality, it continued to preserve its separate identity for a long time. It was still a powerful principality and on one occasion could even defeat Ningthouja king. But on the whole the Ningthoujas proved stronger of the two.

The Ningthouja kingdom became stronger during the reign of king Naothingkhong (A.D. 663-763). It was during his reign that the Thanga-Kambongs (two closely allied people inhabiting on the island of Thanga in the Loktak lake) came under the jurisdiction of Ningthouja Kingdom. Khongtekcha, the elder of the two sons of Naothingkhong, ascended the throne in A.D.763. Before his time, the Luwangs had dwindled in importance. The Khumans, the Angoms and the Moirangs were remaining independent of the Ningthoujas. But it also became increasingly evident that they too remained independent only on sufferance of the Ningthoujas.

The conflict between the Ningthouja and the Khuman began since the reign of King Ayangba (A.D. 821-910). And it continued for some three centuries till the Khuman principality was absorbed in the Ningthouja kingdom. Meanwhile the once powerful Luwang Salai came under the complete control of the Ningthouja kingdom during the reign of King Chenglei Epan Lanthaba (A.D. 949-969). The Luwangs came on a small boat on the stream of Luwangli, but they were all captured on the order of the king. Since this incident the Luwangs could not rise up their heads once again.

Heirem-Khunjans were two closely allied people who settled at the south of Khuman principality. During the reign of King Thawan Thaba (A.D. 1195-1231) the Khumans invited the king to join them in their fight against the Heirem Khunjans. The King accepted the invitation and his army proceeded on boat. The combined forces of the

Ningthoujas and the Khumans defeated the Heirem Khunjans. However, the alliance between the Ningthoujas and the Khumans was short-lived. The King invaded the Khuman principality. The ensuing battle was decisive. The Khumans were completely defeated and their power was crushed. But the principality was not annexed to the Ningthouja kingdom.

The accession of King Khumomba (A.D. 1263-1278) marks another phase in the history of Manipur. Since the reign of Sameirang (A.D.518-568), the Ningthoujas embarked on a policy of conquering and absorbing the principalities of the other clans. What was a dream in A.D. 518 became, practically, an accomplished fact by the end of the 12th century when the Khuman principality accepted the suzerainty of the Ningthouja kingdom by paying an annual tribute in cash. Only Moirang and Angom principalities remained independent. All other principalities were now either absorbed in or dependent on the Ningthouja kingdom. In the case of Moirang Salai also, the Moirangs were defeated whenever and wherever they fought against the Ningthoujas, also called the Meiteis. The Moirangs were defeated twice before they were completely conquered by King Ningthou Khomba (A.D. 1432-1467). The first happened during the reign of King Moiramba (A.D.1278-1302) and the latter during King Thangbi Lanthaba (A.D.1302-1324).

Ningthou Khomba invaded Moirang with a strong force assisted by among others, an Angom hero, Yaiskul Lakpa and Tumu Lanjingba. Moirang was completely defeated. Now, Angom was the only principality remained to be annexed to the Ningthouja Kingdom. But this was accomplished during the reign of King Charairongba (A.D.1697-1709) with the help Kumfel Lanchingba. The conquest of Angom by King Charairongba completed the process of consolidation of the Salai which began vigorously since A.D. 518. Meanwhile the smaller Salais like Sarang,

Leishangthem. Khaba and Nganba completed a process of fusion and emerged into new Salais as Sarang-Leishangthem and Khaba-Nganba who were allied people. With this now the principal *Salais* were reduced to seven. And when the system of *Yek* was introduced the seven Salais became exogamous units which came to be known as Yek Taret (seven Yeks) which prohibits intermarriage inside a Salai (clan). Thus a new political entity emerged out of the fusion of the seven Yeks and it was given the name 'Meitei'. In the latter course of history of Manipur the seven Salais (Yeks) were treated as cultural units which was at one time counted as political units. The introduction of a myth on the birth of the Salais further strengthened the bond of integration among the Salais.

PART I

1

Myth Associated with the Evolution of Meitei Family

A. THE MYTH

Kuru, the Almighty, begins his creation by producing *Atiya Sitapa* from his thigh. Kuru advised his eldest son to create 'Man'. In his venture to create 'Man', *Atiya Sitapa* first creates seven monkeys. Kuru enquires on the attempt of *Atiya Sitapa*. His says he has made it. Kuru comments that the attempt of *Sitapa* is not up to the mark. *Atiya Sitapa* is embarrassed on the failure. *Atiya Sitapa* again creates seven frogs. Kuru is still not satisfied with the creations of Sitapa. Perturbed by the failure in his attempts *Atiya Sitapa* allows to settle the frogs in the valley and those of monkeys in the hills. *Atiya Sitapa* creates 'Man' by imitating the posture of 'Kuru'. And it is named *Kuru Mee*. The one who comes out of the heart of *Kuru Mee* with a dazzling light is named as *Nganpa*. The one who comes out of the long tongue is named *Leishangthem*. *Sarangthem* comes out with an assorted colour from the tongue of Kuru. Luwang is emitted from the head of *Kuru*. The one who comes out of right hand is *Khuman*. The Angom is emitted with whitish colour from the throat. The one who is emitted gently from the right eye is Ningthem. The one who comes out of the testes with assorted colour is Moirang. The *Kuru Mee* is broken into pieces. *Sarang Leishangthem* collects the brain. *Nganba* collects the bones. *Luwang* collects the skin. *Angom* collects the head. *Ningthoucha* collects the testes. *Khuman* collects the fluids. *Moirang* collects the nerves. The breaking up of the body of *Kuru Mee* is called *Sakhai* which latter on changed into *Sagei* (*Yumnak*).

B. TRADITIONAL *YUMNAKS* (SUB-CLANS) UNDER THE SEVEN Salais/YEKS.

In the past this small valley (Imphal valley) of 700 sq. miles acted as melting pot and people who migrated both from the west and east were accommodated to the *Meitei* society by awarding them a new Sagei. However, before beginning the process of assimilating the people who came from East and West there were a fixed number of *Yumnaks* or Sagei for each of the seven Salais. They are varied in number, the largest being 116 in Ningthoucha Salai and the smallest is 16 in Nganba Salai. For Angom it is -47, Chenglei-31, Luwang-57, Khuman-101 and Moirang-64. So, in total there were around 432 Sageis (Yumnaks) for the seven Yeks (Salais). The Sageis are arranged in alphabitical order for each of the Salais.

1. Ningthoucha Salai

1. Akhom
2. Akhongpam
3. Ahanthem
4. Atom
5. Aheipam
6. Changninghenpam
7. Charoipam
8. Chirom
9. Chomchanpam
10. Fairenpam
11. Famtom
12. Ficham
13. Fenlem
14. Heirom
15. Haokhom
16. Heirangkhongcham
17. Heisanam
18. Huirongpam

19. Huitrom
20. Hotam
21. Haoteicham
22. Haopam
23. Hemam
24. Ipushangpam
25. Irom
26. Irengpam
27. Irungpam
28. Keithellakpam
29. Khoirom
30. Khongnam
31. Khumanlampam
32. Khoisanam
33. Kangasenpam
34. Khamlangpa-Sangpam
35. Khuntrakpam
36. Kangasenpam
37. Kongpacham
38. Keisham
39. Khoitongpam
40. Khumancharakpam
41. Khunchahanpam
42. Khangsulakpam
43. Khoinucham
44. Khuntom
45. Khoiriyanpam
46. Khwairakpam
47. Kanghacham
48. Leiyushungpam
49. Loitam
50. Laisangpam
51. Laikangpam
52. Lourangpam
53. Leichonpam
54. Loitongpam
55. Lukram Nong-in Fapam
56. Leimaram
57. Lamleirakpam
58. Leimayokpam
59. Langpokthapam
60. Lourempam
61. Laitoncham
62. Lantham
63. Mairenpam
64. Mayanglampam
65. Mutum
66. Moichem
67. Nahakpam
68. Naokalsangpam
69. Naorem
70. Nongthonpam
71. Namoicham
72. Naoroipam
73. Ngarenyanpam
74. Ningthoucham
75. Nakampam
76. Nameirakpam Moirang Ningthoumayum
77. Naotam
78. Nongmeikapam
79. Nongthonpam Irungpam
80. Pounam
81. Paopam
82. Phourungpam
83. Phatlampam
84. Sanglenmayim
85. Shukhwam
86. Sanoucham
87. Sairem

88. Soyam
89. Shatpam
90. Shatthokpam
91. Shingkhwam
92. Soram
93. Sakolsem
94. Sanasapam
95. Shankaisenpam
96. Shangpam
97. Sanapam
98. Sarensangpam
99. Shingkhangpam
100. Shaikhom
101. Shoukrakpam
102. Thongakapam
103. Taimacham
104. Thingnam
105. Thoutam
106. Thangkangsapam
107. Tenshupam
108. Waikhom
109. Wangkheimayum
110. Wangkheirakpam
111. Wareppam
112. Yenkhom
113. Yangnuyeipam
114. Yumnam
115. Yensenpam
116. Yenkokpam

2. Angom

1. Ayekpam
2. Awang Kheibam Wangkheibam
3. Akoichambam
4. Achoibam
5. Chingangbam
6. Hidam
7. Haiheibam
8. Hongnemshumbam
9. Huirem
10. Ekhei Shangbam
11. Kongbam
12. Khangenbam
13. Keikrunbam
14. Khoimom Tapam
15. Khana Chaobam
16. Khuyonthem
17. Kiyam
18. Kaswam
19. Leitautham
20. Longcham
21. Lairellakpam
22. Laitonjam
23. Laishangbam
24. Mangshatabam
25. Morimayum
26. Mantingbam
27. Nongmaithem
28. Narumpam
29. Ngarenpam
30. Nongthonbam
31. Nakpak Khanpam
32. Ningombam
33. Nganglenbam
34. Nganuppam
35. Ongnam
36. Pongsumbam
37. Potshangbam

38. Putoncham
39. Seram
40. Shairom
41. Shangambam
42. Shangtoncham
43. Tenlem
44. Thongcham
45. Wanglenbam
46. Yumlempam
47. Yumkhaibam

3. Chenglei

1. Ayekpam
2. Chanam
3. Chingakham
4. Haiwam
5. Heiwam
6. Ingûdum
7. Khakokpam
8. Kharaicham
9. Konsam
10. Khoisanam
11. Leishangthem
12. Loushikabam
13. Leitam (Loitam)
14. Langkoncham
15. Maiba Thiyam
16. Meinam
17. Mayanglambam
18. Maibram
19. Naoshekpam
20. Ngathem
21. Potshangbam
22. Shuraibam
23. Sharangthem
24. Shamnoibam
25. Sharakkhaibam
26. Thangcham
27. Tongbram
28. Tourangbam
29. Thumkanbam
30. Wairotpam
31. Yenlangbam

4. Khaba (Nganba)

1. Aheibam
2. Ficham
3. Hentakpam
4. Haopacham
5. Kabowlambam
6. Khaitem
7. Khuducham
8. Khuraicham
9. Meihoubam
10. Nongchenpam
11. Shanchiram
12. Tekcham
13. Thongam
14. Thinbam
15. Wangpacham
16. Yangoicham

5. Luwang

1. Ashangbam
2. Arambam
3. Apucham
4. Arubam
5. Athokpam

6. Chingchabam
7. Fammihanbam
8. Feiroicham
9. Heitham
10. Hicham
11. Haorongbam
12. Khunchan Mayim
13. Kongbam
14. Khunmukcham
15. Khoknam
16. Khoibam
17. Leirongbam
18. Luwangshangbam
19. Laishom
20. Loukham
21. Laikangbam
22. Lairenjam
23. Loicha Yangambam
24. Meiyengbam
25. Moibunglakpam
26. Maisanam
27. Meitram
28. Nongthonpam
29. Ngangom
30. Nongpokpam
31. Nahakpam
32. Naoroibam
33. Nantam
34. Nganbam
35. Nganglom
36. Ningchitpam
37. Pungraijam
38. Shenbangcham
39. Shoupwam
40. Sanlam
41. Shingkhangambam
42. Shambanduram
43. Tinbijam
44. Toibicham
45. Thammangcham
46. Thangcham Saram
47. Thiyam
48. Thouknaocham
49. Thangcham
50. Thauteicham
51. Urepkhinbam
52. Wanglenbam
53. Wakongthem
54. Waikhom
55. Wahengbam
56. Yumlembam
57. Yangambam

6. Khuman

1. Akham
2. Ayam
3. Afram
4. Akangcham
5. Ahongshangbam
6. Ahongbam
7. Asem
8. Amakcham
9. Akiram
10. Amom
11. Chandam
12. Chabungbam
13. Chungkhwam
14. Charoibam
15. Chingtham

16. Fairembam
17. Fancham
18. Heikrucham
19. Hanglem
20. Haopicham
21. Haobam
22. Hentakpam
23. Haorongbam
24. Houwaibam
25. Haowaibam
26. Khamnam
27. Kiyam
28. Konlom
29. Kaborambam (Kabrambam)
30. Khunlem
31. Khoirishumbam
32. Khoirom
33. Kadam
34. Khumanthem
35. Khut-heibam
36. Laipukhram
37. Likmabam
38. Lammabam
39. Langkam
40. Laishram
41. Langheibam
42. Lantham
43. Langkhombam
44. Maibam
45. Mongbicham
46. Maimom
47. Meitalkeishangbam
48. Maibam
49. Mayanglambam
50. Maiphubam
51. Moirengcham
52. Moichem
53. Ngangbam
54. Namram
55. Nepram
56. Ngasetpam
57. Oinam
58. Pukhrem
59. Pangkhaicham
60. Pukhranbam
61. Puyam
62. Panlucham
63. Pangambam
64. Polem
65. Sinnam
66. Shoukaicham
67. Shiyatpam
68. Shamukcham.
69. Shankhom Sinnam
70. Santham
71. Shanshenbam
72. Shakappam
73. Saram
74. Shentam
75. Thoidingcham
76. Thinggujam
77. Thonggrabam
78. Thongbam
79. Thaodem
80. Taibangjam
81. Thongcham
82. Thingkom
83. Thingbaijam
84. Toncham
85. Tourem

86. Toumom
87. Tokpam
88. Thangcham Yaoshem
89. Thangcham
90. Taobam
91. Tenlem
92. Tonthram
93. Thangangshabam
94. Wareppam
95. Wangkhom
96. Yanglem
97. Yangauyeibam
98. Yaithingbam
99. Yumkutum
100. Yampem
101. Yanglem.

7. MOIRANG

1. Akhwaijam
2. Akuram
3. Aheibam
4. Asem
5. Chongtham
6. Chakpafiyam
7. Chakpa Taba Manglem
8. Haorongbam
9. Hitam
10. Haoroibam
11. Kaborambam
12. Konchengbam
13. Kabajam
14. Konkham
15. Keithellakpam
16. Kumabam
17. Kairencham
18. Khuyonthem
19. Khoiyangbam
20. Konchengbam
21. Khoinaicham
22. Keithellakpam
23. Khwairakpam
24. Khomdram
25. Laiucham
26. Lampucham
27. Laikhucham
28. Lisam
29. Laiphrakpam
30. Lairenmayum
31. Leimajam
32. Leimakhujam
33. Menlem
34. Moirangthem
35. Mangkhom
36. Mayanglambam
37. Moifwam
38. Moirangmayum
39. Narengbam
40. Nongthonbam
41. Ngangnem
42. Nungleppam
43. Ningthoukhongjam
44. Namucham
45. Ngangom
46. Nangkham
47. Ngaseppam
48. Okram
49. Pukhranbam
50. Puthem
51. Ponlem
52. Soibam
53. Shingkhangbam

54. Thangcham Shangkhom
55. Thangajam
56. Thangjam
57. Thopchom
58. Wayenbam
59. Wangpicham
60. Wanglenbam
61. Wangkhem
62. Yaikhom
63. Yumkhaibam
64. Yoirenbam

C. MEANING OF YUMNAKS

All the four hundred and thirty two *Yumnaks* of the seven Salais (Yeks) bear a meaning of their own. Yumnak (a synonymous to Shagei) was given most probably by the king in consultation with the scholar in consideration of the profession, habit, nature, post, occupation, etc. of the progenitor. *Yumnaks* were also given considering the incident or occasion in which the progenitor was involved. The following is a discussion on how the *Yumnaks* were given by the king to his subject people.

1. Mangang (Ningthouja) Salai

1. *Yenkhom*:- The first Shagei (lineage) of Ningthoucha clan was given to this Pukok (progenitor) and hence the name Yenkhom. (Yenba = to distribute). In the beginning there was no Shagei. Yenkhom was the first lineage of Ningthoucha clan.
2. *Keithellakpam*:- He was engaged in the duty of guarding market. Keithel = market, Ngakpa = to guard. It was the lineage given in consideration of his post of Keithellakpa.
3. *Khoirom*:- He introduced the trade of bee-keeping. Khoi=bee. It was given in consideration of his occupation of bee-keeping.
4. *Nahakpam*:- He possessed an extraordinary large ear. And hence the name.

   Na = ear, Hakna = Very

5. *Thongakapam*:- He used to climb the bridge. Thong = bridge. And hence the name.
6. *Sanglenmayim*:- This was given in consideration of his duty of guarding the royal house.
7. *Mairenpam*:- This was given to the person who introduced the cultivation of Pumpkin (Mairen).
8. *Phairenpam*:- This was given in consideration of his occupation of weaving who introduced the art of using *Fi-Afaipa*.
9. *Heirom*:- This was given on the merit of the person on many trades and on his managerial skill.
10. *Khongnam*:- The person used to dig canal and hence the name was given. Khong = canal.
11. *Naokalsangpam*:- This was given from the duty of the person of looking after the child of the King.
12. *Taimacham*:- This was given from the occupation of the person of making the *Tai* of the King. Tai is the royal carrier put on the back of elephant.
13. *Naorem*:- Once upon a time king Naothingkhong escaped from the captivity of Selloi Langmai (a minor Salai inhabiting at the foothill of Noingmaiching range). A pregnant young woman named Takyel Pukangbi waited the King on his way passing Takyel pat. The King blessed her two sons. The children became illegitimate but could not be misled. So, from this occasion Naorem was given to them.
14. *Ipusangpam*:- This was given from the duty of guarding the sylvan deity (Umanglai) Puthiba. Puthiba; this deity is the one who engaged in searching the Almighty, the creator of this world. Since he went to the north, he is also known as Laiwangma. The secred places of Puthiba is located in many regions of Manipur.
15. *Leiyusungpam*:- This was given from the occupation of preparing *Leiyu*. Leiyu is the name of a local liquor.

16. *Khumanlampam*:- He was brought up by Keirunghangpi, the wife of King Naothingkhong. Keirunghangpi belonged to the Khuman clan and hence the name.
17. *Khoisanam*:- The line he has drawn on the field he has ploughed is not properly align. So, the name to his lineage.
18. *Sukhwam*:- The person was master on all the trades and hence the name.
19. *Namoicham*:- The name of his grandfather was *Namoi*. So, the name Namoicham was given to him deriving from his grandfather, Namoi.
20. *Mayanglangpam*:- The person was a Lampu of May-ang region. And hence the name.
    Lampu = the administrator of a region.
21. *Naoroipam*:- This was given from the duty of taking care the children of the King.
22. *Kangasenpam*:- This was given from the occupation of rearing *Kanga* (Goose).
23. *Changninghenpam*:- He was beautiful as well as neat and clean as Changning (fruit of a wild plant). And hence the name.
24. *Ngarenyanpam*:- He was a bee-keeper and used to collect a specie of a bee known as Ngarenkhoi. This bee is considered to be dangerous among the Meiteis. This was awarded in consideration of his occupation of bee-keeping.
25. *Loitam*:- He pursued a *loi* who escaped from the custody. Loi = a prisoner. A person who is found guilty of crime was used to exile to a particular area of Manipur. Sugnu, Thanga, etc. were the popular places of exile. So, from that occasion the name was given to his lineage.
26. *Khamlangpa-sangpam*:- Khamlangpa is a sylvan deity (Umanglai) located at Kakching, a village in

the southern part of Manipur valley. The person performed the duty of caring the deity and hence the name.

27. *Irom*:- This was given in consideration of the ability of the person. He prepared bamboo chips by his teeth for use in making the roof; he also collected the required thatch by himself and finished roofing the house by himself. From his ability to accomplish such an ardous task he was given the above name.
28. *Laisangpam*:- He guarded the deity Marjing. This was a sylvan deity (Umanglai). This was given from his duty of guarding the above Umanglai.
29. *Thingnam*:- To make a dam on a drain or a canal is known as *Thingel*. Since he made a dam on the drain he was given the above name.
30. *Akhom*:- Akhom is the name of a deity. Since he used to worship this deity his lineage was named as Akhom.
31. *Khuntrakpam*:- The Pukok (progenitor) was a village Chief and hence the name.
Khun = village, Lakpa = chief.
32. *Kangasenpam*:- This was given in consideration of his duty of rearing *Kanga* (goose) of the King.
33. *Haokhom*:- He might be a Lambu or a general who gathered a large number of labourers from the hills of Manipur for performing certain task for the king. From his ability to collect such a large amount of persons from the hills the above name was given.
34. *Sanaucham*:- His duty was to collect the bone of forehead of the dead king. And hence the name.
35. *Laikangpam*:- He captured a python and dried it in the sun-shine. Since then the name was given.
36. *Wareppam*:- He was a worshipper of bamboo, Wa = bamboo. There was a practice named Khuyon

wakhong shengba. This was a ritual used in worshipping bamboo.

37 *Lourangpam*:- He was a skilled cultivator and hence the name. Lou = paddy.

38. *Yangnuyeipam*:- This was given as the person prepared Yangnu flower for the king.
Yangnu Lei (flower): This is a small herb used in Kwak Tanba festival.

39. *Sairem*:- This was given from his occupation of craftsman. Sai = the lower edge of a thatched roof of a traditional Meitei house. He was specialized in trimming the *Sai* in order to make it more attractive and hence the name.

40. *Akhongpam*:- The grandfather of the person produced a noisy sound while talking and hence the name.

41. *Soyam*:- His duty was to look-after the king at the time of coronation. He used to supervise the ceremony and took care not to make any mistake.

42. *Mutum*:- The grandfather of the Pukok (progenitor) was sleepy by nature. So, the name was given considering the nature of the grandfather.

43. *Heirangkhongcham*:- Heirangkhongfapa is the name of a person born in this lineage. Taking the cue of his name the above name was given.

44. *Heisanam*:- The grandfather performed the duty of preparing fruits of the king. *Hei-sa* = fruits

45. *Huirongpam*:- The grandfather was able to sleep skilfully on a lying dog. And hence the name. Hui = dog.

46. *Kongpacham*:- The Pukok settled on the bank of Kongpa river and hence the name.

47. *Ahanthem*:- This was given in consideration of the duty of the person. The Meiteis once followed the

tradition of secondary burial. He was the first person who used to wash the buried skull of a dead king.

48. *Satpam*:- This name was given as the person has visited a place named Sonlai.

49. *Leichonpam*:- The grandfather of the person held the post of Leichon Lakpa. So, the above name was given in consideration of the post held.

50. *Keisham*:- The grandfather of the person hide in a bush pretending a tiger and hence the name. *Kei* = Tiger.

51. *Irengpam*:- The person became close with the king as the relatives of king visited him. And hence the name was given.

52. *Satthokpam*:- The person engaged in extricating the bones of the buried king. So, the above name was given from his duty. *Satthokpa* = To extricate.

53. *Charoipam*:- The person reared a wild bird named Charoi at home and hence the name was given.

54. *Loitongpam*:- This person engaged in washing the bones of the buried king after passing one year. Lu-Tong = bone. So, the name was given from his duty.

55. *Atom*:- It was given from the name of the person Atom Naha Sangkai Pampa. Sangkai Pampa was the youngest of the brothers and hence the name was given from his position.

56. *Pounam*:- This was given in consideration of the ability and strength of the person who captured wild animals with poles only.

57. *Irungpam*:- The grandfather engaged in preparing liquor. So, the above name was given in considering the occupation of the grandfather.

58. *Lukram Nong-in Fapam*:- At the failure of the king *Nong-in Fapa* to capture a game while hunting, the person carefully captured a bird named *Nong-in* and

offered it to the king. From this occasion the above name was given to the lineage of the person.

59. *Leimaram*:- The person descended from the house in revolving motion to the ground. So, the name was given from his ability.

60. *Nongthonpam*:- The grandfather held the post *Nongthonpa* and from this the above name was given.

61. *Famtom*:- The person got a respectable seat separately on special occasion and hence the name was given from his status.

62. *Hemam*:- The person was handsome and hence the name.

63. *Chirom*:- The person was very talkative, so the name was given for his nature.

64. *Khoitongpam*:- The person possessed a swollen navel and hence the name.

65. *Lamleirakpam*:- The grandfather *Leisok Pampa* held the post *Lamlei Lakpa*. So, the above name was given considering the post held.

66. *Huitrom*:- This was named after the name of Tonpa Huitronpa.

67. *Yumnam*:- The person constructed the coronation hall. The person was a craftsman and the name was given from his occupation.

68. *Leimayokpam*:- The folk name of silk worm is Leima. The person engaged in the occupation of rearing Leima and hence the name.

69. *Khumancharakpam*:- The person toured the jurisdiction of Khuman and conducted judicial activity and hence the name was given from the occupation.

70. *Langpokthapam*:- A relative of the king was sent by him to a place named *Langpok*. It can be a case of exile. So, the name was given from this occasion.

71. *Ningthoucham*:- The person married a relative of the king and hence the name.
72. *Nakampam*:- The person performed the duty of burying the *Naopham* (placenta) of the King. And hence the name.
73. *Shingkhwam*:- His duty was to prepare firewood in the palace. From his duty the name was given.

    Shing = firewood
74. *Soram*:- The name of his grandfather was Satanon. So, the above name was derived from his grandfather's name.
75. *Yensempam*:- His duty was to rear chicken in the palace and hence the name.
76. *Thoutam*:- The person had a habit of ordering jobs to others. So, the name was given considering his habit.
77. *Hotam*:- It was derived from his grandfather's name Hotika.
78. *Sakolsem*:- His duty was to look after the horses of king. And hence the name. *Sakol* = horse.
79. *Sanasapam*:- He was goldsmith. So, the name was given considering his occupation. *Sana* = Gold.
80. *Nameirakpam Moirang Ningthoumayum*:- The conch which he offered to the king was snatched by someone. He tried to capture it by holding the tip of loin-cloth. And his grandfather was the king of Moirang. So, considering the above event and his descendance from Moirang King the name Nameirakpam Moirang Ningthoumayum was given to his lineage.
81. *Paonam*:- He worshipped the deity Paota Hithel. And hence the name. The Paota Hithel is located at the bed of Imphal river which is at the north-eastern side of Kangla. Pakhangba is considered to be the deity associated with this place.

82. *Fourungpam*:- It was given considering his grandfather's post of Fourunghanpa. There was a department which looked after the collected paddy. The head of this department was known as Fourunghanpa. And hence the name.
83. *Sangkaisenpam*:- His duty was to do sentry the nine-roomed house of the king at the palace. *Sangkai* = the royal house. And hence the name.
84. *Sangpam*:- His duty was to guard the Umanglai (sylvan deity) Numit Leima. So, the name was given from his duty of guarding the deity. *Sangpa* = to guard.
85. *Khunchahanpam*:- His grandfather held the post Khunchahanpa. And the name was derived from his grandfather's post. *Khunchahanpa* = village chief, head.
86. *Sanapam*:- The person was greedy for gold. And hence the above name was given. *Sana* = Gold.
87. *Waikhom*:- His duty was to collect paddy husk for the king. So, the name was given from his duty.
88. *Khangsulakpam*:- The person worshipped the spear named Khangsu Naha. And hence the name. It is considered as a legendary spear and believed that it was used in eliminating the demon Moyadana.
89. *Yenkokpam*:- There was a practice named Yelhing Thapa in which the ailments of an ailing person (both physical and mental) was believed to be transferred to the sacrificing chicken. This person once performed the ritual for the king and he was successful. From this event the above name was given.
90. *Ficham*:- He was a skilled weaver. And the above name was given from his occupation of weaving.
91. *Thangkangsapam*:- The person was a producer of wick. So, the name was given from his occupation. *Thangkang* = wick.

92. *Aheipam*:- This was also given from the person's occupation of blacksmith.
93. *Fatlampam*:- This was given from the name of a person named Wangkhei Falampa.
94. *Fenlem*:- This person, while throwing his spear, could not hit the target. So, from his inability to hit the object the name was given to his lineage.
95. *Lourempam*:- His grandfather found missing paddy from his field, and this he believed to be stolen by evil spirit. But some of the paddy was found left and from this event the above name was given.
96. *Laitoncham*:- This person failed to perform the ritual of the deity which he worshipped. Since then he was considered indebted to the deity. And hence the name from that occasion.
97. *Moichem*:- The person was a producer of Moirik. And hence the name. Moirik is the traditional necklace made of small conches.
98. *Haoteicham*:- The person had friendship with Loipi Hao and hence the name. *Loipi* = Loi chanba = tributary. It was those Haos who were treated as tributary.
99. *Khoinucham*:- This was given from the person's occupation of preparing wax.
100. *Naotam*:- This person learned the habit and nature of a child. And so the name to his lineage. *Nao* = Child
101. *Lantham*:- He was fixed to resist the advancing enemy in the battle-field. So, the name was given from his profession of warrior.
102. *Sarensangpam*:- He performed the duty of guarding Sararel. The Umanglai (sylvan deity) Haoba Sararel of Thoubal was guarded by this person and the name was given from his duty.

103. *Kontha Haopam*:- He captured a young Hao (Haomacha) and brought him up. From this the above name was given to his lineage.
104. *Khuntom*:- The person was a worshipper of the Umanglai Khuthongyai. And hence the name was given to his lineage.
105. *Shingkhangpam*:- The person performed the duty of collecting firewood for use in the palace. So, the above name was given considering his duty.
106. *Saikhom*:- The person took part in building the royal residence (Shangkai) by trimming the lower edge of the thatched roof. And the name to his lineage.
107. *Khoiriyanpam*:- He was such a father who produced a child with a long umbilical cord. From this the above name was given to his lineage.
108. *Shoukrakpam*:- The person was in charge of Shaku Wanlong and hence the above name. Shaku Wanlong is a type of pitcher.
109. *Chomchanpam*:- The person was expert in measuring grains who worked in the royal enclosure. So, the name was given to his lineage from his skill.
110. *Nongmeikapam*:- King Khagemba gave the basic knowledge to operate a gun to this person. And the name was given to his lineage from this occasion. King Khagemba ruled Manipur from 1597 to 1652 A.D.
111. *Tenshupam*:- The person was expert in preparing and handling of arrow. He carried it on as his occupation. So, the above name was awarded to his lineage. *Ten* = arrow.
112. *Khwairakpam*:- His grandfather held the post of Khwairakpa. And hence the above name to his lineage.
113. *Wangkheimayum*:- This Yumnak was given by king Mungyamba (A.D. 1562-1597) to his youngest uncle

Chingayangpa. Formerly it was Awangpa Kheipa but later on changed into Wangkheimayum.

114. *Nongthonpam Irungpam*:- His grandfather held the post Nongthonpa. He also prepared local liquor. From this the above name was awarded to his lineage.

115. *Wangkheirakpam*:- His grandfather held the post Wangkheirakpa. His grandfather was in charge of Wangkhei division (Pana). And the above name was given to his lineage in consideration of his grandfather's post.

116. *Kanghacham*:- The person descended from Sek-U Kangta and hence the name.

II. Angom Salai

1. *Yumlempam*:- It was his duty to weave the cloth used in wrapping the skull of the dead king. From his duty of preparing this cloth the above lineage was given to this person.
2. *Nongmaithem*:- This person settled previously in the Nongmaiching hill. But migrated in the valley later than others. From this the above name was given to him. Nongmaiching hill is just on the eastern side of Kangla fort, around 20 km from it. This hill is very much in the valley and is closely associated with the folklore of Manipur.
3. *Hidam*:- He was given the duty to look after the gems of king. And hence the name.
4. *Seram*:- His service to the king was excellent. So, the name was given to him from his virtue.
5. *Narumpam*:- This person served the king physically very closely, even touching his neck. From his closeness to the king the above lineage was awarded to him.

6. *Pongshumbam*:- Man is known as 'Pong', and this person can cast a spell on this Pong. Since then his lineage was named as above.
7. *Haiheibam*:-The person had a good oratory and hence the above name was awarded to his lineage.
8. *Ngarenpam*:- This person offered 'Ngarenkhoi' to the king. So, the above name was awarded to his lineage since then. Ngarenkhoi is a kind of wasp which has a powerful sting and does not bear honey.
9. *Ongnam*:- This person chanted the word 'Ong' and hence the above name was given to his lineage.
10. *Hongnemshumbam*:- This person worshipped the deity Ahong-Achao. So, the name was given to his lineage.
11. *Kongbam*:- This person settled on the bank of Kongba river and he was entrusted to look after the bank of Kongba river. Another literature Yumchangba Sallai says that the name is derived from the name of the person Aata Kongyamba.
12. *Mangshatabam*:- This person performed the duty of guarding the King's crematorium. And hence the name. *Mang* = crematorium.
13. *Ayekpam*:- This person was expert in drawing and hence the above name was awarded to his lineage. Yekpa = to draw.
14. *Wanglenbam*:- The other name of Pung (drum) is Wanglen. The person was a drummer in the palace and hence the name was given to his lineage from his duty.
15. *Chingangbam*:- The person had a raised lip. So, the above name was given to his lineage from his appearance.
16. *Tenlem*:- This person could not hit the target while shooting an arrow. From this occasion the above name was awarded to his lineage.

17. *Leitanthem*:- The person was a stammerer. So, the above name was given to his lineage from his handicap.
18. *Shairom*:- This person learned handling a weapon named Shairong. From this the above name was given to his lineage. Shairong is a kind of arrow in which the cartridge is made of earth.
19. *Khangenbam*:- Khanghan Ahan, Khanghan Yaima; they were brothers. Taking the name Khanghan from them, the above name was given to their lineage.
20. *Keikranbam*:- This person held the post Keikram Hanba and hence the above name to his lineage.
21. *Nongthonbam*:- The grandfather of this person held the post Nongthonba and hence the above name to his lineage.
22. *Nakpak Khanpam*:- This was given from his duty of closely guarding the dead body of the king.
23. *Khoimom Tapam*:- This person settled at a place named Khoimom and hence the above name to his lineage. This place Khoimom is located to the west of Imphal (to the west of Langjing) and at present this is known as Luker.
24. *Thangcham*:- This person was a blacksmith and he made dagger. From his occupation of producing Thang the above name was given to his lineage.
25. *Longcham*:- This person guarded the king with Long in his hand at the coronation ceremony. And hence the above name. Long is a weapon of multiple spikes having a long handle.
26. *Lairellakpam*:- The grandfather of this person was Lairen Lakpa (a priest who knew the ritual to capture a python) and hence the above name was given from this ability of his grandfather.
27. *Awang Kheibam Wangkheibam*:- The person settled at the extreme north and hence the above name to his lineage.

28. *Kaswam*:- Kasom Ahan, Kasom Yaima; they were brothers and Kasom Ahan was the eldest of the two. The above name was given to their lineage considering the position of Kasom Ahan.
29. *Akoicham*:- This person performed the duty of washing the skull of the king in the secondary burial. While washing the skull he showed disgust in his duty and hence the above name to his lineage.
30. *Ningombam*:- The name of this Pukok (progenitor) was Ningol Yaimaba and hence the above name was derived from his name.

    Background: Khamloi Ahongba married Liema Haoreima, the daughter of Khuman King Chingkhong Thong-graiba and gave birth to Kasom Ahalpa, Ningol Yaimaba and Laitol Atolpa. The progeny of Ningol Yaimaba became Ningombam. The descendent of Kasom Ahalpa became Kaswam. And those of Laitol Atolpa became Laitonjam. Kasom Ahalpa married Moirangthem Chanu and gave birth to Yara. Yara married Laishram Chanu and gave birth to Koiya and Keital. From this Koiya became Kaswam and Keital became Akoicham.
31. *Laitoncham*: Laitol Atolpa was the last and third son of Khamloi Ahongba. The above name was derived from Laitol Atolpa.
32. *Huirem*:- The dog owned by this person was not ferocious and remained useless. And hence the above name was awarded to his lineage from the character of his dog.
33. *Laishangbam*:- This person guarded an un-named deity and hence the above name to his lineage.
34. *Ekhei Shangbam*:- This person guarded the Umanglai (sylvan deity) Ikheiren and hence the above name to his lineage.

35. *Achoibam*:- This was given from the character of the person who kept his belongings in a disorderly manner.
36. *Potshangbam*:- This person served at the palace and guarded valuable properties of the king. And hence the above name was awarded from his duty.
37. *Nganglenbam*:- The person was talkative and the above name was given to his lineage considering his nature.
38. *Yumkhaibam*:- This person separated from a joint family and settled himself separately. From this occasion the above name was given to his lineage. Yum = House, Khaiba = to divide or separate.
39. *Ngannupam*:- This person shot down a duck and might be a sharp shooter. Considering his talent in shooting the name was awarded to his lineage.
40. *Khana Chaobam*:- This person worshipped the deity Khana Chaoba and hence the name to his lineage.

    Background:- Wangbren and Khana Chaoba, two deities, are brothers. They are considered and treated as one and the same. Their parentage is: Wangnu Leima Khongchom Fabichaka is the mother and Chingngu Kouparel is the father. So, they are treated as one in most of the literatures. Their place of worship is located at Sugnu, a village at the southern end of the valley.
41. *Khuyonthem*:- This person guarded Khuyon Wa and hence the name to his lineage. This is a legendary bamboo. And the place for worship is at Moirang.
42. *Morimayum*:- This person worshipped the deity named Mori. This is an Umanglai (sylvan deity). So, the name was awarded to his lineage from his worshipping of the above deity.
43. *Shangngambam*:- This person learned land measuring where Shangngam is a unit of measuring

land. From his occupation the name was given to his lineage.

44. *Putoncham*:- The grandfather of this person was the youngest of their brothers. So, the name was given to his lineage considering the position of his grandfather.
45. *Shangtoncham*:- The grandfather of this person was well-built with an admirable height. So, from the physical structure of his grandfather the above name was given to his lineage.
46. *Kiyam*:- This person worshipped the Kiyam deity and hence the name.
47. *Mantingbam*:- This person was well-adept in imitating the habit of others. And hence the name to his lineage.

III. Chenglei Salai

1. *Thangcham*:- This person was a blacksmith and made dagger. In considering his occupation the above name was given to his lineage. *Thang* = dagger or sword.
2. *Tongbram*:- The Pukok (progenitor) was a labourer on earth-work and he raised a place by the earth dug out from a place. From this the above name was awarded to his lineage.
3. *Ayekpam*:- The person was a skilled painter and hence the above name to his lineage.
4. *Suraibam*:- The person was a skilled artisan and industrious too. And hence the name to his lineage.
5. *Leishangthem*:- The myth says that the progenitor detached out of the long tongue of Kuru. And hence the above name to his lineage. *Lei* = Tongue
6. *Khakokpam*:- The person was bald-headed and looked like a fruit named Hei-Khakok. So, the above name to his lineage from his appearance.

7. *Naoshekpam*:- The tongue of the person looked like a fruit named Hei-Naoshek. And hence the name from his appearance.
8. *Ingudum*:- This person used to sleep quietly without cloths. So, the above name was awarded to his lineage from his behaviour.
9. *Sharangthem*:- The myth says that this person detached from the tongue of Kuru in assorted colour. And hence the above name.
10. *Wairotpam*:- This person had a habit of hiring something from others and hide it for his use. So, from his habit the above name was given to his lineage.
11. *Chanam*:- This person was a staff in the palace administration and his duty was to seal the belongings of the king. So, the above name to his lineage.
12. *Yenlangbam*:- Vegetables collection from a garden is called as *Yenlangba*. The grandfather and mother of this person engaged in collecting vegetables. Hence the name was given to his lineage considering the duty of his grandfather and grandmother.
13. *Chingakham*:- The duty of this person was to guard Chinga, a hillock at the southern-edge of Imphal Municipality where the H. No. 39 passes. So, considering his duty of guarding the hillock the name was given to his lineage.
14. *Maiba-Thiyam*:- The person was a medical practitioner and was very attentive while practising his duty. So, considering his occupation and nature the name was given to his lineage.
15. *Shamnoibam*:- This person performed his duty of massaging the head of the king. And hence the name to his lineage. *Sham* = hair, *Noiba* = massage.

16. *Tourangbam*:- In ancient Manipuri to chop a reed is known as Tou Langba and hence the name to his lineage from his duty of collecting reeds for the king.
17. *Thumkanbam*:- The person was a salt-taster in the palace-kitchen. So, from his duty in the kitchen the above name was awarded to his lineage.
18. *Ngathem*:- The person was a skilled fisherman and the name was given to his lineage from his occupation.
19. *Loushikabam*:- The person was a cultivator and he was very ambitious. So, the above name was given to his lineage considering his occupation and nature.
20. *Haiwam*:- The person was very persuasive and hence the name to his lineage.
21. *Leitam*:- The person was labourer on earth-work and hence the above name to his lineage from his occupation.
22. *Meinam*:- This person forcibly extinguished a fire. So, from his ability to extinguish a fire the name was awarded to his lineage.
23. *Sharak-Khaibam*:- This person engaged in pulling out bones from dead body. This person, most probably, might be performing his duty of pulling-out bones from the forehead of a dead king. So, considering his duty the above name was given to his lineage.
24. *Kharaicham*:- This person prepared the royal gate which is known as Kharai. And hence the name to his lineage.
25. *Konsam*:- The person was an artisan and worked on jewellery and hence the name to his lineage.
26. *Langkoncham*:- Langol is a hill on the west and north-western edge of Imphal. It is related with the history and culture of Manipur since early times.

The crematorium of the king was located at Langol. Besides, the deities Thongak Lairembi, Tarung Lairemma, etc. are also located in this hill. The Pukok of this lineage performed certain rites at the crematorium of the king at the completion of a month, a year, etc. And hence the above name to his lineage considering his duty at the crematorium of the king.

27. *Mayanglambam*:- This Pukok held the post of Lambu where the Mayangs settled and hence the name to his lineage.
28. *Maibram*:- The person was a medical practitioner of Moirang and hence the name to his lineage. *Maiba* = medical practitioner.
29. *Khoisanam*:- This person forcibly captured a bee and hence the above name to his lineage. This person might be a bee-keeper. *Khoi* = bee.
30. *Heiwam*:- This Pukok was master in many trades and had the talent in resolving problems. Hence the above name was given to his lineage considering his skill.
31. *Potsangbam*:- This person performed the duty of guarding the valuables of the king and hence the above name to his lineage.

IV. Nganba (Khaba) Salai

1. *Meihoubam*:- This person lighted the fire of the king and hence the name to his lineage. *Mei* = fire, *Houba* = to ignite a fire.
2. *Tekcham*:- The eldest brother of this person was Tekcha Ahan. So, the above name was derived from the name of his eldest brother.
3. *Thong-ngam*:- This lineage was named from the name of the Pukok whose name was Thong-ngai Yumthangba.

4. *Aheibam*:- This person was a blacksmith and he was expert in casting utensils. And hence the above name to his lineage.
5. *Hentakpam*:- This person prepared Hentak (a type of fermented fish prepared from powdered fish) for the king. And hence the name to his lineage.
6. *Haopacham*:- This person was in charge of Hao and hence the above name to his lineage.
7. *Thinbam*:- This person was slow in movement and in understanding things. So, the name was awarded to his lineage considering his slowness.
8. *Yangoicham*:- This person took refuse in the palace and remained as a guest. And hence the name to his lineage.
9. *Shanchiram*:- This person tamed a bull by holding the horns. From his ability and courage the above name was awarded to his lineage.
10. *Kabolambam*:- This person held the post of Lambu for the Kabow region. And hence the name to his lineage considering his status. Kabow is the name of the valley which is in between the eastern ranges of Manipur and the Chindwin river in Burma (Myanmar).
11. *Khaitem*:- The duty of this person was to dissect the dead body of the king's pregnant wife. There was a custom to cremate separately the dead mother and baby. This was due to the belief that the joint cremation would bring perils to the king.
12. *Khuducham*:- In ancient Manipuri *Nau* (oar) is known as Khumu. This person made oar and hence the name was awarded to his lineage considering his occupation.
13. *Ficham*:- This person was a weaver and prepared *Fi* (cloths). And hence the name to his lineage from his occupation.

14. *Wangpacham*:- This Pukok was tall and well built and the name was given from his physical built-up.
15. *Nongchenpam*:- This person was a Maiba (priest) and he performed rituals to bring rains on earth for the Khaba Salai. So, from his occupation the name was given to his lineage.
16. *Khuraicham*:- This Pukok settled at Khurai, a place in the north-eastern Imphal. And hence the name to his lineage.

V. Luwang Salai

1. *Ashangbam*:- This person washed the leg of Pakhangba. And hence the name to his lineage.
2. *Arambam*:- This person bows down while taking bath. So, considering his nature the above name was awarded to his lineage.
3. *Tinbijam*:- This person lived close to the family of Leirongjam. And hence the above name to his lineage.
4. *Leirongcham*:- This Pukok worshipped the 'Lonlei' of the king. From this the name was given to his lineage. *Lonlei* = a headgear worn by the king on certain occasions, e.g. on coronation, on boat race, etc. It is made of gold and resembles the upper portion of 'Thangjing' (a plant in water).
5. *Toibicham*:- This person lived with someone, but later on the relationship was broken beyond repair. From such a situation the above name was given to his lineage.
6. *Apucham*:- This Pukok maintained the 'Naopham' (placenta) of a newly born baby of the king. And hence the name to his lineage.
7. *Meiyengbam*:- This person used to look whether the fire has been lighted or not. From his duty on fire

the above name was awarded to his lineage. *Mei* = Fire, *Yengba* = To look/observe.

8. *Urepkhinbam*:- This Pukok erected the Urep (main pillar) and hence the name to his lineage from his occupation of craftsmanship.
9. *Arubam*:- This Pukok maintained the royal clothings and ornaments of the king and hence the name to his lineage.
10. *Nongthonpam*:- The grandfather of this person held the post of Nongthonpham and hence the name to his lineage.
11. *Pung-graicham*:- This Pukok worshipped the Pung (drum) of the king and hence the name to his lineage.
12. *Ngang-ngom*:- This was derived from Ngang-ngomba, the grandfather of this person. And hence the name to his lineage.
13. *Luwangshangbam*:- This Pukok looked after the deity of Luwang Salai (clan). And hence the name to his lineage.
14. *Wanglenbam*:- Wanglen is another name of Pung (drum). The Pukok was a drummer and hence the name to his lineage from his duty.
15. *Heitham*:- This Pukok maintained the fruits of the king. And hence the name was awarded to his lineage from his duty at the palace. Hei = Fruits.
16. *Fammihanbam*:- The person held the post of Fammihanba and hence the above name to his lineage considering his status.

    Fammihanba used to look after. This officer made the sitting arrange-ment in official functions and thus maintained the hierarchical order in sitting in such functions in which royal dignitaries were present. This post may be termed as traditional protocol officer.

17. *Thammangcham*:- In an incident this person was considered dead and carried to crematorium for cremation. But later on regained his life. From this incident the above name was given to his lineage.
18. *Wakongthem*:- In ancient Manipuri to impose a fine is known as Wakongba. Once this Pukok committed an offence and for this he was imposed a fine. From this occasion the above name was given to his lineage.
19. *Khunchan Mayim*:- From the good deeds of this person the villagers treated him with affection. From such treatment of the villagers to him the above name was given to his lineage.
20. *Kongbam*:- This Pukok lived at a place named Kongba Meirongbi and hence the name to his lineage considering his place of settlement.
21. *Thangcham Saram*:- Sadanon; the grandfather of this person made swords who was a black-smith by occupation. So, considering the occupation of his grandfather the above name was awarded to his lineage.
22. *Khumukcham*:- The grandfather of this person was very disagreeable, so the villagers had strained relations with him. From such strained relationship of the grandfather and the villagers, the above name was given to his lineage.
23. *Feiroicham*:- This person while dividing a homestead, divided it from its breadth. From this the above name was given to his lineage.
24. *Thiyam*:- The name of his grandfather was 'Thikriba' and he was not an easily convincible person. So, considering the nature of his grandfather the name was given to his lineage.
25. *Shenbangcham*:- The bird 'Shenbang' made its nest in the house of this person and hence the name to his lineage.

26. *Waikhom*:- This person collected paddy husk; most probably for use in the palace, and hence the name to his lineage from his duty.
27. *Moibunglokpam*: To snatch *Moibung* (conch) is known as Lokpa in ancient Manipuri. From this the above name was given to his lineage considering that once he snatched a conch from someone.
28. *Shoupawam*:- The name of his grandfather was Shoupu. So, the above name is derived from his grandfather's name.
29. *Maisnam*:- The name of his grandfather was Sana. So, the above name is also derived from his grandfather's name.
30. *Meitram*:- This Pukok could not maintain fire in his hearth and his house was blackout. So, from his laxity in preserving fire the above name was awarded to his lineage.
31. *Yumlembam*:- This person built a house at free of cost for someone. Considering his generosity the above name was given to his lineage.
32. *Thouknaocham*:- This person was guilty of dereliction of duty ordered by the king. So, from his failure to perform assigned duty the above name was given to his lineage.
33. *Athokpam*:- The myth says that this Pukok emerged from Luwang Kuru, the deity of Luwang clan. And hence the name to his lineage.
34. *Hicham*:- This Pukok was a craftsman and he possessed the art of boat making. So, considering his trade the name was given to his lineage. *Hi* = Boat.
35. *Sanlam*:- This person performed rite to a cow. From this the name was given to his lineage. *San* = cow.
36. *Nongpokpam*:- The Pukok settled in the east. So, considering his place of settlement the name was given to his lineage. *Nongpok* = East.

37. *Yangambam*:- This person was very strong and he could defeat others. And hence the name to his lineage.
38. *Singkhangbam*:- This person was responsible for collecting firewood for the king. So, considering his duty in the palace the above name was given to his lineage. *Sing* = Fire wood.
39. *Haorungbam*:- This Pukok worshipped the Haorongbam deity. And hence the name to his lineage.

    Haorongbam Lai is a skin disease which occasionally inflicts in the leg. In the chronic stage the colour is changed with chapped skins. Gradually it spreads to chin and lips. It is believed to be caused by this Haorongbam Lai.
40. *Laisom*:- This person worshipped Uchi Lai. And hence the name to his lineage. On the other hand it is believed that Laisom is the deity who procreated the mouse.
41. *Thangcham*:- This Pukok was a blacksmith and he made *Thang* (sword). So, considering his occupation the name was given to his lineage.
42. *Thaoteicham*:- The person oiled his hair very often and hence the name to his lineage considering his habit.
43. *Nahakpam*:- This Pukok possessed a large ear. So, the above name to his lineage considering his extraordinary ear.
44. *Loukham*:- Meiba Chingba is the traditional method of igniting fire. This person produced fire by using this traditional implement. And hence the name to his lineage.
45. *Naoroibam*:- This person looked after children, most probably those of the king. And hence the name to his lineage.

46. *Wahengbam*:- This person did not keep his words. Considering his character of indecisiveness the name was given to his lineage.
47. *Laikangbam*:- This Pukok captured a python and kept dry in the sun. So, the name was given to his lineage considering his trade.
48. *Nantam*:- This person was very neat and clean. So, the name was given to his lineage considering his appearance.
49. *Lairenjam*:- This was derived from the name of this person's grandfather whose name was Thinpi Lairenchamba.
50. *Loicha Yangbam*:- This person was in charge of the Lois (the exiled persons). So, considering his duty the name was awarded to his lineage.
51. *Nagaupam*:- This Pukok was very much fond of white cloths. And hence the name to his lineage.
52. *Chingchabam*:- This person relished the rock (red) and hence the name to his lineage.
53. *Nganglom*:- This person was a stammerer, so he could not talk properly. Considering his handicap in talking the above name was given to his lineage.
54. *Ningchitpam*:- This person was expert in walking in the backward direction by his buttock. And hence the name to his lineage.
55. *Khiknam*:- This person was expert in using spear and once he captured something by the butt of his spear. So, from this incident the name was given to his lineage considering his skill and strength.
56. *Sampantoram*:- This person maintained the hair of the king. And hence the name to his lineage considering his duty to the king.
57. *Khoibam*:- This person was a priest and performed rites to the bees. So, the name was awarded to his lineage considering his occupation.

VI. Khuman Salai

1. *Akham*:- This person was slow in executing his assigned job. And hence the name to his lineage.
2. *Ayam*:- This Pukok had the habit of offering a large amount of rice in the death anniversary of someone. So, from his habit the name was given to his lineage.
3. *Afram*:- Maiba in Manipuri carries the dual sense of priest and medical practitioner. In this context it is more inclined to medical practitioner, however, he also has the sense of priest. Maiba (medical practitioner) is of three kinds:-
   - (i) *Maiba Napan Lemba* – he cures illness by using mantras (Laiwas).
   - (ii) *Maiba Napfaba* – he cures ailments by applying traditional medicines.
   - (iii) *Maiba Nongkhaiba* – he cures illness by using *Mari-Suba* – a traditional treatment in which the Maiba presses the belly of the patient with a certain order thereby releasing the residuals (both gas and mass) from the body.

   This *Pukok* (progenitor) is a Maiba and he folds in the third category. So, considering his occupation the above name was awarded to his lineage.
4. *Maibam*:- This person learned to become a Maiba and hence the name to his lineage.
5. *Thoidingcham*:- This person was assigned to wash the bones of the dead king, and while performing his duty this person excelled the others in neatness. From this the above name was given to his lineage.
6. *Yanglem*:- This person had an agile physique. So, considering his quality the above name was given to his lineage.
7. *Theng-gujam*:- This person hammered the reeds of the king with a Theng-gu. So, the above name was

given to his lineage from his duty at the palace. *Theng-gu* is a traditional hammer, made of wood.

8. *Pukhrem*:- While dinning on a dish this person used to leave a remains of the served food. So, considering his nature the above name was given to his lineage.
9. *Fairembam*:- This person introduced the art of Lang Faiba in weaving. So, considering his invention the above name was given to his lineage. *Lang Faiba* is a the art of weaving by clubbing two or more threads.
10. *Chandam*:- This person was treated well by the king and hence the above name to his lineage.
11. *Pangkhaicham*:- This person allowed his son to separate from him and establish his own family. From this the above name was given to his lineage.
12. *Mongbicham*:- This Pukok worshipped the *Mongbi Ching* and hence the above name to his lineage.
13. *Ngangbam*:- This person settled at a place named *Khunpham Ngangjeng*. So, considering his place of settlement the name was given to his lineage.
14. *Akangcham*:- This name was given considering the habit of the Pukok who used to observe the belongings of others with raised legs.
15. *Oinam*:- This name was also given considering the nature of the Pukok having left-handedness.
16. *Maimom*:- This person worshipped Maimu Tomshon and hence the name to his lineage. *Maimu Tomshon* = Ornament for decorating hair.
17. *Khamnam*:- This Pukok was the last of his brothers and so, no one was after him. Considering his position among his brothers the name was given to his lineage.
18. *Ahongshangbam*:- This Pukok worshipped the deity Ahong-Achao and hence the name to his lineage.

19. *Chabungbam*:- While feeding a baby this person served the food without grinding it. So, from his nature the name was given to his lineage.
20. *Thong-gram*:- This person performed rites to deities by climbing an Ukrong Thong. And hence the name to his lineage. *Ukrong Thong* = Wooden bridge with thatched roof.
21. *Ahongbam*:- This was given considering the attitude of the Pukok who was liberal in donating or presenting food or grains to others.
22. *Heikrucham*:- This person used to distribute fruits while attending ceremonies and hence the above name to his lineage.
23. *Sinnam*:- This was a person who could slice *Paya* (bamboo chips meant for binding) with a Sangai (a knife particularly meant for preparing bamboo chips, etc.). So, considering his ability to prepare fine bamboo chips the above name was given to his lineage.
24. *Thongbam*:- This person was well-versed in performing the *Mangthong Thingba* rite which he usually performed. And hence the name to his lineage.

    Mangthong Thingba is a rite performed to such a family where death occur frequently. In order to prevent further occurrence of death in that house or family this rite was performed at places near the front door, at the gate and at the crematorium, etc.
25. *Yang-ngouyeibam*:- This person was an artisan and he prepared the ear-ring Yang-ngou Lei for the king. So, the name was given to his lineage considering his duty for the king. *Yang-ngou Lei* is a kind of ear-ring which is worn occasionally in performing rites to traditional deities.
26. *Hanglem*:- This person performed the duty of extracting maggots from dead body. And hence the above name to his lineage.

27. *Kiyam*:- It was believed that a certain ailment was caused by a deity named 'Kiyam Lai'. This Pukok worshipped this deity and hence the above name to his lineage.
28. *Laipukhram*:- The appearance of this person was like a person under the spell of certain evil spirits. So, from his appearance the above name was given to his lineage.
29. *Thaudem*:- The name of this Pukok was 'Thaudei Yumthangba'. So, the above name was derived from his name.
30. *Kollom*:- This person was literate and worked with pen. And hence the name to his lineage.
31. *Soukaicham*:- This Pukok was expert in handling 'Shou' of fish trap. And hence the name to his lineage. *Shou* is device which prevents the fish to escape from the trap.
32. *Ashem*:- This Pukok was expert in many trades and was able to prepare many items. Considering his talents the above name was given to his lineage.
33. *Wareppam*:- This person worshipped Bamboo and was firm in keeping promise. So, considering his nature the above name was awarded to his lineage.
34. *Taibangjam*:- This person was a *Maiba* (priest) who performed *Atai puri thokpa* (concluding part of a ritual to a deity in which the Maiba pray to the deity to bring good health and wealth to the family.) So, from his profession the above name was given to his lineage.
35. *Shiyatpam*:- This person performed the duty of dissecting the dead body of the pregnant wife of the king. And hence the name to his lineage.
36. *Haopicham*:- Once this Pukok was offered to the *Hao* (hill-people of Manipur). And hence the above name to his lineage from this occasion.

37. *Kaborambam* (Kabrambam):- This person held the post of *Lambu* of the *Kabow* region. So, considering his status the above name was given to his lineage.
38. *Thongcham*:- This Pukok was a craftsman and his work on door was a masterpiece. So, considering his talent in making doors the above name was given to his lineage.
39. *Pukhranbam*:- The grandfather of the Pukok held the post of Pukhranba. And hence the above name considering the status of the grandfather.
40. *Meitalkeishangbam*:- This Pukok looked after the charcoal of the king. So, from his duty in the palace the above name was awarded to his lineage. *Meital* = Charcoal.
41. *Likmabam*:- This name was given to the person's lineage in consideration of his trade of preparing necklaces. *Lik* = Necklace.
42. *Maibam*:- This Pukok was a relative of Maibi Khagi Thambistra. In consideration of his relation with the Maibi the above name was given to his lineage.
43. *Thingkom*:- This person was expert in damming streams and drainages and he performed it easily. From this the above name was given to his lineage.
44. *Mayanglambam*:- This Pukok held the post of *Lambu of Mayang* region. And hence the name to his lineage.
45. *Chungkhwam*:- This name was given to the lineage of this Pukok who defended the attack in the battle-field by holding a shield.
46. *Maifubam*:- This person was a Maiba (medical practitioner) and once he quarreled with some one while discharging his duty. From this incident the above name was given to his lineage.
47. *Amakcham*:- In ancient Manipuri a bow is also known by the word *'Mak'*. This name was given to the lineage of this person as he worked on bow.

48. *Charoibam*:- Charoipung is the place of a deity. The above name was given to the lineage of this person as he worshipped 'Charoipung'.
49. *Khunlem*:- This name was given to the lineage of this person as he settled in a deserted village.
50. *Akiram*:- This name was given in honour of the person who came with a captured game.
51. *Khoirishumbam*:- This was given considering the person's trade who used to tie the navel of a new-born baby.
52. *Lammabam*:- This person guarded certain area of Manipur and hence the name to his lineage.
53. *Yaithingbam*:- This person was a drummer in the palace. His duty was to drum the war-drum in the event of a war. So, the above name was given to his lineage from his duty.
54. *Langkam*:- This person was a brave-warrior and once he hunted a head from the battle-field. And hence the above name to his lineage from that event.
55. *Shamukcham*:- This name was given to the lineage of this Pukok who prepared Shamuk. Shamuk is an iron stand having three legs, used mostly for keeping food, utensils, etc.
56. *Thingbaijam*:- This name was derived from the name of this Pukok who was known as Thingpai Shemhongba.
57. *Khoirom*:- This name was given considering the occupation of this person's grandfather who was a bee-keeper.
58. *Namaram*:- As a habit this person used to carry a single item and hence the above name to his lineage.
59. *Haobam*:- This name was given to the lineage of this Pukok considering his place of origin who migrated from a place named Lok-Kha Haokha.

60. *Moirengcham*:- This name was derived from the name of the Pukok whose name was Moireng Shaphaba.
61. *Hentakpam*:- This name was given considering the food-habit of the Pukok who was very fond of Hentak. *Hentak* is a traditional fish culture prepared by fermenting powder fish.
62. *Nepram*:- This name was derived from the name of the Pukok's grandfather whose name was Ne Ne.
63. *Yumkutum*:- This person was expert in roofing a traditional house. And hence the above name to his lineage considering his skill in roofing.
64. *Laishram*:- This person was in touch with deities. That is, he performed rites to the deities. So, from his association with deities the above name was given to his lineage.
65. *Amom*:- This name was derived from the name of the Pukok's grandfather whose name was *Ama*.
66. *Toncham*:- This name was given considering the facial structure of the Pukok who had an extra-ordinary big nose.
67. *Puyam*:- This person performed the duty of carrying the skull of the dead king. And hence the above name to his lineage considering his duty at the palace.
68. *Shankhom Sinnam*:- This name was given considering the occupation of the Pukok who was a cowhand.
69. *Moichem*:- This person wore a necklace made of pieces of conches. And hence the above name to his lineage.
70. *Langheibam*:- This person knew how to prepare a trap. So, the above name to his lineage deriving from his skill.
71. *Fancham*:- This person was handy in preparing Fan (= a wooden seat still in vogue in most of the houses

in Manipur). From this the above name was given to his lineage.

72. *Panlungbam*:- This person was handy in lying a trap by damming a stream. And hence the above name to his lineage.
73. *Lantham*:- This person was left to engage in the war. And hence the above name to his lineage.
74. *Yampem*:- This person was contented in nature and he would satisfy what one did something for him. From his nature the above name was awarded to his lineage.
75. *Tourem*:- This person was an expert in preparing reed crafts. And hence the name from his occupation.
76. *Ngasetpam*:- This name was given considering the character of the person who stealthily relished the fish of the king. Nga = Fish, Setpa = To tear.
77. *Santham*:- This person performed rites at 'Shanlam' (a passage used by the cattle). And hence the above name to his lineage.
78. *Tournom*:- This person performed the duty of collecting reeds for use in the palace. In the past a reed had varied uses. So, considering his duty to the king the above name was given to his lineage.
79. *Pang-ngambam*:- This was given considering the appearance of the Pukok who had a long neck and looked like a *Pangal* (Manipuri Muslim).
80. *Tokpam*:- Once this person offered a Tokpa to the king. From this the above name was given to his lineage.
81. *Shanshenbam*:- This name was given considering the occupation of the person who was a Cowherd.
82. *Kadam*:- This name was derived from a flower named *Kadamba Leinungshi*. This flower is also known by the name Melei Leishana Nungjumpal.

83. *Chingtham*:- The grandfather of this person was a leader. So, as an honour to his grandfather the above name was given to his lineage.
84. *Shakap-pam*:- This person hunted wild beast and shot them down. From this the above name was given to his lineage.
85. *Haorongbam*:- This name was given from the name of the Haorongbam deity which he used to worship.
86. *Thangcham Yaoshem*:- This person was a shepherd as well as a blacksmith who made sword. So, considering his twin occupation the above name was awarded to his lineage.
87. *Thangcham*:- The occupation of this person was blacksmith who specialised in making sword, and hence the name to his lineage.
88. *Khumanthem*:- This Pukok settled late in the area of Khuman Salai. And hence the above name to his lineage.
89. *Wangkom*:- This person dined his food by keeping it on 'Wangkam' (a container made of bamboo). Hence the above name to his lineage.
90. *Taobam*:- This Pukok took refuge in Aheibam (a lineage of Ningthoucha Salai). And hence the above name to his lineage.
91. *Polem*:- The bank raised around the hedge of this person's homestead was magnificent. And hence the above name to his lineage.
92. *Yanglem*:- This person carried loads comfortably. And hence the above name to his lineage.
93. *Tenlem*:- The arrow shot by this person could not hit the target. The arrow became useless. From this the above name was given to his lineage.
94. *Tonthram*:- Once this person jumped down from the top of a tree. From this the above name was given to his lineage.

95. *Hauwaibam*:- This Pukok cultivated beans in large quantity. And hence the above name to his lineage.
96. *Thang-gangshabam*:- This was given from the occupation of the person who made wick.

    Thang-gang = wick.
97. *Khutheibam*:- This person was master in many trades and could prepare many items. From this the above name was given to his lineage.
98. *Langkhombam*:- This person was a warrior who took position at the rear. And hence the above name to his lineage considering his position in the battle field.
99. *Saram*:- This was given from the nature of the grandfather of this Pukok used to speak fast.
100. *Haowoibam*:- This was given from the appearance of the person who looked like *Hao-Nai* (person of low stature).
101. *Shentam*:- This Pukok learned to manufacture coins. And hence the above name to his lineage. Shen = coins.

VII. Moirnag Salai

1. *Chongtham*:- In an occasion this person jumped down from the boat in which he was captured. From this incident the above name was given to his lineage.
2. *Menlem*:- Once this person took shelter hiding behind the throne in Kangla. From this the above name was given to his lineage.
3. *Wayenbam*:- This person was fair in giving judgement. And hence the name to his lineage.
4. *Pukhranbam*:- This name was given considering the post of Pukhranba which was held by the grandfather of this person.

5. *Narengbam*:- Once this person was observing with suspicion on a moving grass. His suspicion became true when he found something hiding in the moving grass. From this the above name was given to his lineage.
6. *Kaborambam*:- This was given considering the post of the Pukok who was a Lambu of Kabow region.
7. *Thangcham Shangkhom*:- This was given from the twin occupation of the person who was a blacksmith (made sword) as well as a milking man.
8. *Nongthonbam*:- This was given in honour of the post held by this Pukok who was a Nongthol of Moirang Kingdom (principality).
9. *Puthem*:- This person looked after the Umanglai Puthiba. And hence the above name to his lineage.
10. *Konchengbam*:- This person arrived late in the village assembly. So, from his habit the name was given to his lineage.
11. *Chakpafiyam*:- This Pukok was a weaver and he prepared the kind of cloth named Chakfi in large quantity. And hence the name to his lineage.
12. *Laiucham*:- Once this person encountered a python (which was considered as a deity). And from this incident the above name was given to his lineage.
13. *Lampucham*:- Lampucham is the name of an ailment which was considered to be caused by a spirit. This Pukok knew the rite to tame this spirit and he performed it. From this the name was given to his lineage.
14. *Wangpicham*:- This was given by judging the physique of the person who was well-built.
15. *Kabacham*:- This was derived from the name of this Pukok's grandfather who was known by the name Kaba.

16. *Ngangnem*:- This was also given by judging the stature of the person who was short as a boy.
17. *Nungleppam*:- This person worshipped the deity Nungthel Leima. And hence the name to his lineage. Nungthel Leima is considered as the consort of Loyarakpa; both of them are deities.
18. *Thanggacham*:- This was given in honour of the Pukok's grandfather who held the post of Thanggarakpa.
19. *Ningthoukhongjam*:- This was derived from the name of the person's grandfather whose name was Ningthoukhong.
20. *Konkham*:- This person remained fencing around his garden. And hence the name to his lineage.
21. *Keithellakpam*:- This was given in consideration of the duty of the Pukok who looked after a Keithel (market).
22. *Yaikhom*:- This person collected precious items, e.g. diamond, jewel, etc. And hence the above name to his lineage.
23. *Okram*:- This was given in honour of the post held by this 'Pukok' (progenitor). And the post was Okrahanba.
24. *Kumabam*:- This person worshipped the deity Kumgi Lai. And hence the above name to his lineage. It was believed that the chronic illness was caused by this deity.
25. *Chakpa Taba Manglem*:- Once upon a time this person survived from the crematorium of Chakpa's. And hence the name to his lineage.
26. *Moirangthem*:- The myth says that this lineage is detached from Kuru with an assorted colour. And hence the name.
27. *Thangcham*:- This Pukok was a blacksmith and he made sword. And hence the above name to his lineage.

28. *Akhwaibam*:- This person settled at the front of the village. And hence the above name to his lineage. In ancient Manipuri a village is termed as Pan, and its modern use is Khun. Pankok, Panyai and Panmei are all ancient Manipuri and meant front, middle and rear of a village respectively.
29. *Namucham*:- This person wore a large number of necklaces. And hence the name to his lineage from his nature. *Ngangkoy* = *Lik* = Necklace.
30. *Wanglenbam*:- In ancient Manipuri a drum is known as Wanglen. This person was a drummer. And hence the above name to his lineage.
31. *Kairencham*:- This Pukok possessed the know-how of making Kairen Kaichau. And hence the name to his lineage. *Kairen Keichau* is a well-decorated coffin meant specially for the king and the noblemen.
32. *Yumkhaibam*:- This person separated from his parents and established his own family. So, the above name to his lineage from this occasion.
33. *Khuyonthem*:- This Pukok settled earlier in the village named Khuyol. And hence the above name to his lineage.
34. *Mangkhom*:- This was given from the duty of the person who exhumed the corpse of the king after completing the period of first burial.
35. *Khoyangbam*:- This was given from the occupation of the Pukok who was a bee-keeper.
36. *Haorongbam*:- This person worshipped the deity Haorongbam. And hence the name to his lineage.
37. *Laikhucham*:- This person worshipped the deity by touching its feet. And hence the name to his lineage from his nature.
38. *Yoirenbam*:- This was given from the name of the office which he attended. And the office was Yoiren

Shang. It is a Department of women priests.

39. *Kongchengbam*:- This person worshipped Koncheng Lai. And hence the above name to his lineage. *Kongcheng Lai* is a kind of skin disease. It is believed that this skin disease is caused by this spirit.
40. *Akuram*:- It is believed that the Lord blessed him with fish and meat. And hence the above name to his lineage.
41. *Lisam*:- This person supplied *Lee* (traditional water container) for the king. And hence the name to his lineage.
42. *Mayanglambam*:- This was given in honour of the post held by the person who was a Lambu for Mayang region.
43. *Thopchom*:- This was given in consideration of the duty of the person who removed the brain of the dead king.
44. *Ponlem*:- This person was an artisian and was excellent in basketwork. And hence the above name to his lineage from his occupation.
45. *Soibam*:- Once this person attempted to become king but he failed in his venture. From this failure the above name was given to his lineage.
46. *Moifwam*:- This person worshipped the Moiching deity which is located at a place named Thoubal. And hence the above name to his lineage.
47. *Laifrakpam*:- Once this Pukok captured a python. And hence the name to his lineage from his bravery.
48. *Lairenmayum*:- Once a python sneaked in his house. From this occasion the above name was given to his lineage.
49. *Ngang-ngom*:- This person was very talkative. So, the above name was given to his lineage from his talkative nature.

50. *Khoinaicham*:- This person worshipped bee. And hence the name to his lineage.
51. *Leimacham*:- This was given from the name of the deity which he worshipped. It was the Leimaching deity.
52. *Wangkhem*:- This was given considering his place of settlement. This person settled at the northernmost of the village.
53. *Hitam*:- This Pukok learned from someone the art of handling a boat. And hence the name to his lineage.
54. *Shingkhangbam*:- This was given in consideration of the occupation of the person who collected firewood for the king.
55. *Haowoibam*:- This was given in honour of the post held by the Pukok. And the post was Lambu of the Hao.
56. *Keithellakpam*:- This was given from the duty of the person who looked after Keithel (market).
57. *Ngangkham*:- This was given from the name of the village Ngangkha Lawai which this person settled.
58. *Aheibam*:- This was given from the occupation of the person who was a blacksmith. He was specialized in casting utensils.
59. *Ngaseppam*:- The duty of this person was to trim fish for cooking, most probably in the palace. Considering his duty the above name was given to his lineage.
60. *Moirangmayum*:- This person settled earlier at Moirang. And hence the above name to his lineage.
61. *Leimakhujam*:- This person was related to the king as his grandmother was the second wife of the king. So, considering his relationship with the king the above name was awarded to his lineage.

62. *Khwairakpam*:- This was given in honour of the post of Khwairakpa held by the grandfather of this person.
63. *Asem*:- This person prepared meat and fish for the king. And hence the above name to his lineage.
64. *Khomdram*:- The duty of this person was to carry food and liquor for the king while on tour. So, from his duty the above name was given to his lineage.

D. ADDITION OF *YUMNAKS* FROM THE EAST

People from the East began to migrate in Manipur since the reign of king Kiyamba (A.D. 1467-1508). This is recorded in the literature *Nongpok Haramlon*. The record continued till the reign of king Mungyamba (A.D. 1562-1597). During this period in total 57 persons migrated from East to Manipur. Among them 16 persons were from Moguang (Myanmar) during the reign king Kiyamba (A.D. 1467-1508), one person from Kashe Shan (Kabow) during king Kabomba (A.D. 1524-1542), seven persons from Kashe Shan (Kabow) during king Chalamba (A.D. 1545-1562), and 33 persons (16 from Kashe Shan (Kabow), 13 from Kachin (Khagi) and four from Yotra) during the reign of king Mungyamba (A.D. 1562-1597). All of them were assimilated to Meitei society by admitting to five original *Yumnaks* and 29 new *Yumnaks*.

All the 34 *Yumnaks* are arranged in alphabetical order:

1. Akhanbam
2. Achoibam
3. Changkhamayum
4. Chafanmayum
5. Chingsubam
6. Chinggangsu Thang-gangmayum
7. Phuritshabam
8. Heikham

9. Kasommayum Changkhamningthoumayum
10. Louriyam
11. Leipaksangbam
12. Monfangmayum
13. Mungyongmayum
14. Nandeibam
15. Ngaseppam
16. Senjam
17. Sangkhubam
18. Huiyam
19. Heibeethabam
20. Hikhambam
21. Konsam
22. Khongbantabam
23. Kabow Thangjam
24. Kabow Sharungbam
25. Khumpongmayum
26. Sendrangmayum
27. Shamchetsabam
28. Sanggaishenbam
29. Sencham Leipaksangbam
30. Thonggabam
31. Usham
32. Yirungbam
33. Yendrembam
34. Yichom.

Out of these, the following, viz., Achoibam, Konsam, Ngaseppam, Sanggaisenbam and Yirungbam are original Yumnaks. The remaining 29 *Yumnaks* were newly introduced to accommodate the new comers from the East who are known as Nongpok Haram.

E. ADDITION OF *YUMNAKS* FROM THE WEST

Migration of people from her immediate neighbours e.g. Assam, Tripura, Cachar etc. began since 12th century. Migration might taken place much before this, however, the amount might be small. Available records indicates that batches of people began coming to Manipur since the days of King Thawanthaba (A.D. 1195-1231). Meitei society provided accommodation to these people either by enlisting them in the original Yumnaks/Shageis (lineages) or by introducing new Yumnaks/Shageis. The original place of the migrants, their place of settlement in Manipur, their lineages in Meitei society, their admission into one of the salais (clans) and their period of arrival in Manipur; all these are discussed in the literature *Nongchup Haram*. The *Nongchum Haram* contains different chapters dealing on the people coming from a specific region. So, the literatures such as, 1) Kshetrilon, 2) Ukhongshanglon, 3) Lairik Yengbamlon, 4) Takhelon, 5) Kumfilon, 6) Mayang Ningthounailon Leimanailon and 7) Mayang Tekkhaolon are the constituents of Nongchup Haram.

1. **Kshetrilon:** During the reign of king Chalamba (1545-62) as many as eight persons from Takhel (Tripura) came and settled in Manipur. They were accommodated in Meitei society by introducing two new Yumnaks, viz.:

(1) Kshetri Khanachaobam,

(2) Kshetrithingbaijam. Those who came during king Khagemba (A.D. 1597-1652) were enlisted into six new Yumnaks, viz., (1) Kshetrishanjimayum, (2) Kshetrimayum, (3) Kshetrihajarimayum, (4) Kshetriudhabamayum, (5) Kshetrimuknaksangbam, (6) Kshetri-dayamayum. Those who came during the reign of Garibniwaj (A.D. 1709-48) were also given Kshetridayamayum and Kshetrikhanachaobam. Those who came during the reign of King Gambhir Singh (A.D. 1825-34) were accommodated in three

new *Yumnaks* viz., (1) Kshetrikashimayum, (2) Kshetriyogimayum and (3) Kshetrikalayanmayum. What is revealed after examining the literature Kshetrilon is that in total 11 new *Yumnaks* (lineages) were introduced to accommodate those who came from the west of Manipur during the reign of above different kings of Manipur beginning from King Chalamba.

The eleven new *Yumnaks* as found in Kshetrilon are:

1. Kshetri Khanachaobam
2. Kshetri Thingbaijam
3. Kshetrishanjimayum
4. Kshetrimayum
5. Kshetrihajarimayum
6. Kshetriudhabamayum
7. Kshetrimuknaksangbam
8. Kshetridayamayum
9. Kshetrikasimayum
10. Kshetriyogimayum
11. Kshetrikalayanmayum.

2. **Lairik Yengbamlon**: As many as 22 persons, mostly from Takhel (Tripura) and Tekhao (Assam) migrated to Manipur during the reign of King Lam Kiyamba (A.D. 1512-1523) and Khagemba (A.D. 1597-1652). Out of these twenty two persons, five came during Lamkiyamba and the remaining 17 during Khagemba. According to this literature these persons were admitted into Meitei society by introducing 16 new *Yumnaks*. They are as follows:

1. Lairikyengbam Yumlembam
2. Lairikyengbam Yengkhom
3. Lairikyengbam Nautan
4. Lairikyengbam Palsangtabam
5. Lairikyengbam Waribam

6. Lairikyengbam Bartuyanmayum
7. Lairikyengbam Yendemthabam
8. Lairikyengbam Chanamthabam
9. Lairikyengbam Chongkhanbam
10. Lairikyengbam Khundrakpam
11. Lairikyengbam Tanyeibam
12. Lairikyengbam Dewanmayum
13. Lairikyengbam Bahumayum
14. Lairikyengbam Shanggomsumbam
15. Lairikyengbam Ukabam
16. Lairikyengbam Yiming Kheibam.

3. Takhenlon (Nongchup Haram):- This literature is a component of *Nongchup Haram* which exclusively discusses the migration of people from Takhel (Tripura). The record begins from the reign of king Ningthoukhomba (1432-98). It is recorded in this literature that in total 73 persons from Takhel migrated to Manipur during this period. Thirteen persons during Ningthoukhomba, 12 persons during Mungyamba (A.D. 1562-97), 33 persons during Khagemba (A.D. 1597-1652), two persons during Charairongba (A.D. 1697-1709), eight persons during Pamheiba (A.D. 1709-1748) and five persons during King Chingthangkhomba (A.D. 1763-98)—migrated to Manipur. All these persons were assimilated to Meitei society by enrolling them in 13 original *Yumnaks* and in 25 new yumnaks. Thirteen original *Yumnaks* are:-

1. Ayekpam
2. Chabungbam
3. Khaidem
4. Meitankeishangbam
5. Ningthoujam
6. Ongnam
7. Oinam

8. Shagolshem
9. Saikhom
10. Sanjenbam
11. Wahengbam
12. Yimkhaibam
13. Yambem.

And the remaining are the newly introduced *Yumnaks* to accommodate those who migrated from Tripura (Takhel). And they are as follows:-

1. Apubam
2. Abujam
3. Chanambam
4. Fishaba Waribam
5. Kabo Potshangbam
6. Kakching Kshetrinandam
7. Kwathabam
8. Khullakpam
9. Khullenmayum
10. Khagitabam
11. Luplakpam
12. Leihaorungbam
13. Lamcharam
14. Loushambam
15. Ningthoushenbam
16. Shampumphabam
17. Takhel Ayekpam
18. Takhel Fourungba Khanbam
19. Thongsangbam
20. Takhel Potsangbam
21. Takhenchangbam

22. Takhelmayum
23. Takhel Perekhongbam
24. Takhel Anoubam
25. Wakanpam.

4. Kumfilon: This chapter deals with the people who migrated to Manipur from Takhel Kumilasar. Eight persons from this place came and settled in Manipur during the reign of King Punshiba and Ningthoukhomba (1404-67 A.D.). These eight persons were admitted to Meitei society by enrolling them in five original Yumnaks. And they are as follows:

1. Khaidem
2. Khangenbam
3. Wahengbam
4. Khumalthem
5. Moirangthem.

5. Mayang Ningthounailon Leimanailon: This literature deals with those migrants from Takhel (Tripura) and who performed menial services for the king and queen. However, the time of their arrival in Manipur is not mentioned. They were 34 in number. All of them were assimilated with Meitei society by enrolling into two original *Yumnaks* and by introducing 29 new *Yumnaks* (lineages). The two original *Yumnaks* are:

1. Khundrakpam and
2. Maisnam.

And the remaining 29 new *Yumnaks* are as follows:-

1. Avanmakalarajmayum
2. Achoumayum
3. Bangsirupmayum
4. Charonmayum
5. Chongkhanmayum

6. Haorokcham
7. Hiyam
8. Hiyam Maibam
9. Kalarajmayum
10. Khullakpam
11. Kumthoimayum
12. Khakihanjabamayum
13. Leimanai Khullakpam
14. Leimanai Punshipam
15. Leimanai Apajam
16. Leimanai Thokchom
17. Leimanai Ngamthoipam
18. Mariktondasharajmayum
19. Moirang Achoubam
20. Mayangleimanai Khundrakpam
21. Ningthoukhongkhullakpam
22. Nakamayum
23. Pukhrambam Kalarajmayum
24. Purarajmayum
25. Tangchaomayum
26. Takhelmayum
27. Takhel Aturammayum
28. Tollongkhomba Hanjabamayum
29. Wakapam.

6. Ukhongsanglon: It is mentioned in this literature that as many as 54 persons from Kachar and Tekhao (Assam) migrated to Manipur at different periods of history beginning from king Khunjaoba (A.D. 1652-66) to king Chingthangkhomba (A.D. 1763-98). Out of these 54 persons, 49 were from Kachar and the remaining five were from Tekhao (Assam). During the reign of king Khunjaoba 36 persons from Kachar came and settled in Manipur. Another five Kacharis also migrated to Manipur during the reign of king Paikhomba (A.D. 1666-1697). During reign of king Charairongba (A.D. 1697-1709) four more Kacharis also migrated and settled in Manipur. As mentioned in this literature the last batch of Kacharis came to Manipur during king Pamheiba (A.D. 1709-1748). And they were four in number. The last batch of five persons from Tekhao (Assam) migrated to Manipur during the reign of king Chingthangkhomba (A.D. 1763-98). All these 54 persons from Kachar and Tekhao were accommodated to Meitei society by admitting them into six original *Yumnaks* and by introducing another 23 new *Yumnaks*.

The six original yumnaks were:-

1. Maibam
2. Thangjam
3. Moirangthem
4. Konsam
5. Fijam
6. Sorokhaibam.

And 23 newly introduced *Yumnaks* are as follows.

1. Andro Shamchetshabam
2. Beishamaym
3. Dolaipabam
4. Fundrei Ningthoujam
5. Fishabam Taotham
6. Gangachangbam
7. Jagoimayum
8. Khoribam
9. Mayangningthoumayum Shajoubamayum
10. Mayagningthoumayum Panjikhanbam
11. Mayanglambam Apanba Fengbam

12. Moiranghanbam
13. Moifengbam
14. Nukram Anoubam
15. Ningthoujam Aribam
16. Ningthoujam Tekhaolambukhanbam
17. Sharungbam
18. Shamchetshabam
19. Thangjam Apanba Fengbam
20. Thangjam Ningthounaihanjabamayum
21. Taotham Fishaba Shammikmayum
22. Uyungbam
23. Watham.

7. Mayang Tekhaolon: This chapter constitutes the main chapter of the literature 'Nongchup Haram'. What is available from this chapter is that migration of people from 'Tekhal' (Assam) began since the reign of king Thawanthaba (A.D. 1195-1231). And the record continues till the reign of king Gambir Singh (A.D. 1825-34). In total 193 persons migrated from Assam and settled in Manipur during this period. All these persons were accommodated in Meitei society by enrolling them in 72 new *Yumnaks* and in 28 original Yumnaks. Four persons during the reign of king Thawanthaba (A.D. 1195-1231). Seven persons during Thangbilanthaba (A.D. 1302-1324), seven persons during Kongyamba (A.D. 1324-1335), 20 persons during Chingurembi Khonglup, 13 persons during Ningthoukhomba (A.D. 1432-1467), 33 persons during king Khagembat (A.D. 1597-1652), five persons during Paikhomba (A.D. 1666-1697), and only two persons during the reign of king Gambhir Singh - migrated from 'Tekhao' and settled in Manipur.

The new 72 *Yumnaks* are as follows:-

1. Anoubam

2. Ashangbam/Ashangwangbam
3. Achanbam
4. Chiyam
5. Chingsubam
6. Dhobiyupanbam
7. Dhobiwatham
8. Dhobihuimanmayum
9. Dhobamayum
10. Dhobaoinam
11. Dhobayangoijam
12. Dhobatanjabam
13. Dhobamongbijam
14. Dhoba Aheibam
15. Dhoba Moichem
16. Dhoba Nongthonbam
17. Dhobathokchom
18. Fishabam/Fijam
19. Fishaba Khullakpam
20. Hautongbam
21. Hidakshungbam
22. Heirungbam/Yirungbam
23. Katem
24. Keisham Yumbirambam
25. Kaklenpaibam
26. Kapocham/Kabajam
27. Khongleimayum
28. Kharibam
29. Keitongbam
30. Khomamayum
31. Khullakpam/Yogimayum

32. Kioniya Thangjam
33. Khongbantabam
34. Laimucham/Leimajam
35. Lambalmayum
36. Mukakmayum
37. Mayang Aribam
38. Mayangchangbam
39. Moibungkhongbam
40. Ngairangpam
41. Naharakpam
42. Nukram
43. Napitmayum
44. Napetmayum
45. Ningthoujam Fundreimayum
46. Napet-hanjabamayum
47. Napet-hidangmayum
48. Namshatakpam
49. Oinam Yendushangbam
50. Pakhanglakpam
51. Pukhrihongbam
52. Pepam
53. Pamchoupam
54. Pechimayum
55. Perekhongbam
56. Rang-gadasmayum
57. Shangaiproukhullakpam
58. Sanasam
59. Sanakhonpam
60. Shanjenbam
61. Shallungfam

62. Sombem
63. Shabaltongbam
64. Shenyeibam
65. Tayenjam
66. Thangjam Lamleirakpam
67. Takhelchangbam
68. Tarangbam
69. Yupingpam
70. Yammingkheipam
71. Yupanpam
72. Yogimayum.

Twenty-eight original *Yumnaks* are:

1. Arambam
2. Achoibam
3. Ayekpam
4. Arubam
5. Chomchalbam
6. Fijam
7. Heikrujam
8. Irengbam
9. Konsam
10. Kiyam
11. Khaidem
12. Laitonjam
13. Maisanam
14. Mayanglambam
15. Moirangmayum
16. Moirangthem
17. Ngathem
18. Ningthoujam

19. Shagolshem
20. Shaikhom
22. Shatpam
23. Shanjiram
24. Thoudam
25. Thangjam
26. Waikhom
27. Wayenbam
28. Yambem.

F. ADDITION OF *YUMNAKS* FROM THE WEST (MEITEI BAMONS)

The Meitei Bamons (the Brahmans) migrated to Manipur in different periods of history which began as early as during the reign of king Kiyamba (A.D. 1467-1508). *Yumnaks* were also given to them considering their ancestral home, their place of settlement in Manipur and their occupation, etc. They were admitted to different *Yumnaks* and they numbered as many as 67; however, they were allowed to retain their respective *gotras*. Their *Yumnaks* are arranged in alphabetical order in the following way. This is followed by the meaning of their Yumnaks:

1. Adhikarimayum
2. Adhikarimayum Anoubam
3. Anoubam Adhikarimayum
4. Anoubam (1)
5. Anoubam (2)
6. Anoubam (3)
7. Aribam Tampaklailatpam
8. Aribam Bishnulatpam
9. Aribam (Shagol-lailatpam)
10. Acharjyamayum

11. Bachaspatimayum
12. Bachampatimayum
13. Bagindramayum
14. Bishnulatpam
15. Brajamayum
16. Brajabashimayum
17. Brahmacharimayum
18. Brahmacharimayum Anoubam
19. Choudhurimayum
20. Dhyandsamayum
21. Furailatpam
22. Gotimayum
23. Gurumayum
24. Gurumayum Angom Lailatpam
25. Guru Aribam
26. Guru Aribam Mayum
27. Gopal Hanjaba Mayum
28. Gosai Mayum
29. Hangoibam
30. Hanjabam
31. Hanjaba Chandrashyam mayum
32. Hajarimayum
33. Hidangmayum – (1)
34. Hidangmayum – (2)
35. Heikaksimayum
36. Kakchingtabam
37. Kanoujimayum
38. Kulinmayum
39. Kongbalailatpam
40. Laipubam

41. Laimayum
42. Laimayum (Anoubam)
43. Lakpam
44. Leikhunchangbam
45. Leihaothabam
46. Loubuktongbam
47. Mathurabashimayum
48. Manoharmayum
49. Mistrimayum
50. Mangkharmayum
51. Pandamayum
52. Pitambar Cheithaba Mayum
53. Radhakundabashimayum
54. Sanglakpam
55. Sanjukimayum
56. Shyamtanumayum
57. Sitarammayum
58. Shijagurumayum (1)
59. Shijagurumayum (2)
60. Shreemayum
61. Takhenchangbam
62. Tinkhakmayum
63. Thongkhatabam
64. Vanchiramayum
65. Waba Hanjaba Mayum
66. Warilibam Waribam
67. Yangkangmayum.

Background of their *Yumnaks* (Lineages)

1. *Kakchingtabam* – This Brahman settled first at a place named Kakching. So, the name of his lineage was given from his place of settlement.

2. *Kanoujimayum* – This was given considering the birth place of this Pukok (progenitor) and his birth place was Kanouj.
3. *Kulinmayum* – The forefathers of this person belonged to upper caste i.e. Kulin. So, the above name was given to his descendants.
4. *Kongbrailatpam* – When migrating to Manipur this Pukok came from the direction of Kongba river. So, the above name to his lineage.
5. *Gotimayum* – This was given from the service of the person to king Garibniwaj who accompanied the prince on the journey to Ganga.
6. *Gurumayum* – This Brahman served as a preceptor of king Chingthangkhomba (Bheigachandra, 1763-98). Hence the above name to his lineage or descendants.
7. *Gurumayum Angom Lailatpam* – This person was a preceptor of Angom clan as well as he served the Angom deity. So, the above name to his lineage.
8. *Guru Aribam* – Brindaban was the name of this Pukok. He also served king Charairongba as preceptor who chanted hymns on Hari. So, the name to his lineage.
9. *Guru Aribam Mayum* – This name was given to the Brahman who acted as a preceptor of king Charairongba.
10. *Gopal Hanjaba Mayum* – This lineage is found missing. So, also the circumstance leading to the name.
11. *Gosai Mayum* – This was given in honour of the Pukok's original title which was Goswami.
12. *Choudhurimayum* – This was given in honour of the Pukok's original title which was Choudhury.
13. *Takhenchangbam* – This was given considering his first place of arrival in Manipur i.e.Takhenkhong.

14. *Tinkhakmayum* – This person might be hairy like the insect 'Tinkhak'. So, the name might be given as a disgust of the person's appearance or character.
15. *Thongkhatabam* – This was given considering his place of settlement in Manipur. He settled near the Singjamei bridge, (Singjamei Thong).
16. *Dhayandasmayum* – This name was given considering the character of the person who was modest and meek.
17. *Pandamayum* – This Brahman arrived during the reign of king Kiyamba (A.D. 1467-1508). The above name was derived from his original title 'Panda'. But this had been merged to the Shagei (lineage) Choudhurimayum either during the reign of King Chandrakirti (A.D. 1850-1886) when the Puya "Bamongi Meihoubarol" (Origin, Tradition etc. of Bamon) was written or before that.
18. *Pitambar Cheithaba Mayum* – Meaning of this lineage is not found.
19. *Furailaptam* – This was given from his friendship with the king of Pong (Shan).
20. *Bachaspati Mayum* – This was given in honour of the post of Bachaspati held by the Pukok.
21. *Bachampatimayum* – This was derived from the "Ba" sound which was the beginning of the name of the Brahaman.
22. *Bagindramayum* – Meaning of this Yumnak (lineage) is not found.
23. *Bishnulatpam* – Meaning is not found but the name reveals that the Brahman was a worshipper of Bishnu.
24. *Vanchiramayum* – Meaning of this Yumnak is also not found. It is also mentioned that the descendants of this Yumnak is not traceable anywhere.

25. *Brajamayum* – This was given considering the birth place of the Brahman which is mentioned as Braja.
26. *Brajabashimayum* – This name was derived from the birth place of the Brahman which was Braja-brindaband.
27. *Brahmacharimayum* - This Brahman was a *Brahmachari*. And hence the name to his lineage.
28. *Brahmacharimayum Ancubam* – This Brahmachari was rather a new-comer to Manipur. So, the above name was given to his lineage.
29. *Mathurabashimayum* – This was derived from the birth place of the Brahman which was Mathura.
30. *Manoharmayum* – This was derived from the name of the Pukok who was Manoharthakur.
31. *Mistrimayum* – This has been merged to Choudhurymayum.
32. *Mangkharmayum* – This was derived from the name of the Pukok who was Mangkhar.
33. *Adhikarimayum* – This Brahman, after his settlement in Manipur, took part in the judicial administration. From this the above name was given to his lineage.
34. *Adhikarimayum Anoubam* – This was given in honour of the post of Adhikari held by the Brahman in Manipur.
35. *Anoubam Adhikarimayum* – The Pukok was a new-comer. But he used the previous lineage Adhikarimayum. In order to make a distinction the word Anouba was added as prefix.
36. *Anoubam* (1) – This Brahman arrived Manipur during the reign of king Pamheiba (A.D. 1709-1748). He was considered as new-comer and hence the name to his lineage. (Anouba = New).

37. *Anoubam* (2) – He came to Manipur during the reign of king Chinglen Nongdren Khomba (A.D. 1825-1834).
38. *Anoubam* (3) – He came to Manipur during the reign of king Gambhir Singh (A.D. 1825-1834).
39. *Aribam Tampaklailatpam* – This Brahman was a worshipper of Tampaklai i.e. Brindabanchandra, Shree Krishna. So, from this the above name was given to his lineage.
40. *Aribam Bishnulatpam* – This Brahman arrived Manipur during the reign of king Khagemba (A.D. 1597-1652). But the meaning of his Yumnak is not found.
41. *Aribam (Shagol Lailatpam)* – This Brahamn arrived Manipur during the reign of king Garibniwaj (A.D. 1708-1748). The above name was given to his lineage because he was a new-comer.
42. *Acharjyamayum* – This was given from the duty of the Pukok who performed 'Puja' for the king.
43. *Yanggangmayum* – This Pukok possessed a lean and thin body. So, he was known as Yanggangba (a thin body) and hence the above name to his lineage. This Brahman settled near the Kongba river. So, later on, from his place of settlement his Yumnak was changed into Kongbrailatpam.
44. *Radhakundabashiyum* – This was derived from the original place of the Pukok which was Radhadkunda.
45. *Laipubam* – This Pukok arrived Manipur during the reign of king Charairongba (A.D. 1689-1709) accompanying a statue of 'Jaganath'. So, from this the above name was given to his lineage.
46. *Laimayum* – This Brahman died as an enlightened person. So, the above name to his lineage in consideration of his personal character.

47. *Laimayum Anoubam* – This Pukok arrived Manipur later during the reign of Beigyachandra (A.D. 1763-1798). His original place was Braja. Since he was a new-comer, so, the above name to his lineage.
48. *Lakpam* – This was given in honour of the post of Lakpa held by the Brahman.
49. *Leikhunchangbam* – This was given from the personal nature of the Pukok who always remained silent and remained aloof from the occasions of his vicinity.
50. *Loubuktongbam* – At the time of his arrival in Manipur this Pukok settled at a rice field (Loubuk). From this the above name was given to his lineage.
51. *Leihaothabam* – This Brahman offered 'Leihao' (a flower with a sweet smell) to the king. From this the name was given to his lineage.
52. *Waba Hanjaba Mayum* – Meaning of this Yumnak is not found. But he came during the reign of king Bheigyachandra (A.D. 1769-1798).
53. *Warilibam Waribam* – This was given in honour of the post held by the Pukok. He was 'Sanglakpa' of Govindaji temple.
54. *Sanglakpam* – This was given in honour of the post held by the Pukok. He was 'Sanglakpa' of Govindaji temple.
55. *Sanjukimayum* – This Brahman arrived Manipur as a 'Sannayasi Yogi', but he married a Meitei woman and became a Sangshogi (a married Shadhu). And hence the above name to his lineage from this occasion. But later on this Yumnak was merged to other Yumnaks.
56. *Shyamtanumayum* – This Brahman worshipped 'Ganesh'. So, from this the above name to his lineage.

57. *Sitaramammayum* – Meaning of this Yumnak is not found.
58. *Shijagurumayum* (1) – This Pukok served king Kiyamba (A.D. 1467-1508) and queen Gomati as their preceptor. And hence the name to his lineage.
59. *Shijagurumayum* (2) – This Pukok arrived later during the reign of king Khagemba (A.D. 1597-1652). So, his lineage was known as Shijagurumayum second.
60. *Shreemayum* – This was derived from the name of the Pukok who was Shreeramdhar Chatterjee.
61. *Hangoibam* – This was given from the nature of the Pukok who used to take bath many times a day like a frog lives in water.
62. *Hanjabam* – This was also given in honour of the post held by the Pukok who was 'Hanjaba' of 'Brahma Shabha'.
63. *Hanjabam Chandrashyammayum* – This was also given in honour of the post held by the Pukok whose name was Chandrashyam. The post held by him was 'Hanjaba' of 'Brahma Shabha'.
64. *Hajarimayum* – This was given considering that the Pukok came to Manipur leading one thousand (1000) persons or he was the commander of 1000 soldiers.
65. *Hidangmayum* (1) – This was given in honour of the post held by the Pukok who was 'Hidang' of "Shree Gobindajee temple".
66. *Hidangmayum* (2) – This Pukok arrived during the reign of king Garibniwaj (A.D. 1709-1748). He was a late comer but was accommodated in Meitei Bamon by enrolling in Hidangmayum second.
67. *Heikaksimayum* – This was given in consideration of their first place of settlement in Manipur which was Heikaksi.

G. ADDITION OF *YUMNAKS* FROM THE WEST (MEITEI PANGALS: THE MANIPURI MUSLIMS)

Shageis were also given to Meitei Pangals (Manipuri Muslims) who settled mostly during the reign of king Khagemba (A.D. 1597-1652). 'Pangal' is a corrupt word of Bengal whom the Meiteis considered that the Muslims came from Bengal. Around 61 Shageis which were given to the Meiteis Pangals (some of which are original Shageis) were based on the occupation, post and place of settlement in Manipur, etc.

The following are the *Yumnaks* (lineage) of Meitei Pangals which are arranged in alphabetical order. This is followed by the background of their Yumnaks:

1. Aribam
2. Ayekpam
3. Bogimayum
4. Basimayum
5. Chesam
6. Dolaipabam
7. Fisabam
8. Firingji Mayum
9. Hidakingkhol
10. Heikha Mayum
11. Heipok Mayum
12. Hawai Engkhol
13. Ipham
14. Kontha Mayum
15. Keikhongta
16. Kaji Khut
17. Keithel Engkhol
18. Khullakpam

19. Khutheibam
20. Korimayum
21. Keinoumayum
22. Komolmayum
23. Luplakpam
24. Loupanmayum
25. Labuk tongbam
26. Lairikyengbam
27. Leishangkhong
28. Longjaimayum
29. Makakmayum Amuba
30. Manjormayum
31. Meraimayum
32. Moijing
33. Maibam
34. Moinam
35. Mayangmayum Anouba
36. Musara
37. Mansam
38. Makakmayum Angouba
39. Mayangmayum (Ariba)
40. Malsam
41. Nongsayaibam
42. Oinam
43. Phundreimayum
44. Phusam
45. Pukhrimayum
46. Shakakpam
47. Sangomsumbam
48. Sairem

49. Sajoubam
50. Singgakhongbam
51. Thangjam
52. Tampakmayum
53. Taothongmayum
54. Thoubalmayum
55. Thongkhongmayum
56. Urepmayum
57. Vukramayum
58. Wangmayum
59. Yumkham
60. Yumkhaibam
61. Yangkhubam.

Backgorund of their *Yumnaks* (Lineages)

1. *Luplakpam* – This was given in consideration of the post held by the Pukok (progenitor) which was Lupalakpa.
2. *Ayekpam* – This was given in praise of the artistic talent of the person who was a master painter and sculpter.
3. *Loupanmayum* – This person was a cultivator of the king. So, from his duty to the king the above name was given to his offsprings.
4. *Yumkham* – This person pacified the quarrel between two brothers who wanted to separate one from the other. From this incident the above name was given to his offsprings.
5. *Vukramayum* – This was derived from their original surname Vukra. With the addition of the 'Mayum' it became a lineage of Meitei Pangal.

6. *Makakmayum (Angouba and Amuba)* – During the reign of king Paikhomba (A.D. 1666-1697) some Muslims led by two brothers (Sunar Ful and Lukhiya Ful) from a place known as Makak came to settle in Manipur. Taking the cue from the place of their origin 'Makak' they were given the above lineage. However, the two brothers separated from one other and became separate lineages. Makakmayum Angouba was given to the elder brother from his fair complexion and Makakmayum Amuba to the younger brother from his shadowy complexion.
7. *Kontha Mayum* – This Pukok (progenitor) migrated to Manipur during the reign of king Khunjaoba (A.D. 1652-1666) and was settled at a place named Kontha to guard the royal granary (*Kei*). From their place of settlement their lineage was given.
8. *Labuktongbam* – This person reached Manipur in 1688 A.D. along with his companions and was given settlement in a rice field which in Manipuri is 'Labuk'. So, his lineage was given this name from his place of settlement.
9. *Fisabam* – This was given considering the occupation of the Pukok who was a weaver. This lineage was detached from the previous lineage 'Khullakpam'.
10. *Keikhongta* – This was given to the group of Muslims who reached Manipur in A.D. 1609 and was settled at a place named Keikhu Keikhong. They were also known as Keikhong Tabam.
11. *Hidakingkhol* – This person introduced the garden of tobacco plants in Manipur. Tobacco is known as "Hidak Mana" in Manipuri and hence the above lineage to his descendents.
12. *Manjormayum* – It was detached from the original lineage Ipham. This was given in honour of the post held by the person who was a Major.

13. *Kaji Khut* – This was also detached from the lineage Ipham. And it was given in honour of the post held by the person who was a Kaji and his descendents came to be known as Kaji Khut.
14. *Mayangmayum (Anouba/Ariba)* – They were late-comers and came during Gambhir Singh (A.D. 1825-1834) and Chandrakirti. The earlier Muslims were treated as Meitei Muslims (Meitei Pangal) but the late comers were treated as Mayang Pangal (Muslim foreigner or Pangal Foreigner). Those Muslims who came during Maharaj Gambhir Singh were given Mayangmayum Ariba (old) and those who came during the reign of Chandrakirti (A.D. 1850-1886) was given Mayangmayum Anouba (new).
15. *Firingji Mayum* – Their original lineage was Nong shayaibam. During the reign of Gambhir Singh (A.D. 1825-1834) three Britishers were visiting Manipur. This Pukok accompanied the Britishers. And from this his descendents came to be known as Firingji Mayum.
16. *Lairikyengbam* – The ancestor of this Pukok was Hindu and known as Lairik Yengbam (Scribe). Later he was converted into Islam but he accompanied his original surname. And hence his descendents came to be known as 'Lairikyengbam'.
17. *Heikha Mayum* – This was given in consideration of the duty of the person who looked after the royal orchard. This was shortened from Heikhong Mayum to Heikha Mayum.
18. *Shakakpam* – This was given in consideration of the occupation of the person who was a butcher. He was one of the soldiers who were captured by king Khagemba in A.D. 1606.
19. *Malsam* – This was also given considering the occupation of the Pukok (progenitor) who was

specialized in making Mals (goods or furniture). This was a short form of Malsaba Mayum or Malsapam.

20. *Thangjam / Thangcham* – Besides being a solider this person possessed the art of blacksmith after his settlement in Manipur. And hence the above name to his descendents.
21. *Tampakmayum* – This person was appointed as 'Tampakyim Nai' of queen Nongthilchaibi of king Charairongba (A.D. 1697-1709). Now this lineage has merged into Khullakpam.
22. *Taothongmayum* – This was given in consideration of their place of settlement. They were the group who settled for the first time at Taothong.
23. *Keithel Engkhol* – The circumstance leading to the naming of this lineage is under investigation. However, a study from the words reveals that it was a garden located in the vicinity of a market. The person might have settled first at this place.
24. *Heipok Mayum* – This was given considering their place of settlement. He was the first Meitei Pangal who settled at a place named Heipokching.
25. *Ipham* – This person lived in a garden of thatch. From his place of settlement the name was given to him by King Khagemba (A.D. 1597-1652).
26. *Khullakpam* – This Pukok was the descendent of Muhammad Sani, the General of the invading Moghul army. He was defeated by the Manipur forces at the Yangoi Karong battle. Khagemba appointed him Khullakpa (Chief) of all the Muslim *Yumnaks* in Manipur. And hence the name.
27. *Khutheibam* – This person was an artisan. So, from his skill king Khagemba gave him the above name to his lineage.

28. *Sangomsumbam* – This person offered milk to king Khagemba as tribute. From this king Khagemba gave him the above name.
29. *Meraimayum* – This Pukok was a descendent of Mir Sahib. From this the above name was given to his lineage by King Charairongba (A.D. 1697-1709).
30. *Yumkhaibam* – This Pukok separated from their brothers and established his own family. From this king Khagemba gave him the above name to his lineage.
31. *Korimayum* – This Pukok offered a dolai (palanquin) covered with copper to king Khagemba. From this king Khagemba gave him the above name.
32. *Aribam* – These persons might have entered Manipur without the notice of the king before the reign of king Khagemba. When king Khagemba gave *Yumnaks* (lineage) to Muslims they were treated as old settlers. From this the above name was given to them by king Khagemba in order to differentiate them from the new Muslim settlers.
33. *Hawai Engkhol* – This Pukok lived at the king's pulse garden. From this the name was given by king Khagemba considering his place of settlement.
34. *Sairem* – This person was the descendent of a Sairem woman who married a Muslim. So, the Sairem lineage was given to him by king Khagemba.
35. *Moijing* – This person settled at the foot of Moijing hill at Thoubal. So, from his place of settlement the above name was given by king Khagemba.
36. *Leisangkhong* – This was also given by king Khagemba considering his place of settlement who lived at Leisangkhong (Wangoi).
37. *Sajoubam* – This was given by king Khagemba considering the physique of the person who was well-built.

38. *Urupmayum* – This was also named by king Khagemba considering his place of settlement who lived at Urup (a village at the south-east periphery of Imphal).
39. *Maibam* – The ancestor of this person was a Maiba (medical practitioner). So, considering the profession of his ancestor the above name was given to his lineage by king Khagemba.
40. *Thoübalmayum* – This was given by king Khagemba considering his place of settlement who lived on the bank of Thoubal river.
41. *Moinam* – The ancestor of this person offered a Moina (a bird) to king Khagemba. From this Khagemba gave him the above name.
42. *Chesam* – This was given by king Khagemba from the occupation of the person who was a paper maker.
43. *Musara* – This was given by king Khagemba considering his original place of settlement, i.e. Musara Barimula.
44. *Phundreimayum* – This person was an artisan and he prepared Phundrei – a technology used by carpenters. From this king Khagemba gave him the above name to his lineage.
45. *Longjaimayum* – This was given by king Marjit (A.D. 1813-1819) considering his place of settlement who lived at Longjai.
46. *Bogimayum* – This person caught an Urok (Egrets) and offered it to king Khagemba. In Hindustani an Egrets is known by the name 'Bagala'. From this incident king Khagemba gave him the above name to his lineage.
47. *Thongkhongmayum* – This was given by king Khagemba considering his occupation who was a carpenter, and he prepared door frames.

48. *Wangmayum* – This person settled at the foot of a tree, named Wang. And hence the name to his lineage by king Khagemba.
49. *Nongsayaibam* – This name was given by king Khagemba considering the nature of this person who always sat in the Sun.
50. *Singakhongbam* – This person was a player of the musical instrument, Pere Singa. From this king Khagemba gave him the above name.
51. *Mansam* – This person was a descendent of a wrestler. This was given by king Khagemba.
52. *Keinoumayum* – This was also given by king Khagemba considering his place of settlement who lived at Keinou (a village in Bishnupur district. Manipur).
53. *Komolmayum* – This person was the descendent of a Konok woman who married a Muslim. From this king Khagemba gave him the above name.
54. *Basimayum* – This person was a musician who played on flute. From this king Khagemba gave him the name to his lineage.
55. *Phusam* – This was given by king Khagemba from the occupation of the person who was a potter.
56. *Yangkhubam* – The original name of this person was Yanglem Khamba who converted to Islam during the reign of king Charairongba. From this background the above name was given by king Charairongba (A.D. 1697-1709).
57. *Pukhrimayum* – This was given by king Khagemba considering his duty in the palace who guarded the royal tank.
58. *Dolaipabam* – This person served at the Dolaipaba Loisang of king Khagemba. And hence the name to his lineage from his service. Dolaipaba literally means orderly.

59. *Oinam* – This person was the descendant of a man of Oinam Sagei (lineage), who turned Muslim. So, king Chandrakirti (A.D. 1850-1886) gave the name considering his original lineage.

H. TRADITIONAL SOCIAL DIVISION OF LABOUR THROUGH THE ASSIGNMENT OF PARTICULAR TRADE TO PARTICULAR *YUMNAK*

I. Assigning of responsibilities to certain *Yumnaks* (lineages) to carry out different jobs in the royal factories, in the royal household activities, in performing rituals to traditional gods and deities, and in prayer service to the sylvan deities and in running the royal office etc., began since the reign of king Naothingkhong (A.D. 663-763). But it was from the reign of king Loyyamba (A.D. 1074-1122) that this practice became an established tradition which even today, even after facing many vicissitudes in history of Manipur, the tradition leaves its vestiges; though in traces, in the Meitei society.

1. Following is the list of lineages who were given the task of weaving the following particular royal clothes:

1. Thingkucham was to weave Mungfi.
2. Lairellakpam was to weave Laifi.
3. Kwaswam was to weave Wana katangfi.
4. Chakpa Thiyam was to weave Laifi tongkap.
5. Chakpalampam was to weave Firel.
6. Kongpacham was to weave Langtomfi.
7. Thongkapam was to weave Yairongfi.
8. Khumallambam was to weave Chanifi.
9. Haokhom was to weave Tongkapfi.
10. Laikhrampam was to weave Sharongfi.
11. Shalchiram was to weave Leirum.

12. Wahengbam was to weave Dolai Kupfi.
13. Kabacham was to weave Dolai Thanafi.
14. Apucham was to weave Firoifi.
15. Haodeijam was to weave Heikoy-fi.
16. Thoitingcham was to weave Singkhal-fi.
17. Thongpam was to weave Laiyek-fi.
18. Kongbam was to weave Prum-fi.
19. Chingngakhalpam was to weave Fakang-fi.
20. Thoutam was to weave Tarau-fi.
21. Thinpam was to weave Pumthit-fi.
22. Taipangcham was to weave Fimu Yekpasung-fi.
23. Yumlenpam was to weave Nong-fi.
24. Wokthiyampam was to weave Khunung Musam-fi.
25. Khoirisumbam was to weave Khunung Chumkhan-fi.
26. Yumnaksangpam Yumnam was to weave Chingkhong- fi Fimu.
27. Khoisanam was to weave Fimu Lal-fi.
28. Singkhangbam was to weave Khunung Mathang-fi.
29. Chingkhwampam was to weave Karon fi fingang.
30. Wangpacham was to weave Sangnu Langmu-fi.
31. Thangkangshapam was to weave Thangli, Shakaram.
32. Ahongshangbam was to weave Khutsu Likhong-fi.
33. Naotam along with Fishaba Yangnu, Fishaba Heisu Naha and Fishaba Khoiriyan was to weave Ningthou-fi.

II. Following is the list of lineages who were given the task to dye clothes in different colours:

1. Langshangbam Akangchampam was to dye Leirel Khoipaklei (i.e. purple).
2. Langshangbam Chingkhwampam was to dye Chingsang Mayumlei (i.e. violet). The dye is

extracted from the plant Chingshang Muyumlei and is mostly grown in the hills, and hence the name is given with the prefix Chingshang. (Chingshang = hill range).

3. Langshangbam Yiroibam was to dye Talla Ureirom Makong Meiri Malba (i.e. deep red blood). The traditional women's costume 'Fige Fanek' is dyed with this colour.
4. Langshangbam Fishaba Nganba Naha is to dye Loirang Thaochu Leipee (i.e. light red). This Loirang Thaochu Leipee is prepared out of the combination of the three colours, e.g. red, white and black in certain proportion.
5. Langshangbam Khulmanthempam was to dye Hikok Nanau Lei (i.e. light blue).
6. Langshangbam Khumukcham was to dye Kumlang Kumpal Lei (i.e. deep black). This colour is prepared from the leaves of kum plant. Kum (Bot. *Strobilanthes flaccidifolius*)
7. Langshangbam Yipushangbam was to dye Chingya Napu Lei (i.e. light yellow) and Taoching Heitroi Lei. Heitroi (Bot. *Flocourtia cataphracta*)
8. Langshangbam Wasiyampam was to dye Wana Katang Manba Shanglen Yichu Lei, (i.e. olive green). It is like the colour of bamboo trees.

III. King Loyyamba fixed responsibilities to the following lineages to look after the following male and female deities:

1. Hakwalthem was to look after Loiyamba (M). (M for male deity).
2. Heirom was to look after Meireima (F). (F for female deity).
3. Irom was to look after Khamlangba (M).

4. Soiyam was to look after Wushoi.
5. Hidam was to look after Yikhei.
6. Shoirenshangbam was to look after Sararen (M).
7. Ningolbam was to look after Wangkol
8. Sarangthem and Leishangthem was to look after Lammabi.
9. Sharotkhaibam was to look after Fou-oibi (F).
10. Potshangbam was to look after Sanglangmei.
11. Moireng Pukhrambam was to look after Kuchu.
12. Ayam Puroicham was to look after Puroi Leima (F).
13. Shoupam was to look after Mawao Leima (F).
14. Heisanam was to look after Panthoibee (F).
15. Khosinam was to look after Petangnga (F).
16. Hoitolkokpam was to look after Hoitol Lairemma (F).
17. Taibangcham was to look after Laikhurembi (F).
18. Konthoucham was to look after Huimureima (F).
19. Ashangbam was to look after Leinao Tabi (F).
20. Chingkhwam was to look after Nungthel Leima (F).
21. Arambam was to look after Shoubon Leima (F).
22. Yenkhom Fishabam was to look after Awangba (M).
23. Luwangshangbam was to look after Luwang Ching.
24. Sinam Laishangbam was to look after Laiyingthouhanba (M).
25. Moirangthem Puthem was to look after Puthiba (M).
26. Mangshatabam was to look after Pureiromba (M).
27. Langmaithem was to look after Tenlongba (M).
28. Yarangyalpam was to look after Thongak.
29. Nakalbam was to look after Chingkol Ningthou (M).
30. Khuraicham was to look after Chingbal Leima (F).

31. Meiyengbam was to look after Yaoreibee (F).
32. Leishangthem was to look after Koubaren (M).
33. Yelkhom was to look after Chakhapa (F).
34. Ningthoujam was to look after Numit Leima (F).
35. Pukalbam was to look after Kouparu (M).
36. Chenglei Laishangbam was to lock after Maraching (M).
37. Moirangthem was to look after Moirang Faktom Ariba (M).
38. Kangpucham was to look after Hongnem Yoikhunjau (M).
39. Chingakhalbam was to look after Chinga.
40. Longcham Feiroicham was to look after Langching (F).
41. Tekcham was to look after Langkol.
42. Langmai Yummatheng was to look after Langmaiching.
43. Ningthoujam was to look after Chingnga Leima (F).
44. Heithou Khongtekcham was to look after Heipok.
45. Chingkhwapam was to look after Laiching Hiyangthou Leima. (F).
46. Thaopicham was to look after Yumchao Lairemma. (F).

IV. In continuation of fixing of duties to the *Yumnaks* (lineages) the following *Yumnaks* were assigned to perform a number duties in the palace which were related with rituals to the deities and other activities in the royal precinct:

1. Ashangbam was to wash the feet if the king.
2. Arambam was to take bath of the king.
3. Leirongcham was to collect flower for the king.
4. Toibicham was to blow the instrument "Tharaochi".

   Tharaochi:- This is a musical instrument made of brass and blown by mouth. It was used on some particular occasions; at the birth of a baby (son) of the king, on the ceremony 'Soraren Laoba" and on coronation ceremony. It was believed that the blowing of this instrument was heralding the heavenly deities and "Maikei Ngakpa" deities on the occasion taking place on earth.

5. Arupam was to perform the work on neat and clean.
6. Lourembam Nangdi Yumuchao Cheng Kap-O.
7. Shinaipa was to prepare "Leiren Leichao" for the queen.

   Leiren Leichao:- It is an ornament worn by the queen on the day of coronation of the king. This three pronged hair-dress was worn by the queen.
8. Konsapam was to prepare "Lollei Luthak".

   Lollei Luthak is also known as Kajenglei. It is a hair dress.
9. Aheipam was to cast a dish named "Nati".
10. Hishapa was to make long seat (made of wood).
11. Thangshapam was to make sword.
12. Feiroijam was to prepare "Laptrei". It is a device for carrying basket (containing fish) or prepared (cooked) food. It is usually kept in the kitchen hanging down from the roof upon the hearth.
13. Moichembam was to prepare necklace of conch.
14. Loukham was to ignite fire by using "Meiba".

    Maiba Chingba; it is a traditional method for igniting fire.
15. Moirangthem was to perform rites to the Umanglai (Sylvan deity) "Hiri Khongshang".
16. Maimuwam was to perform rites to "Maimu Tomshol". It is an ornament worn in the hair.
17. Taipangcham was to perform rites to the deity.
18. Maiba Thiyam was to supply firewood at the death of the king. He was also to take part in the cremation of the king.

19. Loushi Nahakpam was to ignite fire by using "Meiba".
20. Khunthoubam Nahakpam was also to ignite fire by using "Meiba".
21. Meihoubam was to prepare fire.
22. Meiphuwam was to accelerate the fire by blowing.
23. Naokal Sangpam was to look after the "Naopham" (placenta).
24. Apucham was to carry the "Naopham" (placenta).
25. Tokpam was to dig the earth.
26. Tokpuram Thangshabam was to raise the earth to a particular place.
27. Tourem was to supply reed for the king.
28. Naoroipam was to take care the children of the king.
29. Leishangthem was to be included in the advance party in the crematorium.
30. Pukyu Haopam was to arrange the drinks.
31. Wangkhem Longcham was to hold the weapon 'Long'.
32. Ngathem was to perform the rite "Ngami Kouba". Ngami Kouba is a rite to summon the fish.
33. Langkolcham was to attend the cremation.
34. Langtem was to throw a stick named "Lalchei".
35. Langkambam was to collect "Lalchei".
36. Thongpam Nangdi Thongka Thing-O.
37. Laitoncham was an informer and he was to inform the progress made by the advance party in the crematorium to the palace. Only then the corpse of the king was to transport to the crematorium.
38. Shingkhangpam was also included in the group who collected firewood for the cremation.

39. Atom was to perform rite to pacify the deity "Sharei Lai".
40. Yurungbam was to perform "Lal Hoiba".

    Lal Hoiba was included in the coronation ceremony. It was an imitation of pursuing the war captives.
41. Mayanglambam was to perform "Shami Kouba".

    Shami Kouba; it was a ritual performed when the king was to set out for a war.
42. Khumallampam was to look after "Shaya Kot".

    Shaya Kot; it is the place where the items to be offered to the deity is kept cautiously.
43. Langhipam was to prepare the trap.
44. Toumom was to flatten the reeds.
45. Haomukcham was to weave mat.
46. Shatokpam was to weave mat made of reed.
47. Khoirishumbam was to tie the umbilical cord of the boy.
48. Khoiriyanpam was to cut the umbilical cord.
49. Lairencham was to wash the clothes.
50. Thoupicham was to collect banana leaves.
51. Lisham was to make "lee" for the king.
52. Leishawonbam was to make pitcher.
53. Yelwam was to supply chicken for the king.
54. Ngamukappam was to handle the duck.
55. Khuyolthem was to supply goat.
56. Wokronbam was to supply pig.
57. Maiparampa was to perform "Yelkhong Tamba".

    Yelkhong Tamba is a ritual performed by sacrificing a chicken. It was believed that the chicken would carry away the ailment or unwanted fortune of the person.

58. Pongkhaicham was to perform "Sapei Yengba".

    Sapei Yengba: it is a ritual performed by dissecting a chicken or an animal. It was used to predict something by observing the position of heart or spleen of the chicken or of the animal.

59. Akuwampam Nangdi Singpao Tam-U, Uchek-Khol-Tao.

60. Maipam Aframpam was to ignite fire by using "Meiba".

61. Chapungpam was to feed the baby.

62. Ahongsangbam Nangdi Ahong Achao Tam-O.

63. Waleppam was to perform rite to bamboo.

64. Maipam was to perform "Chupshaba".

    "Chupshaba"; it was a ritual performed to unnatural death so as not to re-occur it in the family or in the lineage.

65. Chakfiyam was to cultivate "Chakfi Laisham.

    Chakfi Laisham; it is a hair like plant, used in the rites to deities.

66. Ngang-ngom was to perform "Konyai Hulba".

    Konyai Hulba:- The pieces of gold and silver are included in the rituals of some deities. And the offering is done either at the beginning or at the end of the ritual. It is known as 'Konyai Hulba'.

67. Yelkokpam was to take part in the ritual and his function was to place the egg at the right of the rice.

68. Khumukcham was to control the 'Kei'.

    Kei; These were the persons who performed menial works in palace. Sometimes they were treated as slaves.

69. Ningthoucham was to worship the Umanglai "Kurek Haikhong Yaikhom".

70. Loichayangbam was to worship "chingfou".

71. Ayangpam was to mint coins.
72. Akaram was to prepare meat meant for cooking.
73. Pung-graicham was to drum the "Wanglen Pung" (the royal drum).
74. Lairelpam was to worship "Laikhul".

    A cave under the water is known as 'Laikhul' to the Manipuris.
75. Wakongthem was to worship the Umanglai "Waton Uton Wakalyai".
76. Akham was to shave the hair of the king.
77. Siyatpam was to worship the (mound) 'Pung'.
78. Sathokpam was to dissect the corps of the king.
79. Sharotkhaipam was to open the corpse.
80. Hayingthem was to remove fluids from the corpse.
81. Khaithem was to separate the limbs of the corpse.
82. Hakwanthem was to remove the maggots from the corpse.
83. Halnoibam was to finish the captured maggots.
84. Puroicham was to remove the brain of the corpse.
85. Luwongcham was to observe the skeleton.
86. Amakcham was to hold the bow and arrow.
87. Sharubam was to guard the skeleton.
88. Narumbam Nangdi Narum-O.
89. Khumurong was to make "Long".

    Long is a sieve made of bamboo strips. It is used in fishing as well as in sieving.
90. Luchambam was to wash the skull.
91. Mangsangpam was to guard the crematorium.
92. Wanglenbam was to beat the drum.
93. Kabrambam was to worship "Leishoupung".
94. Seram was to worship 'Ngautong'.

Ngautong; it is the cataract on eye. It was believed that it was caused by an evil spirit.

95. Shampaltaram was to worship the air.
96. Santham Nangdi was to worship Lamshal Latlo.
97. Shangngai Kappam was to beat the drum.
98. Thongkrampam was to worship "Ukrong".
99. Shoukrakpam was to made "Shafu Wanlong".
100. Kharipam was to serve liquor.
101. Leiyushungbam was to measure the liquor.
102. Ngaseppam was to prepare fish.

V. *Tampak Maibagi Mashin (Duties of Tampak Maiba)*: The *Maibas* (priests) belonging to different *Yumnaks* (lineages) were assigned to perform duties to a number of deities along with related rituals. The Maibas belonging to the following *Yumnaks* were fixed to perform the following duties and allied rituals:

1. Kiyampa is to worship 'Kiyam Lai' (Kiyam deity). It is believed that a particular skin disease is caused by evil spirit and named as Kiyam Lai. Illnesses were considered to be the handiwork of evil spirits.
2. Nampucham is to worship 'Nampucham' deity.
3. Asheibam is to sing the song 'Sana Lamwok'.

   Sana Lamwok is a hymn and this was used in the king's seeing off ceremony.
4. Ashem Ngakhakhoi is to sing 'Yakei Ishei'.

   Yakei is the song used in waking up the king often accompanied by 'Pena' – a musical instrument.
5. Khoinaicham is to worship the 'bee'.
6. Sanachirampam is to pull the 'bull'.
7. Paobam is to listen the foretelling of go at 'Paoda Hidel'.

Paoda Hidel is located at Kangla fort. He is to listen attentively the foretelling by god through a Maibee (priest) who is in trance at the ceremony 'Laimang Phamba'.

8. Famdom is to present 'Khongkang Khuda'.

   It is the site where 'Yot Khunet', 'Shel Khunet', is displayed and is such a place where the person who carries the deity is to step on it compulsorily.

9. Laishram is to worship 'Santhong'.
10. Haobicham is to sing song in the lanes.
11. Kampam is to worship 'Tokpa'.
12. Naokhongcham is to worship 'Khong' (drum).
13. Laltham is to sing 'Lalfa Ishei'.

    Lalfa Ishei is the song sung after capturing a wild prey.

14. Kharaijam is to take care of 'Kharaithong' deity.
15. Yimlempam is to worship water.
16. Chakpathiyam is to perform 'Mang-Changba'.

    Mang-Changba:- There was a tradition in which a priest who performs 'Mang-Changba' was to enquire anything to the deceased parents of a person in the dream of the priest. But this was to be held within a few days after the death. This lineage is also to perform 'Meipa Chingba'; this is a traditional technology for igniting a fire. A bamboo chip is pulled vigorously around a bamboo pole and near it dry substances are kept so as to fall the spark on it from the friction of the bamboo pole and chip.

17. Akhongbam is to play the music.
18. Nampam Nangdi Hiyang Koi Chong-O.
19. Heirangkhongjam is to perform 'Kongpa Chengkupshiba'.

20. Thilbam Nangdi Nakthillo.
21. Mutum is to worship 'Lalhampung'.
22. Thingnam is to worship 'Ukrong'.
23. Chingkangbam is to worship 'Chinganglen' (Chingaren).
24. Kharibam is to worship 'Hichakang'.

    Hichakang is the quarter where 'Hiyang-Hiren' (royal boat) is kept.
25. Laishom is to worship 'Mouse'.
26. Shingkom is to sing the hymn 'Langmairol'.
27. Thonggam is to sing the hymn 'Ahonglon'.
28. Shoraisham is to sing the hymn 'Khoichu Lam-Wok'.
29. Chantam is to sing the hymn 'Khongchinglon'.
30. Heisanam is to worship 'Fly'.
31. Thiyam is to worship 'Boat'.
32. Moirang Pukhrambam is to worship the deity 'Tilleng Kangleng'.
33. Apucham is to worship 'Pond'.
34. Nongpokpam is to worship 'cloud'.
35. Waikhom is to collect paddy husks.
36. Akoicham is to perform 'Mikolba'.

    Mikolba or Mikon-Thakonba is the ritual which is performed toward the end of 'Thaban Chongba' festival and 'Lai Haraoba' festival. It is also performed to a person who is in spell after drowning or from a fall in order to return his or her normalcy.
37. Hicham is to collect 'Nungkhong Nunglaobi'.

    This ceremony was performed in the event of a draught. Small pebbles were collected from the gorges of 'Nongmaiching' hill (it is located at some 18 to 20 km east of Imphal) and the rite was performed. There was a belief that rain will follow after this rite.

38. Sallam is to worship 'Langmaiching' (Nongmaiching). He is also to act as 'Tangkhul Sharam Pakhangpa'.

    In 'Lai Haraoba' festival there is a role for 'Tangkhul Shaba'- where Tangkhul is a tribe settling in Ukhrul district of Manipur. And this shows the cultural ties between the plain and hill people of Manipur.

39. Hidam is to prepare 'Sana Lifak'.

    Lifak is a mat made from cane and this is for royal use, and hence the name 'Sana Lifak'.

40. Heitham will perform royal wash and bath.

41. Laishangbam Melleppam is to guard the coronation hall.

42. Khamnam is to perform 'Khamnung Chayom Thaba'.

    It is a part of after-death ceremony and in this rice is offered for the death person at three places-at the courtyard (Khangelpham), beyond the gate and at the crematorium. It shows that the Meitei believes in life after death.

43. Shenshapam is to mould the 'Gong'.

VI. *Yumnak Mashin (Duties of Yumnak)*: Some of the *Yumnak* were assigned to perform the following duties:

1. Namaram is to worship the "Kasha Tel".

   Kasha Tel is kind of bow used in the rituals.

2. Panam Yangkokpam is to worship the "Panam Lai".
3. Pukhranpam is to worship the "Lollei".

   Lollei is a kind of head-gear. It is a crown made of gold and looks like the head of a shrimp. It is occasionally worn by the king in coronation ceremony, in Heikru Hidongba festival, etc.

4. Furitshabam is to perform the duty of stitching with a needle.
5. Putolcham was to carry the skeleton.
6. Sangtolcham was to perform the 'Luthetpa'.

   Luthetpa is a way of decorating the skeleton of the dead king with flowers, etc.
7. Thoudam Heibong Makhong Taba was to worship "Chingkhei Guru". He was to perform "Lai Ekouba" in the early morning.

   Chingkhei Guru; the rising sun in the early morning is known as "Chingkhei Guru".
8. Chingakhampam was to worship the "Chinga" hillock. He was also to guard this hillock 'Chinga'.
9. Lairellakpam was to worship the "Lightening".
10. Nongchelpam was to perform the ceremony "Nong Kappa".

    In some of the rituals shooting an arrow in the skyward is occasionally included which is called 'Nong Kappa'.
11. Moirangthem was to perform rituals on various occasions and to the deities.
12. Naorem was to worship the "Naoshong Fal".

    Naoshong Fal is a wooden seat especially meant for use at the point of delivery. It is meant for the royal family.

VII. There was an elderly women's office in the palace to help the administration. This office was staffed by women recruited from a number of *Yumnaks* (lineages). The woman officer in this office was known by the name "Niyaipi".

Angom was responsible for recruiting a woman from each of the following lineages viz., Kongpam, Yumlempam, Hitam, Hongnemshumbam, Chakparam and Chinkangpam.

Again Longcham was to recruit a woman from each of Luwongcham, Laillelakpam and Kharipam.

Besides, a woman from each of the following lineages were also recruited, namely:

1. Pukhranbam,
2. Khumanthem,
3. Mangshatabam,
4. Narengbam,
5. Meiyengpam,
6. Wahengbam,
7. Lailencham,
8. Yangampam,
9. Khuraicham,
10. Kiyam,
11. Laishram,
12. Haobam,
13. Ngangbam,
14. Loukham,
15. Pungkraicham,
17. Oinam, and
18. Puyam.

VIII. When a baby was born in the palace a number of persons were needed to carry out a number of jobs till the birth ceremony of the child was performed. A host of items were necessary from the very day of delivery till the birth ceremony. For this the king was not to bear the expenses but was to be supplied or made by some selected lineages. And those selected lineages and their bounden duties were as follows:

1. Nahakpam was to ignite fire by using "Meiba".
2. Meiyengbam was to take care of the fire.

3. Meikambam was to blow the fire.
4. Meithoubam was to inflame the fire.
5. Wanggolsangbam was to guard the "Wanggolsang".

   Wanggolsang was an annexe meant for delivery.
6. Nakalpam was to carry the "Naopham" (placenta)
7. Thaotem was to arrange the required banana leaves.
8. Lisham was to made the "Lee".

   Lee is an earthen pot meant for storing potable water.
9. Khwairakpam and Tenshubam was to make the "Sana Leefak".

   Leefak is a mat made of cane. The word 'Sana' is added as prefix so as to signify the mat for use in the palace.
10. Nahakpam and Khulhoubam was to make hanger for hanging cloths and other items.
11. Arubam was to remove the garbage. It was to burry the Naopham (placenta) also.
12. Ashangbam was to wash the face, leg and the limbs.

    The following items - a pot for use in washing, a pot for showering, a cloth, an earthern jar and a cloth for filtering water were also to be procured by Ashangbam.
13. Arambam was to bath the baby.

    Besides these a Khuchai (a pot made of bronze), a Khutei (a loin cloth) and a Phal (a wooden seat) was also to be supplied by Arambam.
14. Naoroipam was to nurse the baby for one month. If the baby was a girl that was to be nursed by a woman from Naoroipam. If the baby was a boy that was to be nursed by a man of this lineage.
15. Nakalpam was to wave the fan.

16. Shatokpam was to perform the ceremony "Chak-Umba".

    Chak-Umba it is a ceremony performed after five or seven months of the birth of the baby.

17. Toipicham was to play the instrument the "Tharaochi".
18. Yirupam was to collect earth from river bed for making earthen pots.
19. Naosham was to make the "Khoilen Thang".

    Khoilen Thang; it is a knife meant for cutting the umbilical cord.

20. Masum was to make 'Kolnafi' and 'Yannafi'.

    Kolnafi, Yannafi; these are clothes used in bringing up a baby. Kolnafi is the one used in carrying the baby at the back of the mother. And Yannafi is the one used in wrapping the baby.

21. Angomchalpam was to make necklace, bangle and 'Khutchup' (a toy worn in the wrist of the baby meant for kissing).
22. Aheipam was to make the 'Khuchai' (a pot made of bronze meant for keeping potable water) and the 'Tengkot' (a bowl).
23. Ayekpam was to make 'Naoshongfal', 'Khomyilfal' and 'Leitafal'. All these are seats made of wood meant for different purposes.

IX. Miscellaneous

1. The lineage Lisham was to collect earth from river bed. This earth was meant to make utensils for the palace. But this was accompanied with a ritual. The required implement in collecting earth and in performing the ritual was to be acquired by Lisham. The items included in the ritual are—two *'Famfi Leiyonfi Firak'* (a cloth), *Konyai* (metal), Khunet yot

(a piece of iron to be stepped on), *Khunet shen* (a coin to be stepped on), *Chafu Iwal* (utensils for cooking), Spoon, Tongs, *Yot shubi* (iron stand-three legged), *Shareng* (a fish), *Ngaten* (a fish), salt, chilli, banana leaf, vegetables, rice, flowers, sugarcane, banana, sweets, betelnut and leaf, *Leishang* (plant), *Leitou Tok* (a digging implement) and *Nahai Thang* (a ritualistic knife); all these were to be acquired by the lineage Lisham.

2. In collecting banana leaf also a ritual was necessary. And this was performed by the lineage "Thoutem". Besides, he was to supply the following items for supplying the banana leaves; Naheithang (a ritualistic knife), Laren Thanggon (a sickle for cutting banana leaves), a cloth for wrapping the banana leaves, 'Fimu khawol' (a kind of shirt), a bell, two cloths, sugarcane, fruits, banana, fruit having smell (odour), Konyai (gold and silver pieces).
3. The lineage Nahakpam was to collect both bamboo for "Meiba" and reeds for making mat. In both these cases also a ceremony was necessary. And this lineage was responsible for performing the ritual as well as the items required in the ritual.

The following item: Meibathang (a chopper), Sanggai (a long handed knife), Yot Khunet (iron piece to be stepped on), Shen Khunet (a coin to be stepped on), two broad clothes, sugarcane, fruits, banana, sweets, Konyai (gold and silver pieces), betelnut and leaf, and Leishang (a flower) are to be acquired by Nahakpam in collecting bamboo for making "Meiba".

Again the following items: Khunet Shen (a coin to be stepped on), Khunet Yot (an iron piece to be stepped on), Konyai (gold and silver pieces), sugarcane, fruits, banana, sweets, betel-nut and leaf, Leishang (a flower) and two broad clothes are to be acquired by Nahakpam in collecting reeds for making mat for royal use.

X. At the birth of a child in the palace some selected lineages were perform their duties beginning from the point the delivery till Chak-umba (rice feeding ceremony). Any attendant in the delivery should not be a widow.

At the point of delivery the lineage:

1. Khulthonpam was to dig the earth for burying the 'Naopham'.
2. The burying of Nopham was to be carried out by Arupam.
3. Ashangpam was to wash the face and leg of the baby.
4. Arampam was to bathe the baby.

The rice feeding ceremony (for royal baby) was held at the completion of three months. The rice was served by the lineage Shatokpam. In this Wangkolshangbam was to sweep the Wanggolshang. And Arambam was to sweep Chapoksang.

XI. *Puroi Leikoyba Mathou Yangkelbagi Mashin:* A tradition which came into force since the king of Naothingkhong (A.D. 663-763) was the involvement of a number of persons from different lineages in performing the burial of dead body of the king.

Beginning from mourning, making of coffin, etc, till the Secondary burial*, all these were executed by persons from different lineages. In this way the mourning was the duty of the two *Yumnaks* viz., Nakanpam and Pamkhaicham.

* Secondary burial; Before the advent of cremation the Meiteis performed Secondary Burial. The corpse of the person was removed from the ground after the completion of one year. The skeleton was washed thoroughly. After this the skeleton was decorated well with flowers, etc.; which is known as "Sharu-Leitengba". The ceremony ends when decorated skeleton was kept inside a big 'Kharung' (earthern jar) and once again buried in the ground. In the course of the ceremony "Yurangba" was also performed. Yurangba is the festivity after the burial which includes local liquor.

The coffin was made by Thongbam. The burial site was dug by Tokpam. The duty of Ayam was to offer rice at the crematorium. He was also to perform the rite "Mangthong Thingba". The banana leaves required in offering rice at the crematorium was to be supplied by Thaudeicham. Chinggangbam was responsible for collecting the necessary amount of firewood for use in the royal kitchen for the burial. A rite known as "Mangthong Hangba" was performed by Ayam after completing one year of burial. This was the rite used in extracting the corpse from the ground. The items included in the rite were, viz., a spade, Nahei Thang (a knife), Khunet yot (piece of iron meant to be stepped on), Khunet shel (coins meant to be stepped on), two broad cloths, rice, flowers, egg, gold and silver, etc.

The burial site was dug by Tokpam. Sathokpam was responsible for removing skeleton. The cleaning and removing of dirts was to be done by Siyatpam, the hair was combed by Akham. He was responsible for removing maggots from the corpse. Sharotkhaibam was to extract the skeleton from the corpse. Washing of the skeleton was the duty of Khoirom. However, most part of the skeleton was washed by the five lineages viz., Loitongbam, Thoitingcham, Longcham, Ahalthem, Akoicham. But the finishing touch was given by Amakcham. Washing was done by using 'Long' (a traditional sieve made of fine bamboo chips). This 'Long' was offered by a tribe known as "Tingshang". The collection of rotten flesh and dirts was the duty of Soukulakpam, Khoipam and Sampantoram. The dirts were collected in an earthern pitcher and buried in the ground. The above two lineages were responsible for making the pitcher. The cloth required for wrapping the thoroughly washed bones was made by Yimlenpam. Hanglem and Kolom performed 'Porom Thopthilba'. The thoroughly washed bones were dried in the sun for five days and buried on an auspicious day.

CONCLUSION

From this brief discussion what has brought to the picture is that the Meitei family that we see today is not a sudden creation of history. Its development is evolutionary in nature as we see in the emergence of Meitei identity. The birth, growth and development of Meitei family is coincident with birth and development of Meitei identity. The seed of Meitei identity which was sown early during the reign of king Sameirang (A.D. 518-568). But it took centuries to mature this identity and the same happened during the reign of king Nougda Lairen Pakhangba (A.D. 34-154) was germinated much latter during the reign of king Charairongba (A.D. 1697-1709) when he annexed the Angom principality to his kingdom.

The traditional *Yumnaks* (lineages) are around 432 in number. But to-day the figure is much more than this. This increase is the result of migration of people from the East and West of Manipur. At one time the Meitei society possessed the potential to accommodate this migrants since it had the capacity to act as melting pot. *Yumnaks* were given to the migrants; some of them were enrolled in the Salais. However, most of them were kept outside the purview of Yek/Salai. The Meitei Bamons and Meitei Pangals falls to this category. Since the Meitei society was not an advanced feudal society the economy could not go beyond the subsistence level.

The traditional social divison of labour as we find in Meitei society is the image of such an economy. As it was not a money economy the compulsory participation of families in running the State administration was an unavoidable. And hence the assignment of certain duties of the palace (which was the hub of State administration) to a particular Yumnak was the only way to run the administration. Such a traditional social division of labour came into force much early since the reign of king Naothingkhong (663-763 A.D.).

However, it was during king Loyyamba (1074-1122 A.D.) that it developed as a social code and became an established order. Such an order survived for a long time. But the demise of kingship put an end to such an order. The arrival of modernisation also hastened its death.

REFERENCES

1. Cheitharol Kumbaba (M.S.)
2. Ningthourol Lambuba (M.S.)
3. Thawan Thaba Hiran (M.S.)
4. Khagemba Yumlep (M.S.)
5. Shang-gai Phammang (M.S.)
6. Ningombamgi Meithoubarol Yumchangba (M.S.)
7. Nongshamei Puya (M.S.)
8. Khagemba Lanfa (M.S.)
9. Nongpok Haramlon (M.S.)
10. Kshetrilon (M.S.)
11. Lairik Yengbamlon (M.S.)
12. Ukhongshanglon (M.S.)
13. Takhenlon (M.S.)
14. Kumfilon (M.S.)
15. Mayang Ningthounailon Leimanailon (M.S.)
16. Mayang Tekhaolon (M.S.)
17. Bamon Khunthoklon (M.S.)
18. Laishara Phamlon (M.S.)
19. Loyyamba Shinyen (M.S.)
20. Mashin (M.S.)
21. Bamon Khunthoklon (M.S.)
22. Bamongi Meihoubarol (M.S.)
23. Oral interview with Padmashri N. Khelchandra
24. Oral interview with Pandit N. Manijao
25. Oral interview with Pandit Ng. Kullachandra
26. Oral interview with Pandit Yaima/N. Ibochouba

27. Oral interview with Y. Ibenton Devi, Maiyoknabi.
28. Oral interview with S. Nilbir, Prof. Pol. Sc. D.M.C. of A/C.
29. Oral interview with N. Ngambi Devi, Maiyoknabi
30. Jhalajit, R.K., *A Short History of Manipur.*
31. N. Khelchandra Singh, *Ariba Manipuri Lon-gei.*
32. Kullachandra and Badar-ruddin, *Meitei Pangal Hourakpham.*
33. Sharma, B. Kullachandra, *Meitei Bamon Hourakpham.*
34. Sabhapatigi Bhasan, Manipuri Sahitya Parishad, 48th session, dated 5-6 June, 1983, N. Khelchandra as Sabhapati
35. Singh, L. Ibungohal, An Introduction to Manipur.
36. Hudson, T.C., The Meiteis.
37. Report of the Expert committee on Other Backward Classes (OBC), Manipur, Names of Sageis (lineages) adopted by the Meitei Pangal, Schedule 1, p. 46.
38. Sageis (clans) of Manipur Muhammadans (Palace Pandits)
39. Manipur State Mussalman Panchayat, 30-11-1932.

2

Traditional House and the Deities Associated with It

(A) TRADITIONAL MODE OF SETTLEMENT

In the past Manipur valley comprising 2238 sq. km was not a place as it is now. Marshy lands and lakes were abundant where the biggest was Loktak lake. So, the habitable areas might not be plenty as it is now. In such a situation the mode of settlement was quite different from today's. Such a mode of settlement might have been influenced primarily by the strategic location of the valley and its demographic situation. Whatever might be the influence the fact is that a homestead was as big as three *paris*, sometimes four *paris* of land where a *pari* is equal to around 2.5 acres. And these homesteads were arranged successively till the last habitable areas. The vestiges of such homestead is still found in the heart of Imphal. Such vestiges are in existence in great numbers in rural areas. Some of them are abandoned homesteads and are converted into paddy fields. But still the boundary of such a homestead is intact.

A part of such homestead was utilized for rice cultivation. But the remaining was meant for the cultivation of different varieties of vegetables, beans and pulses. A number of beans, peas, chouhawai, hawai ashangbi, koli hawai, vegetables; cabbage, mustard plants, gourd, sabot, yendem, chilli, ginger, turmeric, banana plants and potato, etc., were planted in the homestead. Silk worm was reared. Cane sugar was planted. Besides there was a place for thatch garden. However, cotton plantation was not so much popular. The required cotton was supplied from the hills. The dissolution of such homesteads began after the World War II. Since then such a homestead became the home of many families. And families began clubbing together in urban and rural areas of Imphal valley. Such a mode of settlement has become a thing of the past in the urban areas of Imphal.

(B) MAINTENANCE OF HOMESTEADS

It was in this big homestead that Meitei Yumjao stood magnificently at one time. In most of the cases these homesteads were rectangular in shape. A ditch is dug around the homestead. And the earth so collected from the ditch makes a raised earthern wall called 'Leipan' in the inner side of the homestead. The ditch served to drain water from the garden as well as an obstacle to an intruder or to cattle. In strategic areas of the wall spikes made of bamboo or the like is strucked to prevent the cattle or the intruder. It is known as "Shou-Thakpa". It was on this 'Leipan' that bamboo was planted. But bamboo is planted mostly in the western and northern wall of the homestead. In those areas of the Leipan where bamboo was not grown a bamboo fencing was erected.

The Hojang or Konthong (gate) was made in the Chingkhei (north-east) of the Yumjao. A pond was dug in the eastern part of the garden near the eastern wall. The earth so collected from the pond was placed on the eastern wall (Leipan) making the earthern wall nearby the pond little higher than the rest of the Leipan. This raised portion would hide the house and the activities in the courtyard to a new-comer. The area in between the pond and the gate was another place for banana plantation. Banana was planted in the north western area near the western wall of the garden also. The area at the back of the Yumjao was served for piggery. The Amangsang (lavatory) was located at the south-western side of the house. Banana was not planted in the southern side of the house because it was considered inauspicious which would bring bad fortune to the family.

Yumjao and Out-houses

A yumjao of five or four rooms stood in the homestead mostly at the backside of the garden leaving more space in the eastern side of the garden. This Yumjao was surrounded by many out-houses different uses. The back door was placed at the last room which also served as kitchen. The back door was opened at the left wall of the last room. So, the place around the back door was served as 'Lukhak Kom' (garbage).

The left and right sides of the house around the middle of the house was used in making nest for chicken. Awang Sangoi (at the northern side of the courtyard), Makha Sangoi (at the southern side of the courtyard), Mamang Sang-goi (at the eastern side of the courtyard), Shang-gon, Chabokshang, Ya-ongshang, Foukei, Singkei, etc., were the out-houses. Awang Sang-goi and Makha Sang-goi were mostly for decoration of the house. And they were used occasionally at family functions like, marriage, death ceremony, birth ceremony, ear-piercing ceremony, etc. The Mamang Sang-goi was bigger in size and it served a number of purposes. The southern side of it was the place for rice pounding. The loom was placed in the eastern side of it. The loin loom was fixed on the northern wall of the Mamang Sang-goi. The open space between the Yumjao and the Mamang Sang-goi was the Shumang (courtyard). In the centre of the courtyard a shrub (either Tairen or Tulsi) was planted. The circular place around the plant in the courtyard was the 'Thelong': a neat place which is cleaned by scrubbing with a 'Nura' (traditional brush) with water everyday. This 'Thelong' is the place where anything to be distributed to persons present in a ceremony. "Polangkhok (a pole for hanging cloths) was placed in the northern side of the courtyard near the Awang Sang-goi. It was not placed at the right side of the courtyard.

The Shang-gon (cowshed) was placed at the front or at the rear of 'Awang Sang-goi'. Chaboksang (quarter for delivery) was placed on the left side of the house. A quarter for the newly married couple (Ya-ongshang) was placed on the right side of the house. Foukei (granary) was placed behind the 'Makha Sang-goi. Shingkei (quarter for fire wood) was placed on the right side of the house not far-away from Chaksang or the last room. Now such a maintenance of homestead has become a thing of the past. Chaboksang, Ya-ongshang, Shing-Kei, Foukei, Yengkon, etc., are all disappeared. However, a house with 'Mamang Sang-goi' is still plenty in the rural areas of the valley. This is still found in some of the houses in Imphal also. But in the downtown area all these are missing and has no place in the urban setup.

(C) TYPES OF TRADITIONAL HOUSES

The traditional houses can be divided broadly into three types. Five (or four) roomed house for the general people, seven roomed house for the noblemen and nine roomed house for the king.

Five-roomed House

In a five roomed house the open space at the front is *mang-gol* (veranda). The Veranda is divided into Phamen and Naktha, etc. The second room is the place for sons and daughters. 'Ningolka' (quarter for the girls) is on the left side and 'Pibaka' (quarter for boys) is on the right side of the second room. The third room is the 'Phammenka', the place for the father. And opposite to it is the "Maibapham", the place for *maiba* (the priest). The fourth room is the 'Laplenka', the place for the mother. The 'Fungga' or the hearth is placed at the centre of this room in front of the mother's bed. Opposite to the mother's bed is the place for the deity 'Leimaren'. The last room is the 'Laining thouka'. In the south-western corner of this room there is seat for 'Sanamahi' deity. The kitchen was not placed an annexe. It was placed in the north-western corner of the last room.

Materials used in the traditional house

Building materials were limited in number. They were tree, bamboo, thatch, reed, nail chipped bamboo for binding (Paya), rope, rice, straw, cow dung, sand, Leitan (clay), and Leimu (another type of clay), etc.

Implements

The implements used were: Hakmei, Shingjang (axe), Horai (saw), Thangjou (dagger), Paija (chisel), Thenggu, Leplei (screw auger), Guniya (Try square), Sang-gai, Thangon (sickle) and Ulum (weight). The Ulum was very simple and made by binding a piece of earth by a thread. The labeling was made from banana plant. Water is placed on the piece of banana plant blocked by mud on both the ends of it. The leaf of a plant named 'Heirit' was used in polishing the bamboo or the wood as we use 'sand paper' in filing wood or iron in present day's.

Timing of felling Bamboo

There is a definite timing for felling the bamboo for building a house. In local calendar this is most suited in Mera-Hiyanggei (Oct.-Sept.). If it is cut beyond this two months then the bamboo becomes sweet. And insects (mite) can easily attack it. So, the most suitable month is Mera (October). Both the bamboo and Wachet (chipped bamboo) are soaked in the water for one month to two and half months. This cannot be soaked in a longer period, because the Wa and Wachet becomes weak again. Seasoning of the fine bamboo chip (Paya) is done by soaking in the urine of cow. This means to protect it from insects. The other means is to place it above the hearth in the kitchen or in the Fungga.

Architecture of Yumjao

The building of a Meitei house begins with the lying of foundation. 'Yumpham' or the foundation was made by raising earth from nearby area or by digging a pond in the garden. The height of the 'Yumpham' depends upon the location of the place. It was two to three feet in height depending upon the water-level in the rainy season. It was on this 'Yumpham' that the whole structure of a Yumjao stood. Meitei craftsman followed certain rules in building traditional houses which were partly technical and partly beliefs. The first pillar to be erected is the *Urep* (the main pillar or Jatra). This follows the positioning of twenty two other major pillars. In between these major pillars a number of smaller pillars were erected which are known as 'Loy' depending upon the weight it has to carry.

Name of the 22 major pillars:

1. Saitin Atonba, Meiramgi Sum.
2. Loibi Charaihulpa, Loiyu Jatra.
3. Mabtao Ngaklou Ngaiba, Jatra Puba Loiyune (Emingthonggi Loiyu)
4. Langkheimanaoton, Langkhei Paba Loiyune.
5. Salthong Laimahalpa, Sumne.
6. Emupham Lamsilpa, Laithangpa Ukokten.
7. Saruk Loutam Hulpa, Chakhumthangba Ukokten

8. Pal-lem Naoyokpa, Koubru Thangba Sum. (Maningthonggi Loiyu)
9. Mongba Loiren Khomba, Owangthangba Loiyu.
10. Korou Nongchalpa, Maibaphamgi Loiyu
11. Momnu Loutomba, Ningolka Loiyu.
12. Leirak Akhuba, Chingkhei Thangba Sum.
13. Eman Ngaina Namngou, Mangsok Ukokten.
14. Loklou Panam Enamkhang, Famlen Ukokten
15. Tareng
16. Maipu
17. Sentoppa, Faktom Puba Yumbi (3) Ahummak.
18. Langkhei Pungmayon, Chengfu U.
19. Langlel Kongyang Echeisu, Langchei.
20. Mongpasarong Laplenka, Sumang Yurangfam.
21. Mabtao Engngunungchalpa, Jatra Paba.
22. Langcheichara Yiruthek, Jatrane (*Urep*).

The position of the two pillars in the veranda was determined not by architectural design but by traditional beliefs. The space between the right wall of the veranda and the pillar in the Phamen is wider than the space between the left wall of the veranda and the pillar in the Naktha. The belief embodied in this architecture is that the wider gap in the Phamen will bring fertility to family thereby increasing family members. The narrower gap in the Naktha is to lessen the frequent occurrence of death in the family. After positioning the pillars the first part to be put is the long Liokhangs or lower horizontal support beams. This follows the placing of other parts, viz., Khangel (cross beam), Suktu (horizontal support beam), Akhuba (short supportbeam), Khongshangba (long vertical support), Thabakkhang Atenba (cross support beam), Thabakkhang Ashangba (lower cross support beam for roof), Khangabu (upper support), Sanayumbi (vertical support for the main horizontal support beam), Yangbi (main horizontal beam), Yangnam (horizontal beam for securing the roof support) and Uchil-Lokpa, a runner above the Thabakkhang supporting the Hoomdang joining the two Segas.

After installing the frame the next step is to fix the Hoomdangs (lower roof support). While placing the Hoomdang over the Loikhang certain norms were followed based on the beliefs and customs as found in architectural lore. Wamit (eye) of the Hoomdang is not put facing down the ground but it is placed either on the left or right side. The same is followed in erecting pillars. The wamit of the pillar is not placed facing inside the house. This is considered inauspicious. The number of Hoomdangs (in pairs) is determined by the size of the house and they are fixed in number. It is in the sense that they are to be of odd numbers, e.g. 13, 15, 27, 23, etc. The way of counting is the use of (chak-rice, Nga-fish), or (Mei-fire, Eshing-water, Nungshit-air) or (chang-live, Shi-death) where chak-rice, Eshing-water and chang-live are considered auspicious. The Hoomdangs are not placed over the Loikhang in line with the pillars, however, this is relaxed in case of Laplen ka where a single Hoomdang is placed over the pillars which stands in the secluded area of 'Leimren' deity. This is called "Ema Leimaren Shidabi Hoomdang Kokthong Pubi (Nabi)" —the literal meaning is that Ema-Leimarel Shidabi who carries the load of Hoomdang on the head. This gives us the concept of incorporating the symbol of sexual copulation in the architecture, thus cherishing the fertility cult. The placing of Hoomdangs begins from the back of house, not from the front. And it is finished at the front, however, it may finish at the left or right side of the front (veranda). The belief is that when Man is created by God it begins from the buttock, thus enabling to identify whether the person is male or female. When placing the *u-ra* (upper roof support-made of polished bamboo splits) above the Hoomdangs there is no fixed numbers as it is there in the case of Hoomdangs. A thin bamboo chip is woven in between the *u-ras* at places which fall between the pair of Hoomdangs which is known as "Changkhrang". Its function is to reinforce the hold of the *u-ras*. The beliefs continues that Hoomdang represents the ribs. *u-ras* that of flesh and the thatch above the *u-ras* represents the skin. Fungga-Lairu (the hearth) at the centre of the fourth room represents the navel of human beings. Among the major pillars there are eight main pillars (for five-roomed house) which represents the eight openings of the body. Again in a four-roomed house there are six main pillars among the major pillars which represent the five souls and the shadow. Yangbi (main horizontal beam) which rests the Hoomdang and the *u-ra* at the top of the roof represent spinal cord. While placing the bamboo poles like Loikhang, Shuktu, Khangabu Yangbi, etc. they are placed facing the head of the bamboo in the east. They are personified as a sleeping man (Meitei) who is sleeping facing the east. The same is the case in erecting pillars also. If, otherwise, it is considered a man standing upside down which is believed inauspicious. While roofing with thatch sand is sprayed in between which acts as insulater in case of fire.

Plastering of the wall begins from placing the polished bamboo splits vertically and horizontally. In between it the materials Shingut (Phragmites) or Shingnang or Tou are inserted. This stage is known as *"Kairangba"*. The first layer of plastering by mud is known as *"Leipee"*. In this only mud and straw is used. The second layer is also by sand and cow dung. The third layer is also by sand and cow dung but in this sand is more in the proportion. Finishing is done by a fine layer of either *Leitan* (clay) or *Leimu* (another kind of clay).

Doors and Windows

The main door is placed a little to the left, not in the centre or to the right. The back door is at the left walls of the last room. The passage beginning from the main door to the last room is kept open without any door. According to architectural lore the front door is known "Emangthong", and the back door is known as "Emingthong". In common parlance they are known as "Mamangthong" and "Maningthong" respectively. There are two windows on both the sides of the main door. Windows are also made in the second, third, and fourth room, one each on the left and the right wall facing each other. The last room is without any window. "Thongnao" (window) is known "Mihuthong" in the architectural lore.

SOME RULES

(a) Certain rule is followed in making holes for the pillars. The depth of a hole is determined by the distance between shoulder and the tip of male genital organ of the person (owner of the house). It can't be more than this.

(b) *Shaichin* or *Shai* (the lower end of the thatched-roof) should be elongated at least three ft. from the pillars. This calculation is made by observing the inclination of rainfall in Manipur. If it is less than this rains well reach the side veranda and the walls. There is no fixed heights of the houses. It depends on the desire of the person. A high house is known as "Laba Yumsha" and the short one is known as "Amom Yumsha". However, the difference is not much. It applies in the doors also. A little broad door is known as "Amom Thongda" and little higher is known as "Laba Thongda".

(c) *Sanamahi Ka* – The room for the deity Sanamahi should be made smaller than the other rooms.

(d) In the occurrence of death in the family the corpse is carried in the Ashithong (the space between the left pillar and the left wall of the veranda). If the member is a dying person he is carried in the centre of veranda i.e. passage between two pillars in the veranda. If death occurs when a marriage ceremony or death ceremony is undergoing in the family the corpse is passed by making a hole in the wall of the room "Phamen Ka". But this hole is made at the 'Khuya' (the back end of the person's bed) of the bed (i.e. on the right side of the wall).

(e) *U-yung* tree was excluded in building a house. It is believed that lightening will frequently visit the house.

Some Essential Accessories

Pungjei – It is a sharp pointed bamboo split which acts as nails. It is believed that it represents the male genital organ.

Pandali – It is the binding with cane splits. It is used in two places, one-between Khangabu and Yangbi, two-between Loikhang and Loikhom.

Hirukhang – It is like Pungjei but it is longer upto ½ ft. to 2 ft. It is made by sharpening the bamboo split, specially from the head of the bamboo split including the wamit (eye) and is pointed toward the end of the split. It is driven home upto the end with a wooden hammer (Tokshu) at the "Shaijin" (the lower edge of the thatched roof). The purpose is to fasten the hold of the thatch in the *u-ras*.

Saikhang – A polished bamboo chip which is fastened at the eaves by the support of Hirukhang.

Sega – A wooden pole inserted in between the joints of *u-ras* of main part of the house and that of veranda.

Yengai – Yengai or Shandangkha is a triangular bamboo woven structure placed above the front wall of the house but below the roof to serve as ventilator. It is decorated with flowers, birds, houses and other motifs carved from bamboo chips by fixing among the interlacing weaves.

Some Practices

Shagun Thong (passage for the burglar):- In the traditional practice a passage for the burglar known as 'Shagun Thong' was also included in the architecture. The belief around this practice is that if the burglar eats something before stealing the belonging then he stops stealing. So, he eats only when he collects whatever he likes. By so doing the act will cast spell to the sleeping members of the family. If this happens the usual belief is that the act of burglary will repeat again. The burglar usually escapes at the passage (Shagun Thong). If the burglar intends to make the owner rich he will escape by the front door.

Shagun Thong Thingba:- The burglar after executing his mission escapes at the passage (Shagun Thong). But, sometimes he will not escape immediately along with the stolen articles. He will block the passage by the earth around it. If this happens it is usually believed that the family will get rich in the days to come. On the other hand it is also considered that the burglar left something for the survival of the family.

Shenfu :- A locker for the coins was also prepared by making a small hole in one of the secluded pillar, usually near one of the household deity. The hole is made at the upper edge of the joint. When need to remove it another hole is made at the lower end of the joint of the pillar.

In due course of time traces of modernisation is found in the architecture of Yumjao. Shikhong (a horizontal plank at the basement) and Pheiren (another plank criss-crossing the wall) are the latter additions in the architecture. The bamboo supports and pillars also began to be replaced by wooden ones. With this the wooden pillars are placed above fine polished square shaped stones instead of inserting pillars in the earth. However, the Hoomdang (lower roof support), the U-ra (the upper roof support), and the thatched roof survived the changes. Again a bamboo pillar among the wooden pillars was retained in the south-western corner of the house where a secluded place is reserved for the household deity – '*Sanamahi*'.

With the arrival of modernisation the traditional houses are gradually being replaced by modern concrete structures. However, the replacement is not sudden and there is a transitional stage. In this transitional stage the bamboo is completely replaced by wood along with the architectural design. However, the plastering of the wall is still done by mud and the final plastering is done by white-washing. The thatched roof is also replaced by tin roof. In both the transitional house and modern concrete structures the hearth, the Yengai and the place for the deity "Leimaren" is missing. However, in both the cases a secluded place for the supreme household deity "Sanamahi" is still reserved with renewed enthusiasm.

The seven roomed house for the nobleman is a topic which needs further research. The remains of such a house as well as literature on it is scanty. As a result the mode of arrangement of rooms, the name of the rooms, etc. are not traceable. So, the research cannot go beyond the hearsay that a nobleman lived in a seven-roomed house.

The Royal House

Traditionally, the king used to live in a house of nine rooms. Such a house came into existence since the reign of king Naothingkhong (A.D. 663-763). The literature "Kanmgla Houba" says that on the advice of *Guru*, Naothingkhong began to build the Sangai Yumjao (the nine roomed royal house). The name of the nine rooms are available, however, likewise in the seven roomed house, the architecture is not traceable. Such a house disappeared immediately with the abolition of kingship in Manipur. So, the only means is to futher investigate ancient literatures which may remain hiding in the midst of innumerable pages along with a lore on it.

The name of the nine rooms may be mentioned as under:

1. Laining thou Sana Ka,
2. Taracha-Um-Ka,
3. NeNe Yahip Ka,
4. Phadibi Meiring Ka,
5. Emoinu Ahongbee Ka,
6. Leima Arembee Khongham Ka,
7. Pitangnga Leeklu Louthibee Nongga Ka,
8. Angouba Pureiromba Ka,
9. Lainingthou Pakhangba Chatlam Phanshang Ka.

But the nothing is mentioned on the order of the rooms as well as on the rooms for king-queen, prince, princess and household deities, etc.

The Materials

It is found mention that the building materials were strictly selective. Only a few selective trees and bamboos were allowed to include in the building of such a house. Again the places where these materials are to be collected are also strictly particular. Only three varieties of trees, viz., Tumitla, Uningthou and Taimareng were allowed the construction. Bamboos for Hoomdang (lower roof support) were Laiwa, Uyeng and Utang, Paya (bamboo chip meant for binding) was made from Unap and Utang (Local variety of bamboo). The thatch used for roofing was 'Charot Emon'.

Places for collecting the materials

The tree for the main pillar (*Urep*) was collected from a place known 'Chingthang'. The tree for the pillar adjacent to the *Urep* (main pillar) was from 'Wangbren'. The trees for Upa (another main pillar) were Tumitla and Uningthou from Pishum Chinga. The tree for the adjacent pillar was U-Lang from Langjing. The tree for the pillar Upa was Chingthang Taimareng. The tree for the pillar Ukhokten was from Heibok. The thatch was collected from Langmaijing hill. The bamboo meant for the Hoomdang and *U-ra* were collected from Thanga-Karang (islands in the Loktak lake). The tree for the pillar Sanayumbi was collected from Thangjing hill. The tree for the Khangel (cross beam) was from Langgol hill. The trees for the four pillars named 'Maikei' were collected from four villages.

The authentic information on the number of pillars in such a house is not available. However, there are names for eight main pillars and they are:

1. Wangbren,
2. Koubrou,
3. Thangjing,
4. Marjing,

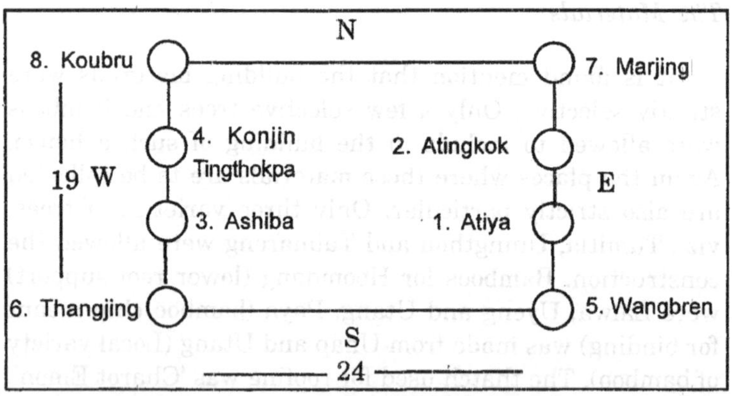

Fig. 1: The possible position of these eight pillars: 1. Atiya - in the right side of the east, 2. Atingkok - left side of the east, 3. Ashiba - right of the west, 4. Konjin Tingthokpa - left side of the west, 5. Wangbren-in the south-eastern corner, 6. Thangjing - in south western corner, 7. Marjing - in the north-eastern corner, 8. Koubru - in the north-western corner.

5. Atiya Sidaba,
6. Atingkok Sidaba,
7. Konjin Tingthokpa and
8. Ashiba.

The names are not given for the remaining pillars. The length of Sanggai Yumjao is 19 Khudups and the breadth is 24 Khudups. The length of the Khangel (cross beam) is 12 Khudups and depth of pillars is 7 Khudups 1 Kaplen 3 Khudon Maphei. The height of the Sangai Yumjao is 14 Khudups 1 Kaplen 1 Kaichou 3 Khudon Maphei. The size of a pillar is 7 wai 3 Khudon Maphei. The depth of the main pillar is 4 Khudups 1 Kap.

Measurement of a Khudup

For a smaller person 1 Khudup is equal to 1 waichou plus the breadth of an index finger. For bigger person; first measure 1 wai; divide it into 16 equal parts. Fold it again into 4 equal parts. Then it is a Khudup.

D. DEITIES IN THE HOUSES

In a traditional Meitei Yumjao a number of places inside the house were reserved for a number of deities ranging from the three principal deities e.g. Lainingthou Sanamahi, Ema Leimarel Shidabi and Emoinu to other minor deities e.g. Saijin Polibi, Santhong Apanba, Thongaren, etc. However, such reserved places were more distinct for the above three principal deities and for the remaining minor deities their places were more or less based on beliefs. For the moment the study is concentrated mostly on the three principal deities.

Sanamahi

To begin with the place for Laningthou Sanamahi is reserved at the south-western corner of the last room which is known as "Laningthou Ka", meaning room for the 'Laningthou'. This room is also known as 'Chak-Khum Ka', meaning room for kitchen. Sanamahi is worshipped everyday in the evening by offering Mekruk (traditional incense) and light. But special offering is made on 'Cheiraoba'—Manipuri New Year day. On this day a variety of vegetables, fruits and flowers available in the season are offered as "Athenpot". It is unaccustomed to offer cooked food and anything dried in the fire to 'Sanamahi'. On the day of 'Cheiraoba' or during the five days beginning from it the old clothes of 'Sanamahi' are replaced by a set of new clothes which is known as "Firoi Hongba". Sanamahi is also worshipped occasionally by an individual when there is a desire to get an offspring or when one wants to cure someone from insanity. The auspicious month for such a worship is "Enga" - June and the auspicious day is "Thanin" - the full moon day. However, with the advent of modern education and scientific knowledge such practices are gradually discarding in the Meitei society.

Leimaren

The place for 'Leimaren' is reserved at the left side of "Laplen-Ka"- the room for the mother (housewife) of the family. 'Leimaren' is also prayed everyday in the evening by offering Mekruk and light. Special offering is made on the day of "Cheiraoba" - the new year day. "Phiroi Hongba" - change of new clothes is also performed during the five days beginning from "Cheiraoba". During these five days the water in the "Eshaifu" - the earthern pitcher, is also replaced by a fresh one. But the water is collected from seven 'Hiden' – the bathing place in a river. On special occasions "Leimaren" is also worshipped not exceeding once in a month. Even the king cannot go beyond this practice. If it is worshipped twice a month it was believed that the country will face a catastrophe.

A host of items is included in such occasional prayer. A gold stick, a silver stick, a bowl, a Khujai (jug), a dish, a pair of bangle, a pair of ear-rings, two pieces of iron, a knife, seven pieces of fire-wood, a Tareng Yot (spinning rode), seven balls of thread, five Tamang, five Langchak, two Langhou Moithap, a set of cloths, a set of cloths for man, an oil lamp, a wax lamp, raw milk, chuhi, honey, five betelnuts and leaves, one Senpak (tray) five kinds of fruits, two hands of banana and a piece of sugarcane. The surface is cleaned by rubbing water on it and the above items are placed on it.

Emoinu

Like the above two deities "Emoinu" is also prayed everyday in the evening. Her place is located just near the "Funga Lairu" (the hearth), but on its south-western side. A small mound is placed at this place to mark the location of Emoinu. Whatever cooked in the family was also offered both in the morning and evening. Like the above two principal deities 'Emoinu' is also worshipped en masse on 12th day of Wakching month (January). For such an occasional worship two 'Athenpots' are prepared which include fruits, flowers, vegetables and other items which are available in the season. One Athenpot is offered to 'Funga Lairu' and the other to 'Lainingthou Sanamahi'. The offering is often accompanied with the chanting of 'Nahairon'. The items included in 'Nahairon' are Tairel, Pungfai, Napu, Nashet, Napi and Shingbi. These are dipped in water and sprinkled on the nearby area including the 'Athenpot'. Only Tairel leaf is used in 'Nahaiba' when the other items are not available.

Nahairol: Ung Hei, Ung Hei, Ung Hei. Lahal Nang Keng Yoi Yoika Melka, Yaika Thousil Thouya Langka. Thouli Thoutil Langpu, Thouli Thapa Pongthou Tamli, Thapa Mapu Lanangte, Numit Pongthou Tamli, Numit Mapu Lalangte.

Yawa Kongkhang, Saki Pongthou Mathang Pichake, Kumcha Pol-loi Thouke, Nongcha Palloi Thouke Ngaluare, Tenare, Ha Ong Tha Nongcha Nong Nong. After offering prayer by chanting 'Nahairol' the two Athenpots are withdrawn with a request to do so from the deities. The Athenpots are well cooked and a part of it is offered to "Emoinu" by preparing "Luk". The cooked food is not offered to Lainingthou. This food is relished by the family. But in these days a visible change is seen in the worship of "Emoinu". In a modern house a traditional hearth is hardly maintained. So, daily offering to her is a thing of the past. However, she is prayed occasionally in a year in every family on 12th day of Wakching month.

(E) RULES AND BELIEFS, AS EMBODIED IN THE ARCHITECTURE OF YUMJAO

Beliefs in Selecting a Place

A homestead may be of different shapes, sizes and of different nature. Depending upon the above conditions it was considered to be auspicious or inauspicious in building a house at a place.

(1) If the south, west, south-west and north-west of the place is higher than the rest, then this type of Engkhol (homestead) is known as 'Samu Namda Taba'. A house to such a place will bring prosperity, long-life and fertility.

(2) If the north, east, south and west end of the place is lower than the most part of the homestead, then such a place is suitable for Brahman, Kshetri, Baishya and Sudra. For a Brahman a place which is inclined to all the four directions is harmless and he can reside there.

(3) If the centre of a place raises like a hump and inclined in all the four directions, then it is known

as "Thenggu Namda Taba". It is suitable to erect a house at such a homestead. It will bring courage and prosperity to the family.

(4) If the place inclines towards the east, south-east and north-east, then it is known as "Hichaba Namda Taba". Such a place is considered unsuitable for living. A family living in such a place will face scarcity and death may occur to his sons and cattle.

(5) If the length of the place falls on east and west, the north and south is little higher and the centre is little lower then rest, then such an Engkhol (homestead) is known as "Lingi Namda Taba". A family to such a place may face death of family members, his enemy will grow and will not get a mental rest.

(6) A place which grows trees, bamboos, creepers, medicinal herbs, grasses in abundance, with plain nature and with fertile soil is best suitable for living. There is no dearth in wealth, and it will bring prosperity and long life to the family.

(7) A place with crack surface with pieces of bones underneath, Leishou Shouba (mound of mites) and with a rough surface is not suitable for living and should be abandoned. A house in such a place will face scarcity, death and sorrows and sufferings. Death occurs to a house on crack surface. Scarcity prevails to a house in a barren soil. A family will always face sorrows and sufferings if it happens to reside at a place with the deposition of bones underneath. And the enemy will prosper if the family resides on a place with a rough surface.

Such beliefs are no longer in vogue among the present Meiteis. It has nothing to do when there is a visible pressure on land, particularly in the urban areas. A man with a piece of land in the urban area is considered fortunate keeping aside all the above beliefs.

Yumpham Mapalgi Maming Amadi Mapham (Name of the nine different foundations and their places in a homestead)

Koubru (N-W) Lola (Donkey) *Yumpham*	Awang (North) Shamu (elephant) *Yumpham*	Chingkhei (N-E) Langja (vulture) *Yumpham*
Nongchup (West) Tampha (gem) *Yumpham*	Sanggai *Yumpham*	Nongpok (East) Phiral (flag) *Yumpham*
Santhong (S-W) Lamhui (fox) *Yumpham*	Makha (south) Nongsha (lion) *Yumpham*	Meiram (S-E) Meikhu (smoke) *Yumpham*

Fig. 2: Name of the nine different foundations

A homestead is divided into nine (almost) equal segments where each segment has a name with their probable fortune. A man has to select one suitable from the nine by observing the day he is born and with the help of other observations for determining suitable and unsuitable place in homestead. The above figure is the representation of the nine segments along with their name and position.

The fortune of each segment is discussed as under.

1. *Firal* (flag) *Yumpham* - A house at this place will bring richness, prosperity and plenty.
2. *Meikhu* (smoke) *Yumpham* – A house at this place will face sorrow and suffering. It will be frequented by quarrel among the family members. Peace and tranquility will be far away from the house.
3. *Nongsha* (Lion) *Yumpham* – The person has to face brave and courageous personalities. He will gain bravery and courage. It is better to live at such a place.

4. *Lamhui* (fox) *Yumpham* – A person with a house at this place will not face a dearth in wealth and food but he may face theft. It is also better to build a house at this place.
5. *Tampha* (gem) *Yumpham* – As suggested by the name itself a house at this place means richness, prosperity and plenty. One can lead a happy life. It is considered as a good place for building a house at this place.
6. *Lola* (Donkey) *Yumpham* – It is not a good place to live. There is dearth of wealth, food and he will gain no fruit of his labour.
7. *Samu* (Elephant) *Yumpham* – It is a good place to live with a house. One will lead a peaceful life with plenty of food and wealth. He will get the fruit of what he labours.
8. *Langja* (Vulture) *Yumpham* – A house at this place will meet sorrow and suffering. There is dearth of food and wealth. Death also occurs frequently. So, one can't lead a peaceful life at this place.
9. *Sanggai Yumpham* – A person to such a place is very selective in his nature and virtues. If he is brave and courageous, noble and open hearted, then it is good for him to build a house at this place. He will gain popularity with a prosperous life. He will gain a number of off springs. A coward and a person with fickle mind cannot live at such a place. He will face downfall. Though considered as a good place among the nine segments of a homestead it is recommended that one should not select this place to build a house for him. It is quite unbearable to stay at this place.

So, after examining all the nature and fortunes of all the nine Yumphams what is considered best is to build the house at the place which touches a little portion of the

Tampha *Yumpham* by the Sanggai *Yumpham*. But this tradition may be following by a few persons only in rural areas. In the urban set-up it has become a thing of the past.

Engkhol Karan and Positioning of Urep (Main Pillar)

Engkhol Karan is a point in the homestead and it is considered necessary first of all to find out this point before doing anything for the house. The importance is given to this point less from architectural aspect but more from beliefs. In order to find out the point, first of all the distance between the western end and eastern end of the place is measured. Divide the distance so measured into half and Karan is the point which falls the half distance. Certain beliefs enhances the importance of this point (Karan).

It is considered inauspicious to place this point near the door. It is also not good to place this point on the line where rain falls from the eaves. If it happens to keep on this line it is believed that a child may slip frequently from veranda to the ground. It is not kept at Khangenpham in the courtyard because death may visit frequently to the family. It is not good to keep at the place of *Urep* (main pillar) because illness may occur to the children of the family. So, what is traditionally followed is to keep the Karan at a distance of a breadth of the calf from the line of rain falling from the eaves. The *Urep* (main pillar) is erected to the east of Karan measured by the breadth of calf in a four roomed house.

Ritual of Urep (Main Pillar)

Certain ritual is followed in positioning the *Urep* to its place. First of all the main pillar (*Urep*) is taken bath and thoroughly clean. Then the pillar is wrapped by a white cloth keeping the left end at the bottom and the right end of the cloth at the top of post. A portion about the breadth of palm or of three fingers at the left end of the cloth is vacated and wrapped it with mango leaves. At this stage the *Urep* is known as "Achiba". At one time it is known as "*Urep* Apanba". The name of the post "Jatra Paba" is "Nongmai Singjaba". The name is "Ekhei Chaiba".

Chant the above words and place a piece of gold on eastern side of the clothed pillar, a piece of 'Tairel' on the northern side, a piece of Chandan on the western side and a piece of Uningthou on the southern side.

Items included in installing the Urep

Among the listed items a fire ritual is necessarily included. Rice, Thoiding, Flower, Tinghtou (a grass) implements, a cloth for the *Urep* and a Khudei (a scarp) for the Urungba, Uyeiba are the items. Besides, two Athenpots (fruits, rice, salt, dry fish, etc.) are also a must in the item. One Athenpot is placed at the head of the pillar and the other at the end. The Athenpot at the head of the *Urep* (main pillar) is meant for the craftsman Maiba (priest). The *Urep* is to be installed with the following words- "Jatra (*Urep*) Pabadi Nongnang Eshing Chaibane, Mamingdi Ekhei Chaiba Koue".

Beliefs embodied in the Architecture

The height of the *Urep* should not exceed beyond the right wall, at the line which falls the rain from the eaves. This may lead to ill health causing running of nose in the family members. The head of the family may die before completing a year. The name of the main pillar in the kitchen (the last room) is "Langkhei Ningthou". It should not be more in height. A more height in this may cause weakness of the housewife. The pillar opposite to it which is at the south-eastern corner of (Chakhumang) which bears the 'Shuktu' is known as 'Korouhanba'. This also cannot be of more height, a more in height in this may cause weakness of head of the family.

It is fatal if someone encounters a spirit at the base of the pillar "Langkhei". So, one must try to avoid this place. One should not touch or lean on it. It is the place where the deity "Leimarel" use to descend on earth. The children of the family should not be permitted to play hide and seek near the pillar "Korouhanba". If one does inspite of this one may be carried away by spirit. The bent of the pillar "Jatra Paba" is to be noted seriously. If the bent is placed facing inside the house then illness may visit frequently to the family. The 'Loy' (minor pillar) at the 'Ningol Ka' facing the pillow should be placed nearer the major pillar reducing the gap in between. This is to be followed in the case of Hoomdang (lower roof-support) also. This gap is known as "Shagun Thong" (passage for the burglar), 'Shagun Thong' is three in number. The gap between the southern "Shuktu" and the Hoomdang is big enough to sneak a person then this is also a "Shagun Thong". The gape occurred between the two 'Lamjeis' (measuring stick) when measuring from the front and rear of the house is wide enough to pass a man-then this is also a 'Shagun Thong'. A 'Shagun Thong' should not be kept closed, this will prevent accumulating wealth. A plenty of space should be left. The Hoomdang at the left side of the veranda should not be placed at the centre of the main door. If it happens then it is termed as "Lan Thong Thingba" (closing the door to wealth). Money may not pay visit the house. So, it should be placed a little to one of the either side.

The pillar near the site of "Leimarel" is the resting place of "Leimarel Shidabi". The main pillar at Chak-khum (kitchen) is the descending place of 'Leimarel'. The gape maintained by the two "Loys" at the southern and western side of "Sanamahi" deity should be narrow. This will lead the deity to normalcy. The Hoomdang placed above the 'Sanamahi' should be kept untie. This may lead in avoiding sorrow and difficulties in the family.

The 'Loy' (minor pillar) next to the 'Chengfu Loy' (the minor pillar which is just at the rice pitcher) will sit above it. The pillar in the "Laplen Ka" facing the pillow is known "Wamit-Tang Warukhoi". It is considered as symbol of "Tengbanba Mapu", the Almighty. It is believed that one will not face dangers such as illness and death if he prays to it before leaving for a journey. The next pillar should be placed a little far away from it. It is considered inauspicious if the eye of the pillar is placed facing south. Place some "Thangmei" (pieces of wood or bamboo produces in the cuts) of the four "Shum" on it. One will not face danger if prayed to it before leaving for a journey. The position of Hoomdang in the 'Laplen Ka' just near the 'Urep' is considered in auspicious if the counting from the 'Shum' ends with 'Thangja' (Saturday) and Nongmaijing (Sunday). The bents at the left and right of the Hoomdang is carefully observed. If the bents and protruding occurs one should not bind it with cane to avoid the bent. If it so does one may face illness and death and may not be free in executing something.

The gap between the Akhuba (short support beam) and the 'Loy' (minor pillar) at the eastern side of the "Laplen Ka" should be made narrow and the same is to be followed in the case of Hoomdang. This is called "Ashithong" (the passage of death). The bent of the 'Loy' should be placed facing the west. It is the passage of the corpse when death is occurred in the family when a death ceremony is going on at the courtyard. The Hoomdang near the "Khangabu Uchin Lokpa" at veranda should not be bound by cane. The 'Sanamahi' cannot bestow the sorrow and suffering to the family. If that is bound by cane then one may not be free in executing something and it is considered inauspicious in doing this.

The Umits (eye) of the Shum (pillar) in the northern side of 'Naktha' (the left side of veranda) and the other Shum (pillar) by the side of 'Sanamahi' deity should not be kept facing inside the house. It tends to shoot. And the house becomes unsuitable for living.

As a rule the place of "Funga Lairu" (the hearth) is fixed in the following manner. On the top of the two pillars separating 'Chak-Khum Ka' (the last room) and 'Laplen Ka' (next to this last room) stands an "Akhuba" (short support beam). Again the "Sanayumbi" (vertical support for the main horizontal support beam) stands above this 'Akhuba'. The 'Funga Lairu' is placed to the east of 'Sanayumbi' by the breadth of a calf or the breadth of eight fingers.

Tree to be excluded in building a house

Trees which are considered inauspicious for use in building a house are - a milk producing tree when the tree is cut, a tree resting groups of birds, a tree broken by wind, a burnt tree, a tree burnt by lightening, a tree hit by meteorite, a tree worshipped by the people, a tree in the precinct of a deity, a tree considered to be the resting place of spirits, a tree growing in the crematorium and a tree climbed by a snake.

Rules for positioning the pillars

A certain rule was followed in positioning the pillars and a person cannot act according to his wishes by installing a pillar from any place of the house. Clearly, there is a beginning and end in positioning the pillars. The first pillar to be installed is the Urep (the main pillar). The next pillar to be followed is Jatra Paba. The third pillar is placed near the 'Chengfu' (rice pitcher). And the other is "Fammen Saitil Tareng". The fourth pillars are Saitil Tareng of Mangsok and Minai Yumbi (Laigi Jatra). The fifth pillar is in the Fammen which bears the "Faktom" of Saitil. The seventh pillar is the 'Ukhokten' and is in the veranda. The eighth pillar is the one which rests the Khangen (cross beam) in the rear side of Mangsok. And the name is 'Ukhokten'. The ninth pillar is located at rear corner of Mangsok. The tenth is at the rear corner of Mangsok. The eleventh pillar (Ukhokten) is the one which bears the "Khangen" (cross beam) at the Fammen in the Veranda. The twelfth pillar (Shum) is at the corner of Veranda in the Fammen side. The thirteenth pillar (Shum) is also at the corner of Veranda in Mangsok side. The fourteenth and the last pillar is the 'Tareng U' at the 'Faktom'. And here ends the positioning of main pillars in a house.

Yum Sangkaba (Inauguration)

The inauguration is held on an auspicious day given by the priest. The belongings of the house is shifted in the house after a day long celebration of the ritual.

The Items and Ritual

An earthern pitcher (*Eshaiphu Erangpul*) with water to its brim is placed at the front of the house. An 'Athenpot' (fruits, rice, fish, etc. for offering) along with a washed 'Firoi' for 'Emoinu Ahongbi' is placed at the "Funga Lairu". A basket full of rice is also placed. On it "Ngari Ngatai" (fermented fish) is placed. Five live 'Ngamu' (fish) is also included. Various kinds of fruits and flowers are also offered. A pitcher known as "Eshaifu" is placed in the 'Leimaren Ka' - room for Leimaren deity. An Athenpot is also prepared for 'Leimaren'. In this - one Sareng, three Ngatel, three Ngahau- all fishes, vegetables and Maroi-Mapang are also offered.

For "Lainingthou Sanamahi" three Athenpots are prepared. List of items is - nine bunch of bananas ending with "Chang", nine betel nuts and leaves, nine pieces of coins, nine flames, Firoi Fingam and three "Chengluk" for "Anam Athou". The ritual "Anam Athou Kokpa" and fire worship is performed. The hymns on 'Sanamahi' is sung and thus the deity is worshipped. Dhup Mekruk (incense) is burnt along with "Khoiju Leikham".

At this juncture the craftsman "Pishatao" will sit at Mangshok. All the implements are laid in front of him. He will wear new clothes and 'Athenpots' are also laid in the front. The owner of the house sits at 'Fammen' in the veranda. All the remaining members of the family are to stay inside the house. The 'Amaiba' (priest) performs his rituals and after this the displayed items of 'Athenpots' is well-cooked. After taking the cooked-food four leaves of thatch from four corners of the eaves is buried in the ground in the north-eastern side of the homestead. A lump of earth is collected from the corner of the homestead and is placed at the secluded place of "Ema Leimarel". After completing the above process then the house is ready to install the belongings of the family in their respective places.

But now the situation is such that in some cases the laying of foundation and inauguration is held on the same day. However, a place for foundation, e.g. an area of a brick is left vacant. And that vacant place is filled up by a brick. And thus foundation is laid on the same day of inauguration.

CONCLUSION

In a traditional Meitei family, each family maintained a homestead of the size not less than six to seven acres. Such large areas enabled the families to maintain a self-sufficient economy of those days. In another sense each family was an economic unit of the Meitei society. Though land was abundant still the society was a stratified one. This is evident by the existence of types of houses, viz. nine-roomed house for the king, seven-roomed for the nobleman, five-roomed for the general (rich) people and four-roomed house for the common man. Still there is a *Khangpok* (hut) for the poor. Customs and beliefs dominated the thinking and the way of life the Meiteis. This had profound influence even on the architecture of the Meitei Yumjao. However, such beliefs and customs cannot withstand the mighty force of modernisation. With the advance of time such beliefs and customs are gradually going to oblivion in the Meitei society.

REFERENCES

1. Shakok Lamlen (M.S.)
2. Kangla Houba (M.S.)
3. Yumsharon (M.S.)
4. Nahairon (M.S.)
5. Kangleiron (M.S.)
6. Sanamahi Phangkhong (M.S.)
7. Leimaren Sekning (M.S.)
8. Leimaren Naoyom (M.S.)
9. Leimaren Phambal (M.S.)
10. Sanamahi Phambal (M.S.)
11. Oral interview with (craftsman) Kh. Thambalngou
12. Oral interview with (craftsman) Ksh. Boro Singh
13. Oral interview with Pandit N. Manijao
14. N. Indramani, *Meitei Yumsharon.*
15. Shahitya, Vol. VII, 27th Edition, Feb. 1976
16. Singh, Y. Budhichandra, *Emoinu: Ahongbigi Likhul Pomit.*
17. Bahadur, Mutua, *Cane and Bamboo crafts of Manipur.*

PART II

3

Marriage and Rituals

In Manipuri society the boys were given the right to make a free choice of their own mate. So mate selection could be done in many ways; through engagement, elopement and by capture. Elopement was done through mutual consent or consent between parents. In the case of marriage by capture there was no marriage service and it was always accompanied with violence; but ultimately settled with marriage. Engagement could be done with mutual consent of the boy and girl or without the knowledge of them; done mostly by the parents. Engagement needs a long process to be followed and still this is in fashion. The bride price was given either in service, in kind or in cash. All these were prevalent in Manipur. In case of elopement the bride price was fixed after the case of elopement was settled between the parents. But according to Pandit N. Khel-chandra the bride price among the commoners was not popular and the custom was not an established one. In the case of marriage with girls of royal family the custom of 'Kwagok-Hanba' (cash payment) was practised. In the ancient past monogamy was the dominant form of marriage. But after 'seven years devastation' (A.D. 1819-1825) which is known as *Chahi Ṭaret Khuntakpa* in the annals of Manipur polygamous marriage began to practice as a means to recover the lost population in the devastation. So, even during the colonial period also both the monogamous and polygamous marriages were prevalent in Manipur. But monogamy was dominant among the commoners and polygamy among the aristocrats. For the aristocrats, it was a symbol of wealth and power. In fact it was used as a means to gain power during those days. And it was the gradual transformation in the concept of the practice in due course of history; from a means to increase population to a means to gain power.

Besides engagement, other forms of marriage were also prevalent in Manipur, e.g. elopement, kidnap or capture, Keina-Katpa and Nambo-Thaba. Engagement was the most popular form of marriage, but nowadays elopement is increasingly popular. Kidnap or capture has no social sanction and is considered a crime. 'Keina-Katpa' is a shortened form of marriage. It is performed in the presence of a few persons including some elderly ones. It is performed only when the relationship between man and woman needs to acquire social sanction. Nowadays it is quite often performed as a punishment to those who are having illicit relationship and having objectionable behaviour. The least popular form was 'Nambo-Thaba'. Here, the persons settled in the girl's house by force. He will come along with his belongings and forcibly stays in the house. It happens to a weak family who are having only one or two old and weak persons. It has no chance in a strong and powerful family. On the other side the girl's family also need someone for their protection and to look after them. But this form of marriage has become a tale of bygone days and there is no news of practicing this form of marriage anywhere in Manipur.

All the rituals and ceremonies of existing types of marriages revolve around engagement form of marriage. Whereas other forms of marriage is the transformation in one way or the other from this principal marriage form. It involves a long process and the tradition is also very old. The essence of rituals in marriage remains unchanged through the ages, although there are some minor changes in dress, container used, etc. The long process of engagement, beginning from communicating message between parents of bride and groom, Waroipot, Heijingpot and finally marriage, all these are found mentioned in the literature 'Panthoibi Khonggul; though in sketchy form.

TRADITIONAL WAYS OF EXPRESSING LOVE

In the current situation there are many ways of expressing LOVE by a boy to a girl. In the traditional Meitei society also there were ways of expressing love to a girl. The traditional society was an illiterate one and the means for writing on paper was out of question. In such a situation varied means might be used in expressing love. Among the means a gift enveloped by banana leaf may be mentioned. Here a banana leaf facing east is cut down and, a 'Tiki' (a dried paste made out of powdered charcoal and cowdung, meant for burning) and a potato is enveloped by it. This packet of banana leaf containing above two items is presented to the girl as a gift. What is conveyed to the girl is that he loves her. The inclusion of 'Tiki' carries the idea that his love to the girl will remain unchanged till his death. What is implied by the inclusion of potato is that he deeply loves the girl. The banana leaf is involved in almost all the rituals and ceremonies of Manipur. And the presence of banana leaf is considered as a symbol of good luck. But in this context the banana leaf represents the mother earth and it says that the boy wants to marry her and ultimately wants to settle on mother earth.

Another worth mentioning tradition is found in the remote Meitei village in Kwatha in the Chandel district of Manipur. In this village small bamboo tubes carved with beautiful designs, which are normally used as Paangngatem (shuttle) for the looms, were presented as love token by the amorous youths to their beloved. The gifts are nonetheless utilized by the girls in actual work when weaving cloths.

But, a girl never parts with the gift, regarding it as precious token from her loved one.

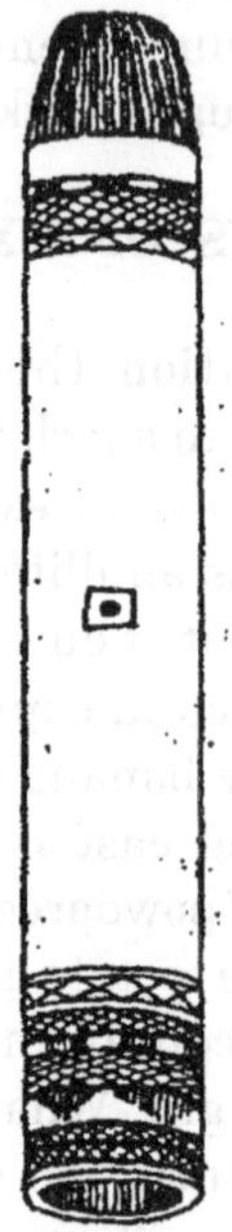

Fig. 3.1: Paangngatem (shuttle) for the looms used by Kwatha youths as love token.

STAGES IN ENGAGEMENT FORM OF MARRIAGE

In the initial stage of engagement it was the role of women. The women of boy's side will communicate to women of girl's side expressing their desire of the girl. At this stage the mother of the boy is not involved in the dialogue. A relative of the boy will indirectly handle the matter. She will communicate everything to the girl's mother on the liking of the boy's parents. The agreed parents of the girl will inform to the parents of the boy on their acceptance of the proposal. They will clarify that the formal process of 'Nupi Haiba' - engagement can be started. Such a clarification from girl's side on their acceptance of the proposal is known as "Yathang Thaba". The next step is the formal meeting of the mothers of the boy and girl. On an auspicious day the women (including mother of the boy) of boy's side will visit the house of the girl. The women (including mother of the girl) of girl's side will response positively and they will welcome the women of boy's side. On this day the formal knowing each other of the mothers of boy and girl commences. On this meeting a formal decision is taken on the acceptance of engagement of her daughter. Even at this stage the decision is not made public, it is a concealed one. But for marriage the decision needs to be made public. Again upto this stage men do not appear in the scene, and it is the monopoly of women. Although acceptance from the father is necessary. On this day an auspicious day is fixed to formalise the decision with the inclusion of elderly persons of both sides. On this auspicious day 'Waroipot Puba' is performed. From this day onwards men come to scene. Elderly persons including the father of the boy will visit the house of the girl. The girl's father will also appear in the scene and he will welcome the guests coming there. On this day the day for 'Heijing Kharai' and marriage is fixed. Till 'Waroipot' any kind of ritual is not included. The sweetmeats brought from the boy's side is distributed to everybody present and they relish it happily. In this way 'Waroipot' formalises the decision of engagement.

But from the day of 'Heijingpot' the process advances to a higher stage. It envolves rituals and offering to deities. Athenpots including fruits, vegetables, sweets are presented to girl's family for the ceremony. In the ceremony 'Waroipot' also the above items are carried to the girl's house. But here a marked difference is visible. Over and above the items, Athenpots are also especially prepared for offering to 'Shagei Shallai Pokpa' deity and 'Lamlai' of the girl's side. A key item in 'Heijingpot' is 'Heijing Kharai'—a basket for ritual use. In this basket including 'Heikru', seven other different fruits are included. 'Heikru' is considered traditionally the leader of all fruits. The other fruits are, Heining, Heiri, Heiyai, Heitup, Heijrang and Heikha. 'Chungou' (white cane sugar) and 'Laphoi' Chang Thokpa' (a hand of banana which ends with odd number when counted in pair) are also essentially included in 'Heijing Kharai'. As mentioned earlier 'Heikru' is considered the elder of the fruits. When placing the fruits in "Heijing Kharai" 'Heikru' is placed at the head of all other fruits. The offering of fruits including 'Heikru' is symbolic of Meitei culture and is a reflection of social status of Meitei women. The underlying idea of offering fruits is that the groom's side is offering something to the girl as a token of bride price. The offering of fruits in the 'Heijing Kharai' in ritualistic form again strengthen the regard and respect extended to the girl. This has brought her as a part of the ritual. In fact the ritual treatment of 'Heijing Kharai' in 'Heijing pot' is itself symbolic of elevating the status of women. Along with Athenpot and 'Heijing Kharai', clothings and ornaments are also brought for the girl. Again special sweetmeats are also brought for the girl and her friends.

The clothes are traditional one only which include a 'Fige Fanek' and an 'Ennafi'. All the items brought from the boy's family are displayed in the 'Thelong' of 'Shumang' (courtyard), where 'Thelong' is the central part of Shumang'. The participants from male side (groom) will sit in the Mangshok (northern or left side of Shumang) and that of female side (bride) will sit in the 'Phammel' (southern or right side of Shumang). The women of boy's side will hand over the clothings and ornaments to the women of girl's side after a thorough examination of the items. In the meantime, the items for 'Apokpa' and 'Lamlai' are carried inside the girl's house and are placed either at 'Fungga Lairu' or at the secluded place of Sanamahi'. The remaining items including the 'Heijing Kharai' are offered to 'Shallai Taret Pokpa Ebuthou' by an experienced person known as

'Piba' or 'Amaiba'. The fathers of the boy and girl will pray to the deity. The Piba or Amaiba will offer the items to the deity on behalf of the two families. After this the father of the girl will sit at Phamen facing north. The father of the boy will sit nearby it facing east and he hands over the 'Heijing Kharai' to the father of girl. The father of the girl will receive the 'Heijing Kharai' by making a 'Figao' (accepting something by stretching one's own cloth). Both the fathers will exchange bowing touching the ground. Again both of them will bow down to the elders of the two Shageis (lineages). The elderly persons (male) of the girl side will sit at 'Phammen'. Those of the boy's side will sit at 'Mang-shok'. After finishing the bowing to elderly persons both the fathers of the boy and girl will sit in their respective seats in their designated sides. After this the items offered to the deity is shared to all those present who enjoy it. The next step is the exchange of 'Kwa' between the fathers of the girl and the boy. Following this they will embrace each other expressing they are 'Ngai-Shen'. In the past embracing each other was a custom, but nowadays this is shortened by the exchange of' Kwa and bowing. The significance of this part is that from that very day they have become relatives. They become 'Eshen' and 'Ebai'. The elder of the two will become 'Ebai' and the younger of them become 'Eshen'. Each one of them disclose their age and then determine the elder and younger of the two. With this the ceremony of 'Heijingpot' is over. In traditional parlance the conclusion of 'Heijingpot' is termed as 'Yumchin kakfei Thare', 'Shumai Urong Khinle', 'Pamel Urai Hak-a'. The meaning is that the conclusion of the ceremony has publicised to all those present that the girl has been owned by the boy's side. Traditionally 'Kakfei Thaba' is a device used in constructing a traditional house. Two or three standing pillars are connected by a 'Wachet' (bamboo piece) as a temporary arrangement known as 'Kakfei Thaba', where the meaning of this arrangement is that nobody is allowed to trespass the area.

'Shumai Urong Khinba' is the erecting of pillar at the courtyard which means a beginning has been made for performing a ceremony or ritual. In the past traditional houses were built by wood and bamboo. Trees were necessary for pillars and beams. And the trees were growing in wild in the community forest. But one needs to groom a tree before felling. He has to wait one year or more for the full growth of the tree. In such a situation one needs to make known to other persons that the tree or trees are under his possession. So, for this he puts a mark on the tree or trees by an axe or dagger. If anybody coming to fell trees in the forest finds such marked tree or trees he will simply avoid them and will try in other trees with no marking. So, likewise, after the conclusion of 'Heijingpot' the girl is under the possession of the boy's family. Now she has become a marked girl like the marked tree in the forest, marked by 'Heijing Kharai' in the ceremony 'Heijingpot'. Everybody present in the ceremony is the witness. She cannot elope with another boy. And nobody can ask or approach to her parents for her hand. If she elopes with someone, then the parents of the girl has to refund the cost of 'Heijingpot'. If such a case happens a sum of Rs. 50/- was fined to the girl's parents. Such a tradition was prevalent till the British rule.

A tradition at Karang, an island on the Loktak lake, is that people put up tall straight bamboo poles, with a lovely cluster of small branches and leaves at the tip, in their courtyard. This has been done to make known to other people that their marriageable daughter in the family is already engaged to her prospective husband.

Apok Asha Thaba

This ritual is mainly performed in the evening. The ritual is held either at 'Mangol' (verandah) or at 'Shumang' (courtyard). Traditionally the ritual was conducted by 'Shagei

Piba' - the traditional head of the lineage. But nowadays with the demise of 'Shagei Piba', an elderly person who is having the knowledge can perform it. The ritual is held conveniently on the day of 'Heijingpot'. The simple ceremony consists of a prayer to 'Shagei Pokpa' and an offering to the deity. The sweetmeats offered is distributed only to the members of the particular Shagei (lineage), i.e. the lineage of the girl. Persons of other lineages are not allowed to enjoy the sweetmeats.

Fig. 3.2: Offering of 'Apok Asha' in the secluded place of 'Sanamahi' deity.

Lamlai Khurumba

It also consists of offering something to the deity who is in charge of the locality. While offering the sweetmeats the face of the person is placed in the direction of the 'Umanglai'. What is offered to the deity can be distributed to everybody present there irrespective of the person belong to the girl's lineage or not. It has no lineage restriction as is the case in 'Apok Asha Thaba' where only those persons belonging to the girl's lineage are allowed to enjoy the sweetmeats offered to 'Apokpa' deity.

Fig. 3.3: A scene of 'Apok Asha Thaba'. (An Amaiba performing the ritual.)

Bor Baton Touba

This is performed on a day in between 'Heijingpot' and 'Luhongba' (marriage). It is held only in the afternoon. As suggested by the title it is a simple ceremony of inviting the Bor (the bridegroom). A boy of tender age, preferably the younger brother of the bride, visits the groom's house

Fig. 3.4: 'Bor Baton Touba' (The groom is receiving the garland of 'Kundo' flower prepared by the bride herself from the boy who is coming to invite the groom for the marriage ceremony.)

guided by an elderly person. At the groom's house he will present 'kwa' and a garland of 'Kundo' flower (prepared by the bride) to the groom with a bowing. The groom, the boy, and the elderly persons all are dressed in traditional attire of white dhotis and shirts. Again the boy also bows to the parents of the groom. And what is implied is that the boy on behalf of the bride is inviting the groom to definitely attend the marriage. This seems to be an addition to Meitei society after the adoption of Hinduism as state religion. The reason is that by inviting the groom the girl makes a request to the groom to definitely present in the marriage ceremony to be held at the girl's residence. And this places the bride (girl) in a subordinate position. This is seemed to be against the tradition of treating women in a comparatively higher status. The ritual treatment of 'Heijing Kharai' in 'Heijingpot' is itself symbolic of elevated status of women in Meitei society.

Fig. 3.5: Offering of 'Phiruk Nungshang' in the secluded place of 'Sanamahi' deity.

Luhongba (Marriage)

On the day of marriage all necessary arrangements are made at the house of bride, including the sitting arrangement. The northern side or left side of the courtyard is reserved for the groom and his father. His mother will sit on the eastern side of the courtyard. On the other side the groom is dressed at the 'Mangshok' of the 'Mangol' (verandah) by an experienced person known as 'Bor Shennaba'. The groom will start his journey by observing an auspicious moment. The 'Bor Shennaba' will guide the groom at every step to be followed in the ceremony. And thus the march begins from his home but with a definite order. In the first place a woman carries the 'Firuk Nungshang' or 'Chengluk Nungshang'. She keeps the Firuk at Phungga Lairu' or at the secluded place of 'Leimarel'. In the second place another woman carries the 'Apok Asha' and she places it at the secluded place of 'Sanamahi' deity. She is followed by the woman who carries the 'Firuk' for 'Lamlai' and she also places it at the secluded place of 'Sanamahi'. The fourth woman carries the 'Mitam Nga' and she keeps it either at

Fig. 3.6: 'Mei Okpa' (Welcoming the groom the fire).

the secluded place of Leimarel' or at 'Sanamahi'. She is followed by another woman who carries the 'Athenpot'. She also places it at the secluded place of 'Sanamahi'. The sixth woman carries the 'Kujapot' and she hand over it to the mother of the bride at the dressing room. These are the clothes to be first used by the bride at her husband's house in the evening. The mother of the groom follows her. In the eighth place the groom follows his mother. This order is to be strictly followed. Again here also, either the 'Bor Shennaba' or an experienced person guides the whole affair.

The groom is welcomed by the party of the bride at their gate with bonfire. This is known as 'Mei okpa'. A torch is made out of strips of pine tree. A herb known as 'Khoiju Leikham' is also burnt. In the past this was known as 'Shingchep Meira Thaba'. This is done to dispel evil spirits from the groom. In the similar manner a person who return from crematorium or from a long journey is also welcomed with fire. This 'Meira Okpa' is performed in three stages. Puffed rice is also sprayed along the fire.

After this the groom further marches toward the courtyard. At the edge of the courtyard the groom is again welcomed by three women led by the mother of the bride by offering 'Kwa'. This is known as 'Maya Okpa'. The groom bows at the 'Shonnabung' - the small mound at the centre of the courtyard where a small herb either Tulsi or Tairen is planted, and return to his reserved place. The 'Piba' or the priest draws the 'Pallandabi Pafan' by flour on the ground where the 'Luhongphal' - the bench, is to be placed for the groom. The bench is placed above the drawing. Now the groom is allowed to sit at the 'Luhongphal'. Then the rite 'Nahei Nashengba' is performed. While sitting on the bench the groom faces east. In the next step the girl is also allowed to sit nearby the groom over a 'Montek' - a soft seat made of cloth. The bride will sit at the north-eastern (Chingkhei) side of the groom. The 'Luhongphal' is placed at western side of 'Shonnabung' or 'Tulsibung'. The mother of the bride comes out and tied the hands of the bride and groom which are placed one above the other. Then the mother of the bride places the 'Kujapot' above the tied hands of the boy and girl. Then father of the bride prays to Almighty for long-life of the bride and groom, and also for their fertility. And he makes a gesture that his daughter has been offered to another 'Shagei' (lineage). The thread binding the hands of the bride and groom is known as 'Langja Taret'. This thread is made out of seven smaller threads and hence the name 'Langja Taret'. The father of the bride bows to both the bride and groom by offering coin or cash on the 'Kujapot'. Then the relatives, brothers, sisters, friends and near and dear ones offer cash at the 'Kujapot'.

The Ingredients of 'Kujapot'

The following items: rice, a hand of banana of 'Changthokpa' (odd number when counted in pair), a 'Heijang' (a fruit), a bud of 'Leishang' (a flower), 'Kwa' (betelnut and leaf), a 'Heijrang' (a knife), a scissor, a 'Kokyet-Feijom' (headgear and *dhoti*), 'Enafi' (a long cloth), and a coin are included in the 'Kujapot'.

Mitam Nga Thaba (Releasing of Fish)

Releasing of fish is performed before removing the 'Kujapot' from the tied hands of the boy and girl. This aspect of the ceremony is executed by three women; two from boy's side and one from girl's side. One of them will hold a lamp, most conveniently in these days a lantern, and will lead the other two. The remaining two women will hold a 'Ngamu' (fish) each in their hands with utmost care so that least pressure is given to the fish while holding them. In the past in place of the lamp a torch made out of pine tree might be serving the purpose. But here the women involved are selective. They need certain qualities to be present in them. In the first place they must be comparatively good looking. They must be mothers of first

Fig. 3.7: Mitam Nga Thaba (Ritual release of fish in the pond.)

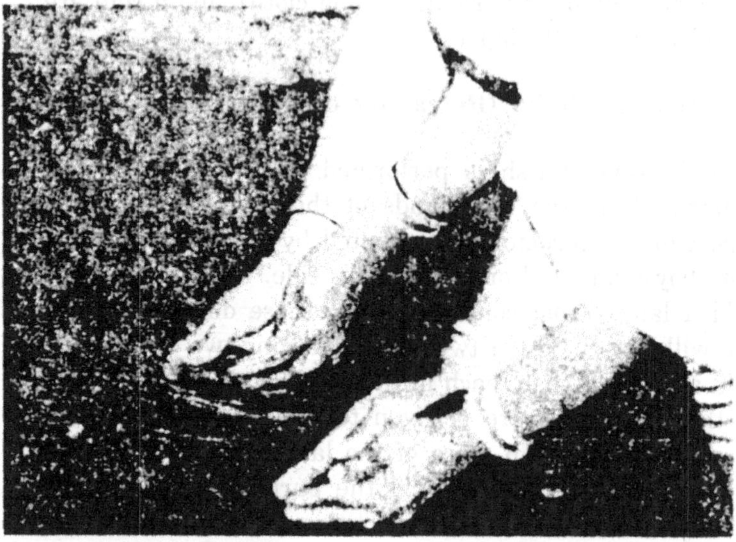

Fig. 3.8: Mitam Nga Thaba (Fishes in the hand at the point of release in the pond.)

born sons. A divorcee is not allowed to take part in the ritual. Further she must also be a woman who is living with her husband. Finally utmost importance is given to the 'Yeks' that the woman affiliated to. They should not be of the same 'Yek' with the girl's family. The last but not the least is that the women should be those who led a couple life by performing rituals of marriage. A varied opinion is available on the significance of Nga Thaba'. The Piba (Athokpam Thoiba) says, this is the scapegoat of the bride and groom. It is believed that any impending sorrow and suffering that may happen to them will be carried away by the two fishes. But Ngangom Ongbi Fatombi (Tombi) of Oinam Awang Leikai gives a different version. The two fishes represents the male and female involved in the marriage. By observing the movement and behaviour of the fishes they will come to some conclusions. If the fishes move in the pond one following after the other it is believed that the couple will lead a happy married life. In opposite to it if one stays and the other moves away in the pond it is believed that the couple will face separation in future. If the female fish follows the male fish the belief is that the family will be a male dominated one. On the other hand if the male fish follows the female fish, again the belief is that the family will be female dominated one. In this way a number of conclusions are derived by observing the movement and behaviour of the fishes.

The three women when coming out of the house along with the fish to be released in the pond, pass through the 'Shonnapung' or 'Mandop'; the central part of the courtyard where the festival is held. In their return trip also they are to come on the same route in a line, i.e. one following the other. They are offered a cloth each by the 'Arangpham' (the manager in the ceremony) before their stepping up to 'Mangol' (verandah). But the cloth offered by the 'Arangpham' is the one brought by groom's side.

The next step is to remove the 'Kujapot' from the hands of the bride and groom. The removal is executed by 'Piba Shennaba' and 'Nupi Shennaba' (the one who guides the bride) and hand over it to the mother of the bride. Then the bride stands up from her seat (Montek, Mondum) and moves around the groom for seven times in anti-clockwise direction, and flowers are showered on the groom intermittently which is known as 'Leichaiba'. Now she puts two garlands at a time on the neck of the groom. After this her task is over and sits on the left side of the groom. Then the groom removes a garland from his neck and puts it on the neck of the bride. The belief behind this is that 'Malem' (the earth) was separated from the Sun. Another name for this 'Malem' (the earth) is 'Chingkhei Apanba'. The name is so given that the sun attracted the Malem (earth) to its fold again but the Malem remained restrained at the last limit of the Sun's gravitation pull or attraction power. In order to acknowledge that the two celestial bodies emerged out of a single body, so the two garlands are using as a symbol

Fig. 3.9: 'Mei Okpa' (Welcoming the bride with fire)

of the two heavenly bodies. Again the act of garlanding the bride by the groom by removing a garland from his neck symbolises that the Malem (earth) was separated from the Sun. This act of exchanging garlands between the bride and groom is immediately followed by the entry of the bride and groom to the house of the bride. There they are welcomed by their respective mothers and offer 'Kangshubi' (a sweetmeat) and 'Kwa' (betel nut and leaf). The girl (bride) also offers the same item to the groom. This is known as 'Kangshubi Lannaba'. Again this act is performed with a certain belief. A belief embodied in the architecture of 'Meitei Yumjao' (traditional house) is that the architecture is derived from human body. On the other hand the human body is like the traditional house. So the entry of the bride and groom to the house after the conclusion of ceremony is symbolic of the belief that the Almighty enters the body of mankind and thus spreads the offsprings.

After the conclusion of marriage ceremony the bride with traditional attire was carried on a chariot (Dollai) to the house of groom. Nowadays, in place of this motor vehicles are increasingly used. In the case of bride also 'Mei Okpa', a welcome with torch is performed in a similar manner at the gate of the groom. But this practice is a very old one. Mention of this is found in the literature 'Panthoibi Khongkul' and the text is:

'Khapa Mayum Nak Yangpa Mashaikonta Tampa Laipu Langna Waithung Larapata Khapa Hoitonpokpam Ningonpi Manutek Ngana Tampa Mahuironpu Shingchep Meira Haichou Thana Lam-okngamye. Chamlou Lamkaroi Pashot Fingou Thana Kapok Famna Hul khapa Pumna Til Shamu Thangchepana LamokNgamye.'

[It says: Panthoibi on her maiden arrival, she was welcomed by her mother-in-law, Khaba Hoidon - Kokpam Ningol Manu Tekngan with a large torch known as 'Shingchep Meira'. On her passage a white cloth was spread and on it puffed rice was sprayed. She was received and warmly embraced by her mother-in-law in the presence of a larger crowd of 'Khaba'.]

On the arrival of the bride at the house of the groom, again a small get-together is performed. Whatever brought from the house of the bride side is again distributed along with those from boy's side to everybody present there. This custom is also mentioned in the same literature 'Panthoibi Khongkhul' and the text in archaic goes in this way:

"Maman Ningthou Khapa Shokchrongpa Kanglei Leipak Mapana Sharel Shanei Ngamta Wanglei Yunei Ngamtarapaki Tara Maikhangnapapu Ngamtarapaki Tamak Khapa Tangcha Yikaikhi. Yangpa Shenkoylakngamlapata Tampa Wangngamlonna Mapal Kanglei Pung Mayonki Lal-Ullakpa Tara chakthompa Sharel Wal-longma, Wanglei khumlongmapu Maikhangnakhiye. Tara Chakyenpasung chakpon Mayeng Tatana chaklemye."

[It says: "At the moment when her father-in-law Ningthou khaba Shokchromba could not introduce all those arriving from Kanglei by offering liquor and meat, and all the khabas ashamed of this failure; Tampa Wangamlon (Panthoibi) served all those present from her dowry which contained a basket of rice, a cane of meat and a jar of liquor. And thus the introduction was accomplished in this manner. The rice was plenty and it surpassed the persons assembled there."]

But here we can observe a sharp difference in the food items brought from the bride to the groom's house. The use of rice, meat and liquor in marriage ceremony is totally ceased to practice in these days. In place of this only sweet-meats are used. After the exchange of sweetmeats 'Ngai-Shen-Konnaba' was repeated again, and the father of the boy and girl embrace each other. And thus ends the marriage ceremony.

Although the marriage ceremony is accomplished on the day of marriage, still there is a ritual to be performed on the fifth day after marriage. This is known as 'Phiruk Nungshang Hangba'. The item carried is also known as 'Chengluk Nungshang'. As mentioned earlier the woman carrying the 'Phiruk Nungshang' leads the marriage procession of the groom and his party. First rice is put in a 'Phiruk (a dome shaped basket) and above it two plates of 'Meitei Thum' (traditional salt made from local brines), two 'Pannao', two 'Shingnao', a fruit with sharp smell and a coin are placed. This 'Phiruk' was offered to 'Phungga Lairu' of the bride's house on the day of marriage. It is left undisturbed till the fifth day after marriage. On this, fifth day after marriage women of groom's side and those of bride's side ritually open the 'Phiruk' known as 'Phiruk Nungshang Hangba'. When opening the 'Phiruk' if an ant or a Kachappi (an insect) is found present inside, it is counted as a good omen. If any one of them is found dead it is counted as an ominous sign. And this is the last ritual performed in Meitei marriage.

Dress

Regarding the dress of a bride in the ancient past a reference can be made from the literature 'Tutenglon'. The literature is an account of the dredger 'Meidingu Taothingmang' who ruled from A.D. 264-364. The dress as mentioned in this literature is found to be very different from to-day. The bride wore 'Leiren Leihao' and feather of the bird 'Langmei'. The hair was also tied into a knot at the tip. In this way a brief picture can be reconstructed from this literature on the dress of a bride in the past. But nowadays the situation is very different. A bride wear 'Kajenglei' (an ornament on the head) and 'Polloi' as lower garment. She also wear rasom shirt and wear many ornaments at the hand and arm.

ISSUES RELATED WITH MARRIAGE

In the ancient past monogamy was the dominant form of marriage. But later on polygamous form of marriage also appeared in the scene, particularly after the Seven Years Devastation (A.D. 1819-1825). Polygamy was practised especially by the members of the royal family, the Raja being allowed four principal wives and any number not exceeding 108 wives of less dignity. In polygamous households custom regulated the attention to be paid to the several wives in order of their seniority. The social reason for polygamy was to get a status in the society where a person with more than one wife was highly esteemed. But in the case of royal family it had political significance, particularly from the point of view of strength. For the aristocrats it was an easy way to get a high social status; and they could do so because of their affluence. Polygamy was practised among the commoners also, but they were following the models of the aristocrats. At present both monogamous and polygamous form of marriage is in practice. However, monogamy is the popular and dominant form of marriage.

The evidence to support the prevalance of polyandry is lacking, but there is the possibility of practicing by someone secretly.

Sororate was not unknown to Manipuri society. Still today in isolated cases a person use to marry with the younger sister of his deceased wife or the younger sister of his living wife. Levirate has no social sanction in Meitei society. It might be practised somewhere in very isolated case. As a rare case in history a mention is found from the literature 'Poireiton Khunthokpa', on the practice of livirate. This is mentioned when 'Poireiton' was asked by his elder brother "Leinung Thongaren" to go for a mission to find a better habitable place. By then Poireiton was a bachelor and he expressed his desire for a pair in the mission. In this 'Leinung Thongaren' advised his first wife "Leima Laikhurembi" to accompany Poireiton but she refused on the ground of her old age. Again, he approached his younger wife "Leima Leinaotabi" and she readily agreed. So, "Poireiton" underwent his mission with "Leima Leinaotabi" with an elaborate preparation.

Manipur followed very intricate marriage laws in the past. And sexual relations among the close relatives were strongly forbidden. Someone who committed it and those who breached the traditional marriage laws were exiled to a specific place. And such places were located to periferal areas of the valley known as "Haojongpan". The 'Haojongpan' in Imphal is located in the village Sairem Khul. It is around 7 km from Imphal on the New Cachar Road. Still "Uyung Trees" are growing in this area. A stone inscription is also found from this site. The people living here wore green turban. As an instance, in 1791 S.E. (A.D. 1869, 12th July, Tuesday), a person was exiled to Haojongpan for being married or having sexual relation with Loitangbam and Paonam; they all belonged to the same clan, Mangang Salai. Again, in 1800 S.E.(A.D.1878, 13th July, Friday), another person was sent to the same place for having sexual relation with Yengkokpam and Sanasam. Both of them also belonged to the same clan, Mangang Salai. But nowadays such law and restrictions are relaxed to a certain extent as the authority to enforce such a custom has vanished in history. Although such a custom and tradition is not altogether rejected, still it has its say in the society. And those who breach such a custom are very few in number and the practice is not still rampant.

Manipuri family is patrilocal in residence. After completing the marriage ceremony the woman is brought to the groom's residence. Then, the original lineage of the woman is lost to her husband's lineage. The children also follow the lineage of the father. Property is also inherited in father's line. Property inherited to the mother is also owned by children. Matriliny is non-existent in Manipuri society. In some isolated cases, the person used to stay at the bride's residence after marriage which is known as "Yaong-inba". But later on the woman had to come to the person's residence.

In Manipuri society early child marriage was not practised and was unknown to the Manipuris. And still it is not practised anywhere In Manipur. But in the past early marriage was pre-dominant. Thirteen years of age was earliest for the girls and 15 years of age was the earliest for the boy's. Nowadays early marriage is gradually diminishing in the urban areas. Widows, except those of the Brahmins, could re-marry, but not with their deceased husband's brother. Widow re-marriage is a socially accepted practice. But they could not perform the same ritual with regular marriage. They were allowed to perform "Apok Asha Thaba", but not "Phiruk Nungsang Hangba".

Inheritance is done through the father's line. Property was not inherited to the daughters. Some movable properties were presented as marriage gift at the time of marriage. But nowadays inheriting immovable properties by daughters is not uncommon. For the unmarried daughters of parents of advanced age the marriage gift were to be arranged by the sons. In the case of a married daughter who returned to her parents house she had to get a plot of land in her parent's homestead. She could stay there till she desire, but cannot sell it. If the parents did not have a male issue then the property would have to be inherited to daughter. Nobody from other lineage could claim it.

Divorce also occured in Manipur society mainly from the reasons of adultery and sterility. But divorce was mainly based on the chastity of woman. The elders of the local disposed the case only when concrete evidences were submitted to them. Nowadays divorce may occur from other reasons also, which may be difference of ideology, status, etc. With the demise of local authorities a person use to approach the law court to get justice at the earliest.

Divorce (Khainaba) Rule

In the past, if a man or a woman wanted divorce, he or she used approach village chowkidar. With the help of village Hanjaba (Head) and other elders, the chowkidar tried to bring about a reconciliation. If a woman wanted divorce to marry another man, her second husband had to pay Nupimamal (price of a woman) of Rs. 50 to the first husband. Although it does not carry the sense of fixing price of a woman like a commodity, but it was imposed in the form of fine. If the husband demanded divorce where the wife was not a fault, the wife could take all movable property with her except his loin cloth. After a divorce the wife's family could demand the return of her original dowry. According to rules, the wife should leave all her children behind except the suckling child.

Adultery was punishable crime. The offending male who received the wife of another man, the offender forced tc pay a fixed sum of Rs. 50 for all strata of population, besides all the fine to the court that tried such cases. Should the offender not be able to pay, his family were siezed and sold as slaves fcr the satisfaction of the claim. Both the male and female offenders were arrested and confined until the claim was settled, after which they were freed.

E. MARRIAGE LAWS

The Meiteis followed very intricate marriage laws. According to these laws marriage between close relatives are forbidden for many generations. Again in some laws the restriction was imposed for a few generations only. In the past these laws were strickly imposed and any one who breached such laws were exiled to a place named "Haojongpan". The interpretation of such laws was the duty of "Pandit Loishang" although the enforcement was in the hand of the state. These laws are found mentioned in the literature like "Salai Taretki Khun-gum", "Salai Poklakpa Langwon" and 'Meihourol Salai Khaiba', etc. At a superficial observation exogamous marriage seems to be the only prevalent marriage laws. But after a closer examination it has found to be a complex arrangement. The laws are mentioned in the following manner: (1) EE Tinnaba or Pudinnaba, (2) Pen Tinnaba, (3) Sairuk Tinnaba, (4) Leinung Pen Tinnaba, (5) *Pi* Tinnaba, and (6) Pellol Tinnaba.

1. EE Tinaba

E Tinnaba and Pudinnaba are one and the same. It means the offspring of the same progenitor. Restriction is imposed in marriage among the offsprings of the same Pukok (Progenitor). In a Salai (clan) there are many Shageis (sub-clan) and majority of the Shageis comes under the purview of EE Tinnaba law. According to literature 'Meihourol Salai Khaiba' Angom Salai has as many as 49 shageis which are considered as the offspring of the same progenitor. And hence all these 49 shageis falls under EE Tinnaba law.

A. The Shageis of Angom Salai are:

1. Yumlembam
2. Langmaithem/Nongmaithem
3. Langmaithem Sangbam
4. Hidam
5. Seram
6. Narumbam
7. Pongsumbam
8. Achuram
9. Haobam
10. Ngarelbam
11. Ongnam
12. Hongnemsubam.

These 12 shageis (sub-clans) are treated as *Angom Ariba* (meaning old Angom).

13. Kongbam
14. Chakpram
15. Mangsatam
16. Ayengbam
17. Wanglem
18. Chingkangbam
19. Tellem
20. Leitanthem
21. Sairem
22. Khangelbam
23. Keikralbam
24. Nongtholbam, Angom-inba
25. Nakpakhanjabam
26. Motabam
27. Thangjam

28. Longjam
29. Lairellakpam
30. Wangkhem
31. Kaswam
32. Akoijam
33. Ningolbam
34. Laitoncham
35. Huirem
36. Moirangloushangbam.
37. Ekheishangbam
38. Achoibam, Angom-inba
39. Potsangbam, Angom-inba
40. Ngalelbam, Angom-inba
41. Emkhaibam
42. Ngannukapakpam
43. Khanachaobam, Angom
44. Khuyolthem-inba
45. Mungkhom
46. Ngasambam
47. Putolcham
48. Sangtolcham
49. Mantingbam.

B. Chenglei Salai E Tinnaba

The following are the Shageis (sub-clans) of Chenglei Salai (clan) which comes under the law of E Tinnaba. They are:

1. Thangjam
2. Tongbram
3. Ayekpam
4. Saraisam

5. Leishangthem
6. Khakokpam
7. Naoshekpam
8. Emkutum
9. Sarangthem
10. Wairokpam
11. Chanam
12. Elangbam
13. Chingngakham
14. Maibathiyam
15. Samnom
16. Tourangbam
17. Thumkanbam
18. Ngathem
19. Loushikam
20. Hairam
21. Leitam
22. Meinam
23. Sarotkhaibam
24. Kharaicham
25. Konsam, Chinglei-inba
26. Langkoncham
27. Mayanglambam, Chenglei-inba
28. Maiparam
29. Khoisanam
30. Heiwam, and
31. Potshangbam Nachou Taba.

C. Ngalba Salai E Tinnaba

The following 16 Shageis of Ngalba Salai are the offspring of the same Pukok (progenitor) and hence comes under E - Tinnaba law. They are:

1. Meihoubam
2. Tekcham
3. Thongngam
4. Aheibam Thongngam
5. Hentakpam
6. HaobamNgalba-inba
7. Thinbam
8. Langtoncham
9. Sanchiram
10. Kabalambam
11. Khaithem
12. Khumukcham
13. Ficham
14. Wangkoncham
15. Khaba Salai Nongchembam and
16. Khuraicham.

D. Luwang Salai E - Tinnaba

The Pukok (progenitor) of Luwang Salai is 'Epuluwang Punshiba'. He married nine wives and according to the literature 'Meihourol Salai Khaiba' some of his wives are 'Eremnaoshangkhu', 'Khongleishang,' Tan Leima, Nusin Leima and Haoku Leima'. All the 57 lineages of Luwang Salai (clan) are the offspring of 'Luwang Punshiba'; and consequently they come under E - Tinnaba law. According to the above mentioned literature the lineages Ashangbam, Meiyengbam, Abucham, Urepkhinbam, Fammihanbam and Wanglembam are the offspring of Eremnaoshangkhu. Arambam, Ngangom, Laichayangbam, Pukraicham, Luwangshangbam, Nongtholbam, Heitham and Toibicham are descended from 'Khongleishang'. Tan Leima Moinu Chanu procreated 'Wakongthem'. Again 'Nushin Leima

Chingnung Haoba chanu procreated 'Khumchanmayum and 'Khhumukcham'. Feiroicham, Moibunglokpam, Soubam, Maisanam, Ngoubam, Thiyam, Meitram, Thamangcham, Emlembam, Thouknaojam and Athokpam are descended from 'Haoku Leima Lamtang Ningthou Chanu'.

The 57 lineages of Luwang clan which comes under E-Tinnaba law are:

1. Ashangbam
2. Arambam
3. Tinbijam
4. Leirongcham
5. Toibicham, Apucham
6. Apucham
7. Meiyengbam
8. Urepkhinbam
9. Arubam
10. Nongtholpam
11. Pungkraicham
12. Ngangom
13. Luwangshangbam
14. Wanglenbam
15. Heitham
16. Fammihanbam
17. Thamangcham
18. Wakongthem
19. Khunchanmayim
20. Kongbam
21. Thangcham Saram
22. Khunmukcham
23. Feiroicham
24. Thiyam
25. Shenbangcham

26. Waikhom
27. Moibunglokpam
28. Soupwam
29. Maisanam
30. Meitram
31. Yumlembam
32. Thouknaocham
33. Athokpam
34. Hicham
35. Sanlam
36. Nongpokpam
37. Yangngambam
38. Shingkhangbam
39. Haorongbam
40. Laishom
41. Thangjam
42. Thouteicham
43. Nahakpam
44. Loukham
45. Naoroibam
46. Wahengbam
47. Laikangbam
48. Nantam
49. Lairenjam
50. Loicha Yangambam
51. Nganbam
52. Chingchabam
53. Nganglom
54. Ningchitpam
55. Khoknam
56. Shambanduram
57. Khoibam.

E. Khuman Salai E - Tinnaba

The following are the lineages which come under Khuman Salai E - Tinnaba law:

1. Akham
2. Afram
3. Maibam
4. Thoitingcham
5. Yanglem
6. Thingkucham
7. Pukhrem
8. Fairelbam
9. Chaltam
10. Pangkhaicham
11. Mongcham
12. Langtem
13. Ngangbam
14. Akangcham
15. Oinam
16. Maimom
17. Khamnam
18. Ahongshangbam
19. Chapungbam
20. Thongkram
21 Ahongbam
22. Heikrujam
23. Sinam
24. Thongbam
25. Yangnuyeibam
26. Hangnem

27. Kiyam
28. Laikhram
29. Thoutem
30. Konom
31. Shoukaicham
32. Ngakhakhoimayum
33. Wareppam
34. Taipangcham
35. Shiyatpam
36. Haobicham
37. Kabarambam,(Khuman- inba)
38. Thongcham
39. Pukhralbam
40. Meitankeishangbam
41. Likmabam
42. Maibam.
43. Thingkom
44. Mayanglabam, (Khuman-inba)
45. Chungkham
46. Maifabam
47. Amakcham
48. Charoibam
49. Khullem
50. Akam
51. Khoirisumbam
52. Lammabam
53. Yaithingbam
54. Langkam
55. Samukcham
56. Thingpaicham

57. Khoirom
58. Namram
59. Haobam
60. Moirengcham
61. Hentakpam
62. Nepram
63. Emkhaibam
64. Emkutum
65. Laishram
66. Amom
67. Toncham
68. Puyam
69. Salkhom
70. Sinaibam
71. Moichem
72. Aheibam
73. Fancham
74. Pallucham
75. Lantham
76. Taurem
77. Yambem
78. Ngaseppam
79. Santham
80. Toumom
81. Pangalbam
82. Tokpam
83. Shansenbam
84. Katam
85. Chingtham

86. Sakappam
87. Haorongbam
88. Lantham
89. Thangjam Yaosom
90. Thangjam
91. Khumanthem
92. Wangkom
93. Aheibam Taobam
94. Yangleibam
95. Pallebam
96. Tellem, (Khuman-inba)
97. Tonthramaibam
98. Thangangbam (Khuman-inba)
99. Khungheibam
100. Langkhabam
101. Soram (Khuman-inba)
102. Hao-oibam
103. Sentam
104. Shinaibam.

F. Moirang Salai E - Tinnaba

The following lineages fall under Moirang Salai E-Tinnaba. They are:

1. Chongtham
2. Mellem
3. Wayelbam
4. Pukhralbam
5. Moirangnarengbam
6. Narengbam.
7. Kabalambam

8. Thangjam Salkom
9. Moirang Nongtholbam
10. Puthem
11. Konchengbam, (Moirang-inba)
12. Keifafiyam
13. Laiyucham
14. Nampucham
15. Wangbacham (Moirang-inba)
16. Kabacham
17. Ngangbam
18. Nungleppam
19. Thangkacham
20. Ningthoukhongjam
21. Konkham
22. Moirang Keithellakpam
23. Okram
24. Yaikhom
25. Kummabam
26. Chakpa Taba Mungnem
27. Moirangthem
28. Thangjam
29. Akhwoibam
30. Namucham
31. Wanglelbam, (Moirang-inba)
32. Kairenjam
33. Moirang Emkhaibam
34. Khuyonthem
35. Mungkhom Maiyangbam
36. Haorongbam

37. Laikucham
38. Yairelbam
39. Konchengbam
40. Akuram
41. Lisham
42. Moirang Mayanglambam
43. Thokchom
44. Pollem
45. Soibam
46. Pukhrambam
47. Maifawam
48. Laifrakpam
49. Lairelmayum
50. Ngangom (Moirang-inba)
51. Khoinaijam
52. Leimayum
53. Wangkhem
54. Hitam
55. Shingkhangbam
56. Hawaibam (Moirang-inba)
57. Kheithellakpam (Moirang-inba)
58. Ngangkham
59. Aheibam
60. Ngaseppam (Moirang-inba)
61. Moirangmayum
62. Leimakhucham
63. Khwairakpam (Moirang-inba)
64. Ạsem
65. Khomdram.

G. Ningthoucha Salai E - Tinnaba.

The following are the lineages which come under Ningthoucha Salai E -Tinnaba. They are:

1. Yenkhom
2. Keithellakpam
3. Khoirom
4. Nahakpam
5. Thongkapam
6. Shanglenmayim
7. Mairenpam
8. Fairenpam
9. Hairom
10. khongnam
11. Naukalsangpam
12. Taimacham
13. Naorem
14. Epushangpam
15. Leiyusungpam
16. Khumanlambam
17. Khoisanam
18. Sukhwam
19. Namoicham
20. Mayanglambam
21. Naoroibam
22. Kangasenpam
23. Changninghenpam
24. Ngarenyanpam
25. Loitam
26. Irom

27. Laishangpam
28. Thingnam
29. Akhom
30. Khuntrakpam
31. Kangasenpam
32. Haokhom
33. Sanaucham
34. Laikangpam
35. Wareppam
36. Lourangpam
37. Yangnuyeipam
38. Sairem
39. Akhongpam
40. Soyam
41. Mutum
42. Heirangkhongcham
43. Heisanam
44. Huirongpam
45. Kongpacham
46. Ahanthem
47. Satpam
48. Leichonpam
49. Keisam
50. Irengpam
51. Satthokpam
52. Charoipam
53. Loitongpam
54. Atom
55. Paunam
56. Erungpam

57. Lukram Nong-in Fapam
58. Leimaram
59. Nongthompam
60. Famtom
61. Hemam
62. Chirom
63. Khoytongpam
64. Lamleirakpam
65. Huitrom
66. Yumnam
67. Leimayokpam
68. Khumancharakpam
69. Langpokthapam
70. Ningthoucham
71. Nakampam
72. Shingkhwam
73. Soram
74. Yensempam
75. Thoutam
76. Hotam
77. Sakolsem
78. Sanasapam
79. Nameirakpam Moirangningthoumayum
80. Paopam
81. Fourugpam
82. Shangkaisenpam
83. Numitleima Shangpam
84. Khunchahanpam
85. Sanapam
86. Waikhom

87. Khangsulakpam
88. Yenkokpam
89. Ficham
90. Thangkangsapam
91. Aheipam
92. Fatlampam
93. Fenlem
94. Lourempam
95. Laitoncham
96. Moichem
97. Haoteicham
98. Khoinucham
99. Nautam
100. Lantham
101. KonthaHaopam
102. Sarenshangpam
103. Khuntom
104. Shingkhongpam
105. Saikhom
106. Khoyriyampam
107. Soukrakpam
108. Chomchanpam
109. Nongmeikapam
110. Tenshenpam
111. Khwairakpam
112. Wangkheimayum
113. Irungpam
114. Wangkheirakpam
115. Kanghacham
116. Khmlangpa-Shangpam.

2. Pen Tinnaba Law

Children of same mother but of different fathers are known as 'Pen Tinnaba'. Such a situation may also arise when a widow (with child or children) is asked by the society or locality to marry with another male. This is known as 'Thangjinnaba' in Manipuri. So the child or children of her first husband cannot marry with the child or children of her second husband. Such a relationship is known as 'Pen-tinnaba'. But this law lapses after three generations and the children can marry with one another.

3. Sairuk Tinnaba Law

This law has a historical origin. It happened from such a situation that the offspring of the same Pukok (progenitor) fused to other Salais (clans) with their lineages. In order to perpetuate their clan indentity the book 'Salai Poklakpa Langwon' was written and at the same time the law 'Sairuk Tinnaba' was developed. According to Pandit Moirangthem Norendra, it is considered that it happened during the reign of Chaoba Shoubonngamba' of Moirang principality. And he gives the historical background in the following manner.

Historical Background

During the reign of 'Chaoba Shoubon-Ngamba' of Moirang principality, the Khaba Salai was ruling at Kangla (Imphal).The ruling king of Khaba Salai (clan) was 'Khwai Nungjeng Piba'. The Kingdom of khaba was destroyed by the allied force of 'Chaoba Shoubon' - 'Ngamba' of Moirang and Ningthemcha Salai. The Khabas run helter skelter, and remained in hiding from the genocidal attack. They fused to any available Salai. So, from such a situation in order to preserve their clan identity the 'Sairuk Tinnaba' law was developed. For the moment the identity of the king of Nihgthoucha Salai cannot be established. But it is generally believed that the king may be 'Nongda Lairen Pakhangba', and it is roughly estimated that the incident occured between the reign of king 'Nongda Lairen Pakhangba' (A.D.34-154) and king Naothingkhong (A.D.663-763) But according to Pandit N. Khelchandra the last king of Khaba Salai who reigned at Kangla was 'Khaba Nongjenba'. At the outset of confrontation 'Khaba Nongjenba' defeated king Nongda Lairen Pakhangba of Ningthoucha Salai who took refuge at Moirang principality. But later on 'Khaba Nongjenba' was defeated by the combined forces of 'Nongda Lairel Pakhangba' (Ningthoucha Salai) and 'Moirang Salai'.

According to the literature 'Salai Poklakpa Langwol' the Sairuk is four in number.

I. During his stay in Moirang 'Nongda Lairen Pakhangba' gave birth to his two sons; (a) Mungyang Chaoba and (b) Tanggru Lummiba. Mungyang Chaoba became the progenitor of Mungyangjam' lineage. And his younger brother' Tanggru Lummiba' became the progenitor of 'Loirenjam' lineage. This two lineages were fused to 'Moirang Khuwang Salai'.' Khuwang' is the name of a person. He belonged to original Moirang Salai. It means the two lineages were fused to his Salai (clan). This two lineages are of the same' Sairuk' with Ningthemcha clan. And the two lineages cannot establish marriage relationship with Ningthoucha Salai. To be more specific 'Mungyangjam' and' Loirenjam' cannot inter-marry with the hundred and sixteen (116) lineages of Ningthoucha Salai. Now the lineage' Loirenjam' is extinct.

II. Ningolbam and Laitonjam of Angom clan are of the same Sairuk with the lineages of Kouba Anganga' of Moirang Anouba' (New Moirang). The above two lineages cannot establish marriage relationship with the lineages of Kouba Anganga' of Moirang Anouba'.

Moirang Ariba (old Moirang) and Moirang Anouba (New Moirang)

Moirang Ariba

These are the lineages of Moirang Salai who settled first at Moirang. They are the descendants of Ngangningshing. (The parentage of Nganghunthok and Ngangningshing is Urenkhuba). Ngangningshing became the ruler of Moirang principality and in such a favourable situation Ngangningshing invited the children of his brother Nganghunthok to settle at Moirang. 'Kouba Angang' is the son of 'Nganghunthok' and as he came from 'Koubru' (a range in the northwestern side of Manipur, still preserved as a sacred place of Manipur and pilgrimage is held every year) the prefix 'Kouba' is used. Ngangningshing was inviting the party of 'Kouba Anganga' and not his brother 'Nganghunthok'. The party of' Kouba Anganga' after their settlement at Moirang principality came to be known as 'Moirang Anouba' (new). Their settlement at Moirang occurred around the reign of Thinggri Nachaoba'. After the death of 'Thinggri Nachaoba', the throne remained vacant as there was no able person to rule the Kingdom. In order to meet the situation 'Koub'a Anganga' was invited along with is party to settle at Moirang and to become King of Moirang principality.

The lineages of Moirang Anouba Kouba Anganga.

1. Thokchom
2. Pollem
3. Soibam-Pukhralbam
4. Soibam
5. Maikham
6. Laifrakpam
7. Lairelmayum

8. Ngangkham (Moirang-inba)
9. Laithangbam
10. Khoinaijam
11. Leimajam
12. Wakhem (Wangkhem)
13. Hidam
14. Shingkham
15. Haowoibam
16. Keithellakpam
17. Ngaseppam (Moirang-inba)
18. Ngangkham
19. Aheibam
20. Moirangmayum
21. Leimakhujam
22. Khwairakpam.

III. Sarangthem, Leishangthem, Haurokcham and Konthoujam of Chenglei Salai, and the lineages of 'Khaba' and 'Nganba' Salai are of the same 'Sairuk' with the 44 lineages of Moirang Ariba (old Moirang).

The lineages of Khaba are:

1. Nungjenbam
2. Khuraijam

The lineages of Nganba are:

1. Meihoubam
2. Tekcham
3. Khundongbam
4. Thongam
5. Aheibam, Thongam

6. Hentakpam
7. Haobijam
10. Shanchiram
11. Kabarambam
12. Khaidem (Khaithem).
13. Khunujam
14. Fijam (Nganba-inba).
15. Wangbijam
16. Wakanbam.

The four lineages: Sarangthem, Leishangthem, Haurokcham and Konthoujam of Chenglei Salai, two lineages of Khaba; Nungjenbam and Khuraijam, and 16 lineages of Nganba Salai i.e. the above 22 lineages cannot intermarry with the 44 lineages of Moirang Ariba.

The lineages of Moirang Ariba (old) are:

1. Moirangthem
2. Chongtham
3. Mellem
4. Wayenbam
5. Pukhralbam
6. Moirangnarengbam
7. Narengbam
8. Kabalambam
9. Thangjam Sankhom
10. Moirang Nongthombam
11. Puthem
12. Konjengbam, (Moirang-inba)
13. ChakpaFiyam
14. Laiyujam

15. Nambujam
16. Wangbijam,(Moirang-inba)
17. Kabajam
18. Ngangna
19. Nungleppam
20. Thanggajam
21. Ningthoukhongj am
22. Kongkham
23. Moirang Keithellakpam
24. Sharungbam
25. Okram
26. Yaikhom
27. Kumabam
28. Chakpa Taba Mangnom
29. Thangjam
30. Akhwaibam
31. Namujam
32. Wanglenbam (Moirang-inba)
33. Kairenjam
34. Moirang Yumkhaibam
35. Khuyonthem
36. Mungkhom
37. Khoiyangbam
38. Haorongbam
39. Laikhujam
40. Yoyrenbam
41. Konjengbam
42. Akuram
43. Lisham
44. Mayanglambam

IV. The lineages Achong Yumlembam, Hidam, Langmaithem and Tellongshangbam of Angom Salai(clan) are of the same 'Sairuk' with the lineages of khaba Salai. The above four lineages are the descendants of one 'Khaba Manao Hunba'. They had been fused to Angom Salai. Though these lineages are found in Angom Salai they cannot intermarry with the lineages of Khaba Salai.

In isolated cases Loktonbam and Mungyangjam are of the same 'Sairuk'. Mungyangjam is basically Ningthoucha Salai but had been fused to Moirang Khwang Salai. Again Naorem and Chenglei salai are of the same Sairuk. In this case also 'Naorem' is basically 'Chenglei', but king Naothingkhong recognised him as his son and fused to Ningthoucha Salai.

4. Leinung Pen - Tinnaba

Leinung literally means underground, but in the present context it means secret. This relationship was established when the maternal grandmother married to different persons and the children of the maternal grandmother with different persons' are within this prohibited degree - 'Leinung Pentinnaba'. The children cannot establish marriage relationship as they belong to the same Mapen, i.e. the same maternal grandmother and hence they fall under 'Leinung Pentinnaba' law. The following are the lineages which falls under this law.

I. *Kasabam.* Akoicham, Ningolbam, Laitonjam and Huirem of Angom Salai (clan) are within the prohibited ambit 'Leinung Pentinnaba' with Khoknam, Sampanduram, Khoibam of Luwang Salai (clan).

II. The lineages:

1. Thangjam
2. Tongbram
3. Saraisam

4. Leitanbam
5. Thumkanbam
6. Ngathem
7. Mayanglambam (Chenglei-inba)
8. Loushibam Leishan-gthem Khakokpam
9. Maibarambam
10. Naoshekpam
11. Emkutum Meinam
12. Heiwam
13. Sharangthem
14. Wairokpam
15. Chanam
16. Sarotkhaibam
17. Maiba Thiyam
18. Sanmom
19. Konthoujam
20. Haorokcham
21. Thangjam Yupanbam
22. Wakanbam
23. Konjengbam
24. Loktonbam
25. Yangkoicham
26. Hemmoibam and
27. Amom (Cheglei-inba) of Leishangthem Salai are within the law 'Leinung Pentinaba' with Haorangbam, Konchengbam, Laikhucham, Okram and Lisham of Moirang Khwang Salai.

III. Hicham and Sallam of Moirang Salai are within the law 'Leinung Pentinnaba' with Oinam, Maimom, Langheibam, Moichem and Laishram of Khuman Salai.

IV. The lineages:

1. Thokchom
2. Soibam Pukhralbam
3. Soibam
4. Shingkhangbam
5. Moirang Keithellakpam
6. Thangjam Ngangkham
7. Moirangmayum
8. Aheibam, (Moirang-inba)
9. Lairelmayum
10. Laifrakpam
11. Khoinaicham
12. Leimacham
13. Moirang Khwairakpam and
14. Hidam of Moirang Anouba Salai are within the prohibited ambit of 'Leinung Pentinnaba' with the lineages:
    1. Khuyonthem.
    2. Mungkhhom,
    3. Khoirangbam.
    4. Lisham,
    5. Moirang Lairelmayum.
    6. Toupokcham.
    7. Putolcham, and
    8. Shangtolcham of Moirang Ariba Salai.

V. Akham of Khuman Salai, Nongchenbam, Khuraicham of Khaba Salai and Meihoubam, Langngam, Khamnam, Thinbam, Langkonjam, Shanchiram and Khaibam of Ngalba Salai are within the law of 'Leinung Pentinnaba'.

5. *Pi*-Tinnaba Law

Pi-Tinnaba literally means having the same mother; where *Pi* is mother and Tinnaba means the same. The situation arises when the mother married to different persons belonging to different Salais. So the children of the same mother with fathers of different Salais cannot establish marriage relationship among themselves. The lineages which come under *Pi*-Tinnaba law are the following:

1. Atom of Ningthoucha Salai and Meikam of Khuman Salai belong to the same *Pi* (mother).
2. Paonam of Ningthoucha Salai and Khakokpam of Chenglei Salai belong to the same *Pi* (mother).
3. Ankokpam of Ningthoucha Salai of Takyel Mapal (a place) and Wangbacham of Ngalba Salai belong to the same *Pi* (mother).
4. Leimapokpam of Ningthoucha Salai and Oinam of Khuman Salai of Sawombung (a place) belong to the same *Pi* (mother).
5. Haokhom of Ningthoucha Salai and Salam of Luwang Salai of Lamlai (a place) belong to the same *Pi* (mother).
6. Charoibam of Ningthoucha Salai and Pukhralbam of Moirang Ariba Salai belong to the Same *Pi*.
7. Irom of Ningthoucha Salai of Chingngamakha (a place) and Laishram of Khuman Salai of Loklaobung (a place) are of the same *Pi* (mother).
8. Yumnam Shalthibam of Ningthoucha Salai of Leishangkhong (a place) and Moirangthem of Moirang Ariba Salai of Shamurou (a place) are of the same *Pi* (mother).
9. Shiyatpam of Khuman Salai and Ningthoukhongjam of Moirang Ariba Salai are of the same *Pi* (mother).
10. Langkoncham of Ngalba Salai and Charoibam of Ningthoucha Salai of Kongbapalli (a place) are of the same *Pi* (mother).
11. Amakcham of Khuman Salai Ariba and Tenshubam of Ningthoucha Salai are of the same *Pi* (mother).

12. Huidrom Uya Tabam of Ningthoucha Salai and Langkoncham of Ngalba Salai are of the same *Pi* (mother).
13. Haobam of Khuman Salai and Wangkhem of Angom Ariba Salai are the same *Pi* (mother).
14. Mungkhom of Angom Salai Ariba and Leishangthem of Chenglei Salai of Lakok (a place) are of the same *Pi* (mother).
15. In the past no restriction was imposed in marriage among Angom, Hicham and Salam. But since the generation of Shikonglamthaba the restriction had been imposed and there can be no intermarriage among them.
16. Akham of Khuman Ariba Salai and Arubam of Luwang Salai are of the same *Pi* (mother).
17. Salam of Luwang Salai and Langpoklakpam of Ningthoucha Salai belong to the same *Pi* (mother).
18. Thounaojam of Luwang Salai and Maibam of Khuman Salai Ariba belong to the same *Pi* (mother)
19. Thounaojam of Luwang Salai of Laimanai (a place) and Konthoujam of Chenglei Salai of Khomitok belong to the same *Pi* (mother).
20. Huidrom of Ningthoucha Salai of Leishangkhong (a place) and Fammihanbam of Luwang Salai are of the same *Pi* (mother).
21. Emnam Shalthibam of Ningthoucha Salai and Fammihanbam of Luwang Salai belong to the same *Pi* (mothe
).
22. Salam of Luwang Salai and Emnam Moibunglokpam of Ningthoucha Salai are of the same *Pi* (mother).
23. Leimapokpam of Ningthoucha Salai and Hijam of Luwang Salai are of the same *Pi* (mother).
24. Ngangom of Moirang Achouba Salai and Huidrom of Ningthoucha Salai of Leishangkhong (a place) are of the same *Pi* (mother).

25. Salam of Luwang Salai of Thangmeipal (a place) and Keisham of Ningthoucha Salai of Lambun (a place) are of the same *Pi* (mother).
26. Wangkheirakpam of Ningthoucha Salai and Hao-oibam of Khuman Salai of Moirangkhom (a place) are of the same *Pi* (mother).
27. Paonam of Ningthoucha Salai and Khetrisana-simayim of Nongchup (west) are of the same *Pi* (mother).
28. Haobam of Ahallup Lakpa Senapati of Khuman Salai and Thangjam of Nongtholba Funga of Angom Salai are of the same *Pi* (mother).
29. Waikhom of Thoubal Taba (a place) of Ningthoucha Salai of Nongchup (west) and Waikhom of Luwang-inba are the same *Pi* (mother).
30. Ngangom of Yairipok (a place) of Luwang Salai and Sansenbam of Ningthoucha Salai of Nongchup (west) are of the same *Pi* (mother).
31. Hijam of Yairipok (a place) of Luwang Salai of Nongchup (west) and Sanabam of Ningthoucha Salai are of the same *Pi* (mother).
32. Laishram of Uchekon (a place) of Khuman Salai and Kshetri khana Chaobam of Nongchup (west) are of the same *Pi* (mother).
33. Laishram of Uchekon of Khuman Salai and Kshetrisalchimayum of Nongchup (west) are of the same *Pi* (mother).
34. Ngangom of Luwang Salai and Kabakengkoimayum of Kaba (Kabow) are of the same pi (mother).
35. Keisham of Yairipok (a place) of Ningthoucha Salai and Fougeishangbam of Moirang Anouba Salai are of the same *Pi* (mother).
36. Waikhom of Thoubal (a place) of Ningthoucha Salai and Sansenbam of Khuman Salai are of the same *Pi* (mother). Both of them are Nongchup (west).

37. Sanasam of Ningthoucha Salai and Oinam of Khuman Salai are of the same *Pi* (mother).

    The genesis of Sanasam: Meitei Ningthou' Thangbi Lanthaba (A.D. 1302-1324) married Yumkhu Chanu and gave birth to 'Kwakpa Thawanthaba'. Kwakpa Thawantha-ba married Mayang Ningol (a woman of western origin) Chingurembi and gave birth to Hotika and Hodang. The lineage of Hodang became Sanasam and that of Hotika are Pebam, Hodam and Ngathem.
38. Ngairangbam of Ningthoucha Salai and Khullem of Haorang (a place) of Khuman Salai are of the same *Pi* (mother). Both of them belong to Nongchup (west).
39. Yengkhom of Damu Shubidar of Ningthoucha Salai and Shamchet Saba Konthoumitong Laiphamlakpa are of the same *Pi* (mother). Yenkhom of Ningthoucha Salai, Konthoujam of Chenglei Salai and Shamchetabam of Kaba (Kabow) cannot establish marriage relationship.
40. Paonam Pandit of Ningthoucha Salai and Ashangbam Pandit of Luwang Salai are of the same *Pi* (mother). This two lineages belong to Pitinnaba Anouba and they cannot intermarry for two generations. However, this is relaxed from the third generation onwards.

6. Pellol Tinnaba

One cannot establish marriage relationship with the girls of maternal grandmother's lineage. These girls falls within the law Pellol Tinnaba.

CONCLUSION

Traditionally the Meiteis are follower of manogamous form of marriage. One obvious reason of this might be the level of production or economic condition of Manipur. However, this character of the Meiteis was forced to transform by an event of history which is popularly known as 'Chahi-Taret Khuntakpa'—seven years devastation. Polygamous marriage is still prevalent in Manipur but its popularity is gradually eroding.

Till today engagement form of marriage is treated as the most noble and prestigious form of marriage. But because of involvement of a long process in engagement people are resorting to arranged elopement. And this considerably shortens the process of marriage leading to saving of time and money. In the long process of engagement there are stages which works to elevate the status of women. This is evident in the early stage of engagement where women monopolises the affairs to a certain extent. However, the involvement of men affirms the decision taken among women of boy's and girl's side. Another stage signifying the elevation of status of women is the ritual treatment of 'Heijing Kharai' in 'Heijing Pot' ceremony. Basically 'Heijing Pot' is a ceremony of presenting a gift for the bride containing mainly fruits. But ritualistic presentation of the gift which also stands as a token of bride price, certainly elevate the status of women. Now they are treated at par with the deities involved in the ceremony. A tradition of sitting arrangement on the day of marriage is the reservation of left side (northern side) of courtyard (Shumang) for the groom's side (for elders) and the opposite for bride's side (for elders). However, this is an extension of sitting arrangement on verandah where the owner gets 'Phamen' side (the right side) and the visitor gets 'Naktha' the northern or left side of verandah.

Bor Barton Touba - Invitation of Bor (groom), a simple ceremony held a day before marriage is seemed to be an addition after the introduction of Hinduism in Manipur. This simple ceremony implies a request to the groom to definitely present in the marriage ceremony. But this act stands against the tradition of elevating the status of women which are testified in different stages of engagement. At different stages of marriage, 'Mei Okpa' - welcome of groom and bride by fire, is held at the gate of bride and groom. But this component part of marriage is similar in content with 'Mei Okpa' - welcome by fire, performed in cremation ceremony. Although we find a little difference in form; in case of marriage the practice is more ceremonial. In case of marriage also the practice is held to ward off evil spirits from the persons of bride and groom.

A discussion on the marriage laws brings us to the conclusion that the Meiteis followed a very intricate marriage laws. Pandit Loishang interpreted the laws and the same was enforced by the state. However with the demise of traditional state, the kingship, the Pandit Loishang' also ceased to exercise its responsibility. So, nowadays no due importance is given to the above intricate laws. However, still the Meiteis abide by the E Tinnaba or Pudinnaba law or exogamous marriage with traditional value and importance.

REFERENCES

1. Panthoibi Khonggul (M.S.).
2. Tutenglon (M.S.).
3. Poireiton Khunthokpa (M.S.).
4. Cheitharol Kumbaba (M.S.).
5. Meihoulon Salai Khaiba (M.S.).
6. Salai Taretki Khun-gum (M.S.).
7. Salai Poklakpa Langwon (M.S.).
8. Khagemba Yumlep (M.S.).
9. Nongban Ponbi Luwaoba (M.S.).
10. Oral interview with N. Khelchandra, Uripok, Imphal.
11. Oral interview with Prof. Ch. Budhi - Anthropology dept. M.U.
12. Oral interview with Athokpam Thoiba, Nongmeibung, Imphal.
13. Oral interview with Mayanglambam Thabal, Kakching

14. Oral interview with Ngangom Ongbi Fatombi - Oinam Awang Leikai.

15. Oral interview with Mutua Bahadur, Keishampat.

16. Oral interview with Moirangthem Norendra, Khongman, Imphal.

17. *Introduction to Manipur* - S.L. Ibungohal.

18. 'Manipuri Samajda La Shijinnabagi Fajaba Shaktam khara: - A seminar paper prepared by kh. Sharoj Devi, Kwakeithel, Imphal.

19. *Leima Yenglingeida khunu Kaba* - N. Manijao,

20. *Cane and Bamboo Crafts of Manipur* - M. Bahadur.

21. *Statistical Account of Manipur* - Brown R.

22. "Manipur and its Tribes" - T. C. Hodson, *Journal of the Society of Arts*. Vol - III No. 2733, London, 1905.

23. *The Meiteis* - T.C. Hodson.

24. *Feminism in a Traditional Society* - Sircar, M. Chaki.

4

Traditional Family Education and Institution

As suggested by the title the education to be discussed here is far different from formal education which is imparted in a four-walled room. In formal education there is teacher and taught, i.e. the pupil. In the context of family education the parents are the teacher and the children are the pupils. It has nothing to do with the varied disciplines as is the case in modern education. So naturally education imparted was limited to moral and social education. The do's and don'ts in the execution of daily domestic routine is also another chapter. In material side vocational training with regard to agriculture, maintaining homestead and weaving are the probable areas of worthwhile. As Manipur remained in war like situation for centuries together the training of martial art might be a compulsory one.

In olden days, family was housed in a traditional house of four or five rooms. As the education was imparted in a traditional house certainly the architecture, arrangement of rooms and location of household deities might be having direct or indirect impact on teaching and learning. As there was no atmosphere for teaching with writing materials naturally only medium of teaching was oral. A supplement to the oral medium was playing with parents. In due course of playing with children the parents slowly instills the moral lessons.

As teaching and learning was carried out in the house and out-houses a description of the types and location of out-houses, the arrangement of rooms in the main dwelling house, etc., may suggest the nature of education to be discussed. The open space just at the front of the Yumjao (main dwelling house) is the 'Shumang' (courtyard) where a traditional house generally faces east. This 'Shumang' is surrounded by out-houses, viz, Awang Shanggoi (on the left side of Shumang), Makha Shangoi (on the right side of Shumang) and Mamang Shangoi (on the east of Shumang). Besides there are other out-houses like Chabokshang, Ya-ongshang, Foukei, etc.

In the centre of the courtyard a shrub (either Tairen or Tulshi) was planted. The circular place around the plant in the courtyard is the 'Thelong'; a neat place which is cleaned everyday by scrubbing with a 'Nura' (traditional brush) with water. This 'Thelong' is the place where anything to be distributed to all those present in a ceremony is placed. It is also the place for performing rituals of certain ceremonies like 'Na-Hutpa' (ear-piercing), etc. Among the three major out-houses, Awang Shangoi and Makha-Shanggoi were mostly for decoration of the house. They were not meant for everyday use. The 'Mamang Shanggoi' (the out-house in the east of courtyard) was bigger in size and it served a number of purposes. The right side of it was the place for rice pounding. The traditional weaving loom was placed in the eastern side of Mamang Shang-goi. The loin loom was fixed on the northern wall of it.

Again coming to Yumjao (main dwelling house) of five roomed, the open space at the front is Mang-gol (Verandah). The Manggol is divided into Phammen, Naktha and Mangshok. The space around the right wall of Verandah is the 'Phammen' (the house faces east). And the space around the left wall of Manggol is 'Naktha'. The area on the right side of the front door stretching upto 'Phammen' is Mangshok'. The second room is the place for sons and daughters, where 'Ningolka' (quarter for the girls) is on the left side and 'Pibaka' (quarter for the boys) is on the right side of the second room. The third room is the Phammenka', the place for the father. And opposite to it is the 'Maibapham', the place for Maiba (priest-cum-medical practitioner). The fourth room is the 'Laplenka', the place for the mother. The 'Fung-ga' or the hearth is placed at the centre of this room in front of the mother's bed. The place for the goddess 'Emoinu' is placed near the western side of this Fung-ga. Opposite to mother's bed is the place for deity 'Leimaren'. Both the father's and mother's bed are placed on the right side of their respective rooms. The place for 'Maibapham' in the third room is on the left side of the room, which is an open space. But the place of 'Leimaren' in the fourth room is a secluded place. The last room is the 'Lainingthou-Ka, the room for the supreme household deity. In the south-western corner of this room there is seat for 'Sanamahi' deity. The kitchen was not placed as an annexe. The north-western corner of the last room was utilized as kitchen. There were only two doors in the house. The front door opens the second room to the Mangol (Verandah). The last door was placed on the left wall of the last room. So the middle of the house was open straight till the last room which facilitates the entry of sunrays of early hours.

Generally, a house is a place for shelter. But traditional Meitei house is more than a mere shelter, it is the embodiment of a temple. Traditionally all the leading gods and goddesses are housed in the traditional Yumjao. However, in due course of time a marked change is visible in this as the household deities like 'Sanamahi' and 'Emoinu' are now publicly worshipped in temples. Most of the rooms in a four or five-roomed houses are housed by different deities. To begin with the place near right side of the front door is treated as the place for deity 'Thongaren'. Basically

'Thongaren' is 'Sanamahi'; according to its location it has changed its name to 'Thongaren'. The edge of Mangol almost in line with the front door is also place for worship and offering. The worship and offering is done only in morning after cleaning the place with water and offer a light with insence stick or the like, flower and water. No major deity is located in the second and third room. But the fourth room is the abode of two major female deities, i.e. 'Leimaren' and 'Emoinu'. Lastly the supreme household deity 'Sanamahi' is placed in the secluded place of the fifth and last room i.e. at the south-western corner of the room.

With the above arrangement in background the children are given traditional family education. The children are taught to pray to god since early morning. The children are woken up and brought to Mangol (verandah) and taught to pray to god with folded hands. It is usually done at the edge of verandah. It is no other than but praying the Sun god. For children who can do service to deities, their service is more in the evening. They are taught to pray and offer light in their respective locations. They will clean the places for 'Thongarel', 'Leimarel', 'Emoinu' and 'Sanamahi' with water by rubbing with hand. Now they are taught to pray one after the other by offering light and traditional incense or the like with words of asking wealth, health and long life. But for 'Emoinu' a small amount of cooked rice is also included in the offering, and wealth is also asked from her.

The boys are taught not to enter the girls room, i.e. the 'Ningolka' and vice-versa. A mother gives her advice to her daughters on the different observations to be made during their menstrual period. They give psychological treatment when their daughter feel depressed. They are taught not to get mating during their menstrual period, on their birthdays and in day time when they lead a married life. They should not allow to touch their cloth by their husbands during day time. But it bears a different meaning which is different from merely touching a woman's clothing. It implies mating in day-time. Again on the other side the boys are taught to treat a woman as his mother while cooking and doing service for her husband. The girls are taught that traditional method of paddy husking (Fou-Shuba) is good to a woman of advance pregnancy. This help in placing the baby (faetus) in its proper place. It also reduces pains in delivery.

Fungga, the hearth is an important place for traditional family education. It is centre for teaching the children by parents on the codes of 'Emoinu' - which are basically the art of maintaining a house. There is a popular saying that 'Turen Leingoidagi Yumballonna Henna Kuppi' - meaning the art of maintaining a house is very complicated and finer than grains of sands in the river. A small fire is made at the 'Funga' (the hearth) and children are allowed to sit around it. The elderly person used to narrate the folk-tales as well as the code of 'Emoinu' in the evening before meals. During day-time children remain outdoor and it is a difficult task to assemble them for teaching and imparting moral lesson. But the 'Fungga' with a small fire in the evening give the advantage to gather the children for teaching and advising on good deeds. Here the parents teach on high moral character, on how to behave to seniors as well as to juniors which in Manipuri is known as 'Thakshi-Khashi', on truthful living, on development of mind and body and on the cultivation of a competent citizen.

Code of Emoinu

In the early morning before leaving bed, a person will chant the name of Almighty. The person will keep his/her hairs and clothings neat and tidy. Then the person will compose his mind and play deep breathing. Before stepping down from bed the person will touch ground by his fingers first. Then the person will play breathing again and find out the free side of the nostrils. Then the person will step down from bed by the left or right led depending upon the side which has free breath. In this also the person will remember the name of Almighty. Then the person will walk upto the edge of Mangol (verandah) and will pray the Sun god. This follows the clean sweeping of house. After brushing the teeth a bath is taken. An offering containing water, fruits, flowers and light are offered to deity 'Mangang'. The days work of the family begins only after this offering. A similar offering containing fruits, flowers and fire are offered to deity 'Luwang' at noon. In the evening another clean sweeping is done after day's work. Again the offering is repeated in the evening, this time to deity 'Khuman'. This follows chanting the name of Almighty with a brief rest before commencing evening work. The Fungga (the hearth) is needed to keep neat and clean. It is believed that the three deities; Mangang, Luwang, and Khuman are embodied on the three legs of 'Yotshabi' (the three legged iron frame used in the hearth for placing containers above) placed above the hearth. One should not touch it by leg and should not walk over it. With this discipline in mind one has to perform fire worship offering rice, etc. The one who observe this will be blessed by 'Emoinu'. At this secluded place of 'Emoinu' everyday a small amount of cooked food is offered to Her. After accomplishing night work one will pray the supreme household deity 'Sanamahi' and goddess 'Leimaren'. Only those who go to bed by remembering the name of Almighty will be blessed wealth and long-life by 'Emoinu'. This code of 'Emoinu' is taught to children by elders of the family.

While dining in kitchen the father use to sit at southern side and western side. While sitting at the western side the father's place will be near the pillar 'Langkhei Ningthou'. It is the central pillar in the western wall of kitchen where there may to be odd number of pillars, e.g. five or seven pillars. He will face either the north or east. The mother and children use to sit on the northern side of kitchen facing south (near the backdoor). The children are taught not to sit at the father's reserved place in the kitchen. Again a child is not allowed to sit at 'Haudongchakthafam' or 'Minaichakthafam'. This place is located somewhere near the eastern side of backdoor. The father use to sit at 'Phammen' at Mangol (verandah). Again, here also the children are taught not to sit at this reserved place.

A person after his day's earning will offer the earned money first to 'Langkhei Ningthou'. But he will keep it beneath the pillow. Then he will offer it to 'Sanamahi' deity as 'Sanamahi Yaikonfurel'. When drying paddy on 'Foura' (a broad and round basket for drying paddy) a woman should not stop on the 'Foura'. Women are taught not to collect fruits by climbing themselves on trees. The vegetables are believed to be asleep during the night. In a tight situation if she intends to pluck vegetable in night she is taught first to awake the plants by uttering the words – 'Houro' 'Houro'.

There is a designated place for keeping broom when not in use. Traditionally it was placed at the north-eastern corner of the last room, i.e. 'Lainingthou Ka'. The children are taught to keep the broom at this place only. And the way to keep is to place the broom up standing on the handle. Normally in a house sweeping is done one in the early morning and one in the evening. During the day time also one use to sweep whenever it is necessary. In the case of sweeping in early morning all the dirts are swept out of the house. And opposite is the case in evening, where all the dirts are swept inside the house and are kept in a heap near the 'Fungga'; the hearth. The dirts are removed in the next morning. This provides the advantage to find out if any valuable is crept among the dirts. So the language used is also different. In the case of morning one will address 'Wai Shittok-U'- meaning sweep out the dirts. For evening one will say 'Wai Shitchillu' – sweep inside the dirts. 'Shumchit' (the broom) is considered unsacred. So, if the broom touches someone while sweeping the person will step upon the broom at least once. So, the children are taught to obey the above traditional norms. Again the children are taught to sweep slowly while sweeping by pressing the tip of the broom on the ground so that the dirts could not scatter away here and there. The children are taught not to sleep below the 'Khangen' (lower horizontal beam) of a traditional house. In the past the area around the house was covered by thick grass. So snake was plenty. Intrusion by snakes in the house was not uncommon. As this was the situation there was chance of a snake slidding above the 'Khangen'.

The basic training of martial art was imparted at house by the father. Higher stages like 'Thenggou' etc. were taught at another designated place by a renowned teacher. The steps required in cutting or felling trees, pulling trees and bamboos from its grove were also taught. Cultivation of vegetables in homestead was taught along with cultivation of rice and other crops in the field. For girl children the art of spinning, weaving and the use of implements like 'Ta-ot', Ta-mang' and spinning wheel, etc. were taught by the mother and other elderly women. Tareng, the spinning wheel, is known by another name 'Sheeleima'. An insect which lives on trees is known by the name 'Sheeleima'. It is a thread producing insect. 'Sheeleima' (Tareng) might have been derived from the name of this thread producing insect. The girl children were taught to worship the 'Sheeleima' (Tareng) the spinning wheel before commencing their day's work. Dance remained an inseparable part of Meitei life. And as such the art of singing and dancing, though in rudimentary form, was taught by the parents and elderly persons of the family. Although for the advance stages the child needs to be sent to an advance trainer.

Shinnaipham Kaba: The only known family institution

This institution was mainly for girl children. They used to assemble in a house in the 'Ningol Ka' – the left side of the second room in a four or five roomed traditional Meitei Yumjao (traditional house). Girls of four or five families of the locality would assemble in the night in the presence of an elderly woman. Number of girls cannot be more as the room was not big enough to accommodate them all. But this assembling of girls was held in rotation from one house to another on different days. In a big village groups were made by girls of four or five families. And there was competition of their work among the groups. A small fire was made in the room and the room was lighted by a Meinam (torch). An elderly woman would guide the girls in their work. But here as a principle a divorced woman is not allowed to participate in the gathering. In the course of their work, conversations and talks were held among themselves, and with the elderly woman. In the midst of such talks and conversations, the elderly woman in the guise of jokes would impart the art of managing a home and the codes to be observed during this menstrual period before and after their married life. In short social education was given to the girls by the elderly women along with valuable advices. The girls were also given vocational training. The girls used to go along with spinning wheels and other implements including raw materials for use in their work. But here no weaving was done. Here the girls were taught the art of extracting thread from raw cotton and finally twisting in Langchak (bobbin). It envolves different stages in the form of ginning, carding, cotton rolling (Moithap Taba), spinning (Lang Naiba), winding and finally twisting. Ginning is done with the help of a wooden machine known as 'Kaptreng'. The seed removed cotton is dried in the sun. The carding is done inside a basket which is locally known as 'Lashing Kapon'. An instrument known as 'Huitri' is used for straightening the fibre of cotton. After the cotton is straightened, it is now ready for the next stage, i.e. Moithap Taba-cotton rolling. The well straightened cotton is spread over a flat wooden stool. Then a Lang-gom (*smithea* sp.) stick measuring about a palm's length is placed in the centre of the stool, with the hand pressing on it, the cotton is rolled and then Lang-gom stick is removed. This process is known is Moithap Taba (cotton rolling). These rolled cotton are made of bundle of 15 each and then are ready for spinning. The spinning is done with Tareng i.e. spinning wheel and Tareng yot - spindle. The spun thread is prepared in Langkhai-hank so that it can be transferred to Langchak (bobbin). For this two roads measuring 25 cm known as Tawot are needed. After the process of 'Langkhai Sagatpa' (winding) comes the stage of twisting. For twisting a 'Tareng' (spinning wheel) and a 'Masa' is necessary. Finally the thread from 'Masa' is twisted around a wooden or bamboo bobbin which is fitted to the spinning wheel through a Tareng yot (spindle). This long process is taught to the girls.

As discussed earlier Fungga (the hearth) is the centre for teaching the children on the code of 'Emoinu' – which is basically the art of maintaining a house. Besides it is also the centre for imparting moral and social education to the children through falk-tales. The tales are many, some are plain and simple which are meant for delighting and amusing the children. Others have their value in moral and social education. The medium is traditional - the oral and the environment is delight and amusement. The following is a selection from the numerous tales which has moral and social educational values. And here the mode of delivery is first to present the tales in brief and to point out the educational value of the tales in concluding remarks.

THE TALES

Lai-Khutshangbi

Long long ago there lived a fairy named 'Lai-Khutshangbi - fairy with long hands. This fairy visited the house of 'Shashi' - a boy of minor age, at odd hours in the day time when most of male are out for their daily work.

Before entering the house he will first enquire from Shashi's mother whether her husband has been out for work or not. If there is shashi's father in the house he will not enter the house but will vanish in the nearby forest. But he will visit Shashi's house the other day at the same odd hour. Whenever he comes to know from Shashi's mother that her husband has been out for work he will enter the house. And he will create havoc in the house. The misbehaviour of 'Lai-khutshangbi' was narrated to Shashi's father by his mother. Shashi's father was enraged on hearing the misconduct of the fairy and decided to punish the fairy. He sharpened his Thangjou (dagger) and suggested to his wife that he would remain in home tomorrow to take revenge on the fairy. Further he suggested that she should tell the fairy that he has been out for work whenever enquired by 'Lai-khutshangbi'. As planned earlier both husband and wife remained waiting the fairy, the man hiding near the window with the sharpened dagger in his hand. Fortunately the fairy visited Shashi's house and in the previous manner enquired whether there is Shashi's father or not. Shashi's mother welcomed the fairy by disclosing that her husband has been out for work. Unhesitatingly the fairy approached the window and inserted his extra-ordinarily long arm. Without losing any time Shashi's father chopped off the long arm of the fairy. The fairy vanished in the nearby forest with her cut-off hand.

Lesson

'Lai-khutshangbi' is symbolic of a person of bad character who misbehaves to other's wife. In common parlance also 'khutshangbi' is the one who misbehave to women. The message is now clear – person of bad character, a person who misbehave to others wife is severely punished.

Shanshennaha (Cowboy)

Once upon a time there was a 'Shanshennaha' (cowboy) in a village. He used to look after cows of the village whenever his turn came. On his duty days he will collect the cows of the village and will feed them in the field. In the evening he will lead the cows to their respective house. But one day the boy decided to play a joke to the fellow farmers working in the rice field. So he screamed to the villagers. And shouted tiger, tiger-it is going to hurt the cattle. The villagers, unmindful of his joke, rushed to rescue the endangered boy. But there was no tiger and it was found to be a lie only. Embarrassed by his joke the farmers returned to their fields much to their annoyance. One day the real tiger appeared and approached with an intention to attack him. This time also the boy shouted for help from the farmers. The farmers, disgusted by the previous incident, did not respond to his frantic appeal, instead remained working in the field. Unfortunately, the tiger killed the boy.

Lesson

Here the message is clear and simple, but valuable. Telling a lie is not good. Sometimes it may cost one's life as testified by this tale.

Pebet Amasung Houdong Lamboiba (Pebet and cat monk)

Long, long ago there lived a Pebet (a small bird) and Houdong Lamboiba (cat monk). One day the cat monk captured the Pebet along with her seven children and kept in his captivity. The cat monk, ridiculously, asked the Pebet, 'How beautiful is he?. The Pebet replied, he is as beautiful as a garland of Ngari (fermented fish), a basket full of paddy to its brim and a Warak Tayal (a creeper with a red inedible fruit which grows mostly in a bamboo grove)'. Satisfied with the praising words of Pebet the cat monk went for his mission in search of food. In the absence of the cat monk the Pebet trained her children on the art of flying. She trained them to fly gradually from one tree top to another, from a bamboo top to another and from one

'Langkhong' (trench) to another. She patiently waited for the full growth of her children. When her children are well trained and attained their strength she advised to free themselves from the captivity of cat monk in an opportune moment. Meanwhile the cat monk returned from his mission and repeatedly enquired the beauty of his appearance. This time the Pebet with full confidence of her children to fly, challenged the ridiculous nature of the cat monk. And replied, 'You are as ugly as a big cat'. Enraged by the unexpected reply the cat monk gestured to attack Pebet and her children. The Pebet instantly gave the signal and in response to it all her children except the youngest escaped from the captivity of cat monk. The cat monk brought up the 'Pebet Macha Heitombi' – the youngest child of Pebet, in the manner as her mother brought up her. The cat monk thoroughly bathed her early in morning and basked her in morning sun. She was fed with fine rice with the intention to use her as food when she was fully grown up. But unfortunately 'Pebet Macha Heitombi' also escaped from the captivity of cat monk on an opportune moment.

Lesson

It contains a suggestion on how to fight a mighty enemy. The tale seems to be developed as a social wisdom at a critical historical moment when Hindu colonialism reached Manipur and became state religion in early part of eighteenth century. Houdong Lamboiba—the cat monk is symbolic of the invading Hindu culture and the Pebet and her seven children that of resisting Meitei identity which is a compound of seven Salais (clans) or Yeks.

The suggestion here is dialectical in nature though traditional. For fighting a big enemy one needs a lot of preparation on the side of man, materials and strength. To be more specific a lot of training is necessary as trained by Pebet to her children. But training should begin from simple lessons and gradually to more rigorous ones. In the like manner the struggle needs to be time consuming and should begin from simpler actions and should gradually proceed to more intensive one.

Hannuba Hannubi Pan (Arum; bt. *Arum indica* or *Calocacia indica*) Thaba (Old man and woman planting Pan).

Once upon a time there lived an old man and woman. One day, when they were planting Pan, some monkeys visited them in the garden and enquired on the method of planting. For a good harvest of Pan in a night's time the monkeys suggested a new method of planting. According to their suggestion the old man and woman peeled the Pan and cooked in the kitchen. The well-cooked Pan was wrapped by banana leaves in pieces (packets) and planted in the prepared bed. In the night the monkeys came in the garden and removed the cooked Pan, ate them all and in place of it they planted wild Pans grown nearby the garden. In the next morning the old man inspected his garden only to find out full grown Pans. He collected a few pieces and showed to his wife. To their astonishment both of them praised the monkeys and decided to test the fresh Pan stems after offering to 'Sanamahi' deity. The old woman cooked the fresh stems of Pan and prepared 'Eromba'—a popular local dish, out of it. The old man tested it to his full mouth. But their expectation and euphoria was dashed to the ground as the fresh Pan was a wild one. It created an intolerable irritation in the mouth of the old man and shouted, 'Hentak'! Hentak! (it is a fermented fish item prepared from powdered fish). Immediately the old woman handed over a piece of roasted 'Hentak' to the old man. The old man got relieve of the irritation, but decided for revenge. So he unfolded a plan to revenge the monkeys to his wife. Accordingly the old man pretended a dead man and laid to rest at 'Khangenpham' in the courtyard. He was surrounded by a number of sticks erecting around the body which can be used as weapon. The old woman mourned the death of her husband. On hearing the mourning the monkeys visited their house to enquire. She told the monkeys that the old man was dead after eating the fresh stems of Pan. The monkey walked upto the corpse of the old man, but suddenly they faced a violent attack of the old man. The monkeys ran helter skelter to the nearby jungle. After this the old man and woman led their normal life.

Lesson

Here also, the tale is a collective wisdom of Meitei society developed in eighteenth century when there was active Hindu colonisation in Manipur. The old man and woman are the personification of the old but degenerating Meitei culture whereas the monkeys, since they are alien to human being, they represent the alien Hindu culture. By cheating and decieving the Hindu cultural colonisation was executed. But as a price of their cheating and decieving the colonizer faced the same fate as the monkeys faced at the end.

CONCLUSION

The family education imparted to children was traditional in its form and content. Among many places like verandah, courtyard and 'Shangoi' (out-house); the 'Funga' (the hearth) occupies the most important place for teaching children. In its warm environment the children were trained morally and psychologically. For the Meiteis the traditional house is the embodiment of a temple with a number of household deities at their designated places. So while living in the house a child is taught to behave like a person living in a temple. As that was a traditional society the teaching could not go beyond the traditional knowledge of world. And there was no scope of scientific understanding of the world. The code of Emoinu is basically the art of household management. Following the code means following a strict daily routine work with strict punctuality. Again the term 'Yumballon' has wider implication than the code of Emoinu. Besides the code it also include the individual behaviour and character (including sexual behaviour), the etiquette to be maintained among the family members and also the discipline (Thakshi-Khashi) to be maintained in the family members, etc.

REFERENCES

1. Oral interview with Ningombam Manijao, Palace Compound, Imphal.
2. Oral interview with Prof. S. Nilbir, Khurai, Imphal.
3. Oral interview with Moirangthem Noren, Khongman, Imphal.
4. Oral interview with M. Bahadur, Keishampat, Imphal.
5. Oral interview with Yumnam cha Budhichandra, Pishumthong Ningom Leirak, Imphal.
6. Oral interview with Dr. Mangi Ningomba, Kanchipur, Imphal.
7. *Emoinu Ahongbigi Tungnapham* – compiled by Yumnamcha Budhichandra.

5

Terms of Address within the Kinship and Outside

In addressing a person of consanguine relation or a person related due to marriage the sound E is prefixed. For example, Epa for father, Eyamba for elder brother and Eche for elder sister, etc. This is used for to a person who is related due to marriage. As for instance Ebai for brother-in-law, Enempok for mother-in-law and Ekupok for father-in-law, etc. However, due to contact with Hindu culture a change is observed in the traditional terms of address. And the change goes in this way: Baba for father, Dada for elder brother, Khura for uncle, etc. The traditional terms of address is a close knitted one and the use of prefix 'E' implies a close blood relationship among the persons of consanguine elation or relation developed due to marriage. The royal families follow a different way of terms of address. Epa-Ebungo for father, Ema-Ebemma for mother, Eyambung for elder brother, Echa-Ebemma for elder sister, etc. which are still in usage.

The terms of address among the consanguineous relation and the relation developed out of marriage can be examined in the following manner.

Epa Father, addressed by both man and woman to man.

Ema Mother, addressed by both man and woman to woman.

Epan This is addressed to father's elder brothers and mother's elder sister's husband. This term can also be used for to mother-in-law's brother if he is older than one's father. This is addressed by both man and woman to man. Now in place of Epan, Pajihan, Pajiyaima, Pabunghan, Pabungyaima, etc. are also used to denote eldest, elder Epan.

Eton, Khura Uncle—This is addressed to father's younger brothers and mother's younger sister's husband. Eton is used in showing relationship and as well as in addressing. Likewise khura also has the same implication. Thus Eton, khura is used in addressing a man younger than one's father whether related by blood or not. This is addressed by both man and woman to man. In place of Eton or khura, Kaka is increasingly being used in these days.

Mamma This is addressed to father's younger or elder sister's husband and mother's elder and younger brothers. Mamhan is addressed to both father's elder sister's husband and mother's elder brother. Mamma is addressed to father-in-law's younger brother which is also addressed as Ekuton. Mamma is addressed by both man and woman to man.

Eku This is addressed by a person to his father-in law and by a woman to her father-in-law. 'Ekuhan' is addressed to elder brother of father-in-law and Ekuyaima, Ekuton to younger brothers of father-in-law. This is addressed by both man and woman to man. But now-a-days this is hardly used. A man addresses Paji or Pabung or Baba to his father-in-law. Likewise a woman also addresses Paji or Pabung or Baba to her father-in-law.

Emhan This is addressed to father's elder brother's wife and mother's elder sisters. In short wife of Epans are Emhans. This is addressed by man and woman to woman.

Ene, Enem This is addressed to both father's elder and younger sisters as well as to mother's elder and younger brother's wives. 'Enehan' is addressed to elder and 'Eneton' to younger one. This is also addressed to father-in-law's elder brother or younger brother's wife. 'Enempok' is addressed to mother-in-law. Nowadays 'Enempok's' is reduced to showing relationship not in addressing. This is often replaced by 'Ema' – Mother. Ene, Enem is addressed by both man and woman to woman.

Endon This is addressed to wives of Khuras, Etons, mother's younger sisters and mother-in-law's younger brother's wife. This is addressed by both man and woman to woman. 'Endomcha' is often used in place of 'Endon'.

Tada, Eyamba, Ebung—Tada or Eyamba is addressed to elder brothers, father's brother's elder sons, wife's elder sister's husband, and to husband's elder sister's husband. All the elder sons of Khuras and Epans are Tadas or Eyambas. Tada is used by both man and woman to man whereas Eyamba is used by man to man. The use of Tada seems to be of recent origin which may be a derivative of Hindu culture. A woman addresses 'Ebung' to their elder brothers and father's brother's elder sons. With the increasing use of Tada in place of 'Ebung', 'Ebung' is now reduced to showing relationship rather than addressing. Tada or Eyamba is also used to elder persons who are outside kinship relationship. And hence they are used in showing kinship relationship as well as in addressing. As for instance, in addressing an elder the word Tada is prefixed to one's name, i.e. Tadachaoba, etc.

Enao Enao is often used in showing relationship but less in addressing someone. They are often call by name. Enao is addressed to younger brothers, wife's younger sisters husband, all the younger sons of Khuras and Epans (man to man), husband's younger brothers and to maternal uncle's younger sons (woman to man). This is also addressed to one's younger sisters, all the younger daughters of Khuras and Epans and to husband's younger brother's wife (woman to woman).

Ebai Ebai is addressed to one's wife's elder brothers, elder sister's (including father's brother's elder daughter's) husband and to father's sister's elder sons. This is used to all the elder sons of Mamma's and Ene's. This is addressed by man to man.

Eshen Eshen is addressed to all the younger brothers of the above relationship. This is used in addressing man to man. But Eshen is often used in showing relationship but less in addressing. For addressing one uses the name of the person.

Eteima Eteima is addressed by man to woman. This is addressed to elder brother's wife, Khuras's and Epan's elder son's wife, wife's elder sisters, mother's brother's elder daughters and to father's sister's elder daughter. This is also addressed to all the elder daughters of Mammas and Enes.

Enaoṇupi This is addressed to all the younger of the above relationship (man to woman). And this is also addressed to wife's younger sisters, husband's younger brother's wife, and to younger sisters (including father's brother's younger daughter, i.e. younger daughters of Khuras and Epans). This is also used in addressing woman to woman. 'Enaonupi' is often used in showing relationship not in addressing someone. In addressing them they are often called by names.

Etei This is used in addressing woman to man. Etei is addressed to one's husband's elder bothers, father in-law's brother's elder sons and to father's sister's elder sons. Eteihan, Eteiyaima is used to the eldest and elder Etei. But the present trend is to call by name to 'Eteis' with the prefix of Tada.

Eche Eche is addressed by both man and woman to woman. This is addressed to elder sisters, elder daughters of Epans and Khuras and to wife of Ebai (man to woman). Again this is addressed to elder sisters as in the above and to husband's elder brother's wife, i.e. wife of Etei (woman to woman).

Echan This is addressed to younger sisters including father's brother's younger daughters, i.e. younger daughters of Epans and khuras and to wife of Eshen (man to woman). This is also addressed to a woman's younger brother's wife and to husband's younger sisters (woman to woman). Echan is also mostly used in showing relationship but less in addressing.

Enama This is used in addressing woman to woman. This is addressed to elder brother's wife, Khura's and Epan's elder son's wife, husband's elder sisters, husband's father's brother's elder daughters, and to mother's brother's elder daughters. 'Enamahan' is the eldest of the 'Enamas'.

Emou This is used mostly in showing relationship rather than addressing. This is used in addressing man to woman and woman to woman. Son's wife, brother's son's wife and husband's sisters daughters are also 'Emous' (woman to woman). 'Emous' are often called by name.

Echa Likewise 'Emou', 'Echa' is used in showing relationship not in addressing. They are called by name. 'Echa' comprises sons and daughters, brother's children, wife's sister's children, husband's brother's children and sister's children. They are addressed by man to woman and woman to man.

Epwa 'Epwa' is also used in showing relationship. When calling them they are called by name. Younger brother, younger sons of Khuras and Epans and husband's younger sister's husband are referred as 'Epwa' (woman to man).

Emak 'Emak' is used in showing relationship not in addressing a person. Daughter's husband including those of brother's daughter's, sister's son and wife's brother's son are referred as 'Emak' (man to man). 'Emaks' are often called by name.

Eya 'Eya' is also used in showing relationship rather than addressing a person. They are often called by name. Daughter's husband, husband's brother's daughter's husband, husband's sister's sons and brother's sons are referred as 'Eyas' (woman to man).

Eshu 'Eshu' is also used in showing relationship not in addressing. When calling them they are called by name. 'Eshu' is grandson and grand daughter. Children of son's and daughters are 'Eshu'. Children of sons and daughters of Khuras and Epans and children of sister's son and daughter are also 'Eshu'.

Epu, Epubok, Epudhou– 'Epu' or 'Epubok' is grandfather.

This is addressed by both man and woman to man. 'Epudhou' is great grandfather and this is also addressed by both man and woman to man.

Eben, Ebenpok, Ebenthou– 'Eben' or 'Ebenpok' is grandmother. And is addressed by both man and woman to woman. 'Ebenthou', is great grandmother (man and woman to woman).

Purennakakpa– It is the seventh generation counting backward from father. This is rather used ironically. He is almost equivalent to a Shagei's Pukok (progenitor).

The literature 'Mingou Thagou' discusses in brief on the way of addressing to the king and his kin by his subject people. This custom is found to be in fashion since the reign of king Khagemba (A.D. 1597-1652), king Paikhomba (A.D. 1666-1697), king Charairongba (A.D. 1697 to 1709) and continued till Garibniwaz (A.D.1709-1748).

The King was addressed as 'Laiyingthou'. The son of 'Laiyingthou' was addressed as 'Ebungshija'. And his daughter was called as 'Ebemma Shija'. The daughter of Maharani the chief queen, was addressed as "Ebemma Shija Sana Tampha'. Her son was addressed as 'Ebungo Sana'. Maharani was addressed as 'Leimaren'. The other lower queens were addressed as 'Ebemma'. King's elder and younger brother's sons were addressed as 'Epunganingthoumacha'. When enquiring anything to the king the salutation 'Sana Khuya' is used. In replying to a call by a king one uses the salutation 'Hoi or 'Hao'. The literature also defines the word 'Ebungshi' which says that he is the one who can command me. The same idea is carried to the word 'Ebemma Shija'.

WIT TEST

Wit Test is popular among the children of the Meiteis. They play on this test when they sit around a hearth in the evening. However, here a process of teaching and learning is involved where the elders are the one who teaches the young ones. This is not a game of mere hide and seek but it certainly involves the exercise of intellect of the child. In a sense it is a way of sharpening the intellect of the child. Again such tests are oral in nature and so far a written account is not available. And it testifies the prevalence of a healthy oral tradition. Such riddles are of various types beginning from very simple to highly literary and complex ones. Following is a selection from the various riddles.

1. Lairabasu Sana Loiba Enak-Khunbasu Sana Loiba karino?

Riddle: A poor man also own gold and a rich man also own gold. What is it?

Key: Meinee - It is fire. Fire is owned by all the families, both poor and rich.

2. Soraren-gi Machanupa Sori Soraba Mamai Awang Pangna Chaktaba karino?

Riddle: Sori Soraba, the son of Soraren, searches its food with his face in the north. What is it?

Key: Soralune - It is a fish-trap known as' Soralu'.

3. Loibi Chinggi Chingleibakta houba Shingngen Leirang Magi Ma-U Tabu Yenglaga Pakhang Oibagi Shalloi Shajei Manba Lei, Shingngen Leirang Magi Leina Tabu Yenglaga Kairi Yenkhong Manba Lei, Singngel Leirang Mana Pomlingeidana Likkolgi Tharo Ma-ong Manba Lei, Shingngen Mana Amuk Hanna Shatlagana Lupa Pathap Manba Lei, Ashi karino?

Riddle: It is a flower which grows on the hill. The stem resembles the whip of a cowboy. Its petal resembles the claw of a cock. When the flower is in bud it looks like a lily. And when it is bloomed it is silvery in colour. What is this flower?

Key: Lashing - Cotton.

4. Palem Panthougi Shumang Mathoukonda Houba U. Ma- U Tabu Yenglaga Tulsi Bina Devi Manba Lei, Mana Tabu Yenglaga Taoba Fluireiton (Huigi Leiton) Manba Lei, Mana Amuk Hanna Shatlagana Pakhang Oibagi Lugun Gaitree Manba Lei, Kari Leino?

Riddle: It grows in the courtyard of her father. The stem resembles that of 'Tulsi' plant. The leaf looks like the tongue of a dog. But when it blooms it looks like the beads of'Lugun' (the sacred thread). What is that flower?

Key: Petruk lei - It is a flower named 'Petruk Lei'.

5. Loibi Chinggi Chingleipakta Houba Shingel Leirang, Ma-U Tabu Yenglagana Liklai Yumbi Manba Lei, Leina Tabu Yenglagana Kaoren Shangi Shankhong Manba Lei, Singngen Mana Pomlingeidana Ningol Magi Khutningthou Manba Lei, Shingngen Leirang Mana Amuk Hanna Shatlagana Nakong Chakra Ma-ong Manba Lei. Loktakishu Hennarei, Napomgishu Ngannarei, Kari Shingngen Leirangno?

Riddle: It grows in the hill. The stem is like a pillar. The petal looks like the foot of a cow. When it is in bud it looks like the ring finger. But when it blooms it resembles the ear hole. It is more pretty than a gorge and it shines on the hill-side. What is this flower?

Key: Chingthrao - A flower in the hill named 'Chingthrao'.

6. Lamlena Patki Patyaida Houba Shingen Leirang, Magi Leina Tabu Yenglagana Panthou Oibagi Khutshu Thanglen Manba Lei, Shingel Mana Pomlingeidana Ningol Oibigi Shinaichei Manba Lei, Shingngel Mana Amuk Hanna Shatlagana

Kori Kombandong Lamjen Korika Pakhang Ethak Kanna Lei, Momnu Koloi Paochel Lei, Kari Leirangno?

Riddle: It grows in the open field. The leaf of the flower looks like a sword. When it is in bud it resembles the 'Shinaichei' (a stick used in weaving). When it blooms it can excite a youth. It is used in sending message to someone. What is this flower?

Key: Kombirei - It is a flower named 'Kombirei'.

7. Kangkha Lemphu Karino?

Riddle: What is that 'Lemphu' under a cot. [Lemphu is the root of water lily etc.]

Key: Houdong Mathi - It is the faeces of a cat.

8. Kalengi Nungsha Phuina Sharagana Leirang Shida Shishina, Leirang Nada Nashinna, Ma-U Tabu Yenglagana Panthougi Tongjei Manba Lei, Leina Tabu Yenglagana Chapna Lakoi, Manba Lei,Shingel Mana Pomlingeidana Ningol Oibigi Egani Langdum Maong Manba Lei, Shingel Mana Shatlakandana Shelotki Tengkot Manba Lei, Ashi Karino?

Riddle: In the hot summer the flower pretends as dead the stem looks like the smoking pipe, The leaf looks like a cut out circular banana leaf. When in bud it resembles a thread ball. When it blooms it resembles a bowl. What is that flower?

Key: Thambal - Lotus.

9. Kalen-gi Nungsha Phuina Sharagana Leirang Shida Shishina Leirang Nada Nashina, Ma-U Tabu Yenglagana Panthougi Tongjei Manba Lei, Leina Tabu Yenglagana Kaoren Sankhong Manba Lei, Shingel Mana Pomlingeidana Ningol Oibigi Egni Langdum Maong Manba Lei, Shingel Mana Shatlakandana Shilotki Tengkot Manba Lei, Ashi Karino?

Riddles: In the hot sun of summer the flower pretends as dead. The stem looks like the smoking pipe. The leaf resembles the foot of a cow. When in bud it looks like a thread ball. When it is in bloom it resembles a bowl. What is it?

Key: *Tharoni* - It is Lily.

10. *Leinung Sana* Karino?

Riddle: What is underground gold?

Key: *Yaingangni.* - It is turmeric.

11. *Leinung Upu* Karino?

Riddle: What is underground box?

Key: *'Leipak-hawain?.* It is groundnut.

12. Mameishu Makokshu Mana Panba Karino?

Riddle: What is that which has ear on both the head and tail?

Key: *Ennaphini* -It is the long cloth 'Ennaphi' which has a similar design at both the ends.

13. Kakla Kaklaga Shangdorakpa karino?

Riddle: What is that which becomes longer when it is cut again and again?

Key: Khongban - a trench.

14. Hakchangda yaoba kannadaba organ macha amani, louthaklabashu yai. Masigi maming ashi syllable ahumna shai. Ahanba syllable ashina fungada, chakhumda shijinnaba item amani. Anisuba syllable ashina hakchangi part amagi mamingni. Ahanba syllable ashiga anishuba syllable ashiga pullaga eshingda leiba thawai panba meena chanaba nga amagi maming oi. Aroiba syllable ashina hakchanggi organ amagi mamingni. Syllable ahum ashina pullaga mathakki kanadaba organ adugi mamingni. Organ adu karino?

Riddle: It is tiny organ in the body which can be removed. Its name is composed of three syllables. The first syllable is the name of an article which is used in the hearth. The second syllable is the name of a part of the limb. Joining the first and second syllable forms the name of a fish. The last syllable is the name of an organ of body. When joining the three syllables, the name of the above useless organ comes out. What is that organ ?

Key: Waikhumit - It is the tiny worn out skin particularly in the fingers. First syllable is wai -it is the paddy husk. Second syllable is khu - it is the knee. The first and second syllable is Wai+Khu i.e. Waikhu = it is the crab. Last syllable is Mit - it is eye. First + Second+ last syllable is Wai + Khu – Mit i,e. Waikhumit = it is the name of the above useless worn out skin.

15. Lam amagi mamingga thaban amagi mingga ani ashi punshillaga khunggang amagi maming oiba karino?

Riddle: Joining the name of a region and the name of a Manipuri month makes the name of a village in Manipur. What is the name of the village ?

Key: Kabowakching. It is a village in Manipur in the Bishnupur district, not very far from Nambol. Kabow is the present Kabow valley and Wakening is the Manipuri month which mostly falls in January.

16. Fambaga leppaga fambana henna wangba sha adu karino?

Riddle: What is that animal which is taller when sitting than standing?

Key: 'Huini'. It is a dog.

17. Mayana charaga mabukna faiba karino?

Riddle: What is that which eats through mouth but defecate by belley?

Key: Chakkri. It is a grinding machine used in grinding paddy to produce rice.

18. Makhoida khujinna shiklaga mamit pangba karino?

Riddle: What is that which open its eye when pressed on the navel.

Key: Torchlight.

19. Mama amana macha mayam ama pok-ee. Adubu machashing adu echa amata haide. Manao, Manao, hai. Asi karino ?

Riddle: A mother produces a number offsprings. But none of them is called a child. Instead she call them younger brother, what is this?

Key: Pan-ni. It is arum. In Manipuri, the daughter arums are called Manao, i,e. Pan manao where Manao in Manipuri is younger brother.

20. Mamma amana macha yangkhei pok-e. Machashing aduna mammada kaoramlaga loina shikhi, masi karino?

Riddle: A mother produces as many as fifty children. But all of them kill themselves by kicking to the mother, what is it ?

Key: *Meikhet,* it is matchbox.

21. Charabasu tengkot than chadrabasu tengkot than, karino ?

Riddle: The amount of food remains the same before and after eating it. What is that food?

Key: *Tharoini.* It is the curry of snail.

22. Thawai chang karino?

Riddle: What is the Thawai chang?

Key: *Merukni.* It is the measuring pot for measuring rice for cooking.

23. Mamma namthibina macharadhikapokpa karino?

Riddle: What is that a ugly mother producing a beautiful daughter?

Key: Chigongleini. It is tree with a bad smell but it flowers beautifully.

24. Machinnacharagamanamnafaiba karino?

Riddle: What is that which eats by its mouth but defeacates on its back?

Key :- *Arramdar.* - It is the Planes.

25. Udana purakle uramlabadi purakloidabani, karino?

Riddle: I have brought it on not seeing it, but I should not have brought it if I saw it.

Key: Tingkhang yuba. It is the injury done by spike.

26. Chabasu machinda faibasu machinda, karino?

Riddle: What is that which does both eating and defecating on its mouth.

Key: *Pitchkari.* It is a pump for sprinkling liquid including water.

27. *Kachin Laimu* karino ?

Riddle: What is *Kachin Laimu* ?

Key: *Chafu amubani.* It is a black pitcher.

28. Mapal Kangdrum mahei thangshang karino?

Riddle: What is that tree which flower like a ball but produces long fruits?

Key: *Yongchakni.* This tree flowers like a ball. But from the ball like flower it produces long fruits.

29. Ma-u taba yenglaga makri langdum manba lei, leirang mana pomlingei kaorel shalgi nakhang manba lei, leina tabu yenglaga taoba huirei manba lei, kari leirangno?

Riddle: The stem is like a bobbin, when the flower is in bud it looks like the nose bridge of a cow, and when it flowers the petals looks like the tongue of dog. What is this flower?

Key *Khongunmelei* ni. It is a kind of orchid.

30. Pij aringei Kappa, pij adraga kappa tokpa karino?

Riddle: It cries as long as it is fed, but stop crying when it is not fed.

Key: *Kaptrengni.* It is the ginning machine for separating the cotton seed from the raw cotton. In the process of separation the raw cotton is fed to the machine and produces a crying sound. And it stops when it is not fed the raw cotton to the machine. And this forms the background of the riddle.

CONCLUSION

Traditionally the terms of address underlies a close blood relationship in the consanguine relation as well as outside this relation. The prefix of sound 'E' which literally is 'blood' is itself symbolic of such close knitted relationship. Still some kind of flexibility is visible in such a strong bond of relationship. The use of *Baba* for *Epa*, *Dada* for *Eyamba*, Paji for *Epa*, *Khura* and uncle for *Eton* and *Bhabi* for *Eteima* is testimony to such flexibility. However, the revivalist among the Meiteis again adopted the use of *Eyamba* for brother, *Epa* for father, etc. In fact there are strong under currents in Meitei society criss-crossing the territory with opposing ethos.

REFERENCES

1. Minggou Thagou (M.S.).
2. Oral interview with Mayanglambam Thabal.
3. *Notes on Meithei (Manipuri) Beliefs and customs,* J. C. Higgins (I.C.S.), Vice-President, Manipur State Darbar, Edited by Dr. John Parratt- 1998.

4. Oral interview with Athokpam Thoiba, Nongmeibung Academy Road, Imphal.
5. Oral interview with Ph. Gopal of Andro Khunou Leikai.
6. Oral interview with Ph. (Ongbi) Salam Ningol Chandrabali of Andro Khunou Leikai.

6

Beliefs, Practices and Superstitions

The Meiteis perform a number of social and traditional practices since olden days which are based mostly on beliefs, customs and superstitions. The reasons of some practices are simply inexplicable. Whereas some practices have their value in imparting some kind of discipline to the members of the community in the form of utilisation of their agricultural products, etc. The beliefs and superstitions are so strongly embedded in the minds of the people that modern scientific education has least succeeded in dispelling those beliefs and superstitions. However, the rapid urbanisation and the continuous blows of modern education through radio, TV, newspapers and other electronic media is gradually breaking the very foundation of such beliefs and superstitions. In rural setting there is environment for survival of such practices and beliefs. For convenience of discussion the issue can be discussed under heads, e.g. (1) Beliefs, (2) Practices and (3) Superstitions.

A. BELIEFS

The beliefs being discussed here are not discussed as a system. It is a collection of beliefs which are found in the way of life of the community that are lying scattered here and there in everyday life of the people. So naturally the task is to arrange those collected beliefs into an order and no logical sequence is applied in arranging them. We can examine them in the following manner.

1. It is believed that a mother is nearing to another round of pregnancy if her crowling child looks back through its crowling legs.
2. Sembrang (a bird) used to nest in the house mostly in the front porch (Verandah) of house. Their nest is made of mud. The belief goes in this way that if this bird (Sembrang) enters a house for its nest the family of the particular house will become affluent. Nestling in the front porch of the house is vulnerable to attack by children of the family. So such a nest in the house signifies the peaceful living atmosphere of the house. If such atmosphere does not prevail there is likelihood that the bird will not nestle in the house.
3. Earthquake is not infrequent in Manipur. Whenever earthquake occurs people use to shout "Chak-Nga," "Chak-Nga" (Chak = Rice, Nga = Fish). The belief behind this is that earthquake is the act of supernatural force which brings disaster to earth. The shouting of the words is the act of praying to supernatural force for prosperity in place of disaster.
4. An infertile woman consults Maiba (priest), Maibi (priestess) and Panji (astrologer) for a baby. With their advice she visits different deities and prays for a baby. She does this with the belief that the deity will bless her with a baby.
5. Thundershowers are very frequent in Manipur particularly in March and April. It is believed that a thunder increases the height of plants, particularly vegetables. If there is lightning in the night accompanied by rain the belief goes that in next morning the vegetables will grow higher.

6. Manipur is a cold place. During the winter the mercury hovers around sub-zero level. Although, there is not snowfall in the winter but one can experience ground frost in plenty. If there is excessive amount of ground frost in the winter it is believed that a plenty of rain will follow in the coming rainy season (June, July).
7. People use to forecast something by watching the behaviours of birds, insects and animals including ants and birds. If the birds and ants nestle their nest in the lower level of trees it is widely believed that the coming season will be stormy. The idea is that nestling in the lower level will protect the nest from being blown away by strong wind.
8. In Manipur fruit bearing trees flowers beginning from January and the flowers appear in full in the month of February. In this context also by observing natural phenomenon there is the tradition of forecasting the weather of the coming season. And the observation is made mainly on mango tree. If mango trees flowers in plenty the belief goes that the coming season will be windy.
9. In the past Manipuris used to put salts in a small 'Chafu' (earthern pitcher) in the kitchen. Salts remain dry in the pitcher in most of the seasons but in rainy season it melts into water. If the salt in pitcher melts rapidly and if ants along with foods and belongings climb to a higher place it is believed that a flood will follow soon in the near future.
10. Twins are frequent in bananas. A woman who has the capacity to deliver babies does not take a twin banana. She is forced by the belief that a woman who takes a twin banana is likely to deliver twin babies.
11. Lightning is very frequent in March and April in particular in Manipur. It was widely believed that

lightning was the act of heavenly deities. It was also believed that a lineage named 'Sorarenshang-bam' prepared a number of 'Nongmei Shingjang' (lightning) every year and offered to the deity 'Soraren'. The number of 'Nongmei Shingjang' lost from such offering was considered the number of lightning that has to occur in the year.

12. A harmful practice which is still prevailing in Manipur particularly in remote areas is the prevention of the baby in using mother's milk in the postnatal days. It was considered unfit for the baby. Forced by this belief the baby was fed by another woman who is known as 'Khom-enbi'. The 'Khom-enbi' used to feed the baby for days together till the mother produces her own proper milk. Gradually this harmful practice is losing its ground. And the credit for discarding this harmful practice goes to enlightenment of people by modern education, health workers, newspapers and electronic media by elaborating the nutritional value of breast feeding during postnatal period.

13. Cocks use to crow at definite intervals of time in the night. Sometimes a cock may crow at any time breaking this time intervals. It was widely believed that such a cock will bring bad fortune to the family. So what is usually practised is to eliminate the cock and use as food.

14. In the event of death of a member (male/female) of a couple in their old age, there is a belief that the living member (male/female) is either 'Eshing= water', or 'Nga=Fish. If the surviving person is 'Nga=fish', he/she will follow the death. And he/she is bound to die soon. On the contrary if the surviving person is 'Eshing=water', he/she will live for a longer period.

15. Wearing amulets in the arm is widely practised in Manipur. And amulets are of different purposes based on the beliefs. What is common to Manipuris is to put a piece of mother's Fanek (Female lower garment) and a piece of Kurao (the bark of a tree). It is widely believed that this amulet will protect the person from any kind of danger.
16. Sometimes a hen, a duck or a cat lays their eggs or deliver their baby in the house. If any one of them enters the house with a motive to lay eggs or to deliver their baby, it is believed as a good omen and one will not disturb them.
17. It is believed that a family living in a house built without any bamboo can never be a happy one. For the Meiteis, if one is to start a house then there should be a bamboo grove growing on his plot of land.
18. The growth of a bamboo grove is believed to foretell the fortune of a family. For this reason bamboos are planted by the elders of the family, and never by the youths. It is believed that if a youth plants a bamboos seedling, his life span will be curtailed.
19. Again, it is believed that if a bamboo flowers, then it is a bad omen for the head of the family owning that particular bamboo grove.
20. But for the villagers of Leimaram, however, the flowering of bamboo is believed to bring good fortune if proper rituals are performed. So the villagers clamour for the flowers. When a bamboo flowers, some people take a portion of that bamboo and put in the curry that is being prepared for the family's meal. When partaking the curry, one remarks; "O" Bamboo! As you flower thus, let me who are to bring good fortune to the person eating the food.
21. Meiteis used to pluck the tender leaves of the bamboo on Cheiraoba, the Meitei New Year's day (celebrated

in April), and add them to a dish called Utee. This is believed to prevent the bamboo from flowering. Besides, eating such a dish is good for a family as to avoid a dark fate. However, the dish is not taken by the males.

22. If and when there is a 'full' cluster of leaves and tiny branches on the tip of a bamboo plant, it is believed as an ill omen for the owner of that bamboo grove, since such type of bamboo resembles the chandwa bamboo used in the funeral pyre.
23. The bamboo that flowers is never used in the construction of house. But in the case of twin bamboo plants in the grove, it is believed that the owning family is blessed with good fortune.
24. If a new sprung bamboo grows up much more higher than the rest of the older plants, it is believed that the particular year shall be a happy one for the family owning that grove.
25. Bamboo with nodes are thought to be just like human beings, by the Meiteis. Bamboos are imagined to "sleep" as humans do and hence the bamboos that are incorporated into the framework of the house are taken as 'sleeping' (inside the house as the humans do).
26. When a bamboo grows up, the length of the internodes is generally uniform. If there is an irregularity in the length of the internodes, e.g. if the length between two certain nodes happens to be quite short, then it is regarded as something bad and is not used as Urep or main pillar of the house. The reason is that since the said bamboo is being 'handicapped' in its growth due to some fault in it, a person using such a bamboo is believed to become one with the bamboo and, therefore, is liable to experience deformity in his body. The occurrence of two nodes growing quite

near to each other in the stem of a bamboo plant, is referred to as 'Shabon Lonba'.

27. In the past, midwives (usually Maibis) used to cut the umbilical cord of new born babies with 'Wakthou' (bamboo blade) made from the Utang bamboo. The reason for cutting the umbilical cord with the Waakthou is mainly due to a belief that just as a bamboo grows up gradually in uniformity, so may the tender child grow up healthy in uniform stages.
28. A notable custom of the Meiteis is the use of Paya as waist belt, tied over the Phanek (the lower garment of Meitei women), by the women when they go out to attend a funeral. The two ends of the Paya are tied in a knot, which is placed on the front of the body. The Paya is tied in such a way that the two protruding ends of the knot point upwards. This seems to be a tradition that has been handed down the generations. After the funeral is over, the Paya is unknotted and the tongue is cleaned with it, then it is cast into the fire. Thereafter, the women sanctify themselves by dipping in the water and return to home. The underlying belief is that this act keeps away evil spirits and prevent death from occurring twice in that particular family.
29. If ropes made from the Utang bamboo are used for tethering cows, it is believed that the cow shall gradually lose their strength.
30. In the case of a cow suffering from pain in its leg, a piece of Utang bamboo is cut and a lid is provided on the open end of the cut bamboo tube. The belief is that if a died lizard is put inside the bamboo tube and tied on the neck of the cow, then the cow shall be cured of the pain.
31. Further it is believed that 'barren' cows are enabled to give birth if fed with the leaves of the Utang bamboo.

32. In the case of a dog bite, it is believed that if the new leaves of the Utang bamboo are pounded into paste and applied to the wound, the medicine sucks out poison injected into the body from the dog's bite. Yet in some other places, it is believed that after scraping off the outer layer or skin of a Utang bamboo tube, and after pouring water into it, if gently pressed on to the bitten part, the person shall be cured of the dog bite.
33. If a dog is subjected to 'Huigang Thangba' with Utang bamboo it is believed that the dog is bound to die. 'Huigang Thangba' is the practice of tying a robe around the neck of a dog, and then attaching a hollow bamboo tube to the rope by letting the rope flow through the tube.
34. It is believed that brushing teeth with Utang paya curtails the life-span of the teeth.
35. The Utang bamboo is also profusely used by the people who practice Black-magic. The Utang bamboo is believed to be an incarnation of the Gods. Bards sing to glorify this belief.

    The creator, Guru Shidaba, after getting His two sons to create this world, thought of testing them to see which of them could perceive Him as the Father. Assuming the form of a cow, He floated down the river Awang Chaokhong Hiden. The two sons dragged it up and enquired of their mother about it. After being informed by Ema Leimaren that it was the Guru, they used up the various parts of the cow to create several things. Thus, the Utang bamboo was created from the nails of the cow.
36. There is a belief related to the number of can splits used for tying and strengthening the circular rim of the Yangkok (winower). The belief is that the number of cane splits thus used corresponds to the

count of 'Chak Nga Chak' or chang shee chang' (*chak* = rice, *Nga* = fish and *Chang* = live beings, *Shee* = dead beings). The basket which a count ending on the 'chang' or chak' number is chosen for use. It is believed that a household which uses such Yangkok shall experience prosperity and happiness in life.

37. The Yangkok used in the household is never left lying around outside the house when not in use. This underlines the belief that a Yangkok is the 'Thawai' or 'soul' of the household; and the soul cannot be separated from the body (i.e. the house). But this belief seems to be imposition of disciple in using Yangkok.

38. In the event of a baby born to a Meitei family a ritual known as 'Epan-Thaba' is held on the sixth day of the child's birth. Wherein the child is placed on a Yangkok usually the one that is used in the household by the midwife (Maibi). It is done for the well-being of the child, so that it may have a bright future.

39. The Meitei house-builder identifies two sections in the Verandah of a house with the setting up of pillars at certain points along the Verandah (front porch). The pillar on the right side of the Verandah marks a section known as Phamen, and that on the left side of the Verandah marks another section known as Naktha. The Phamen is reserved as a resting place for the elders of the family, and the Naktha is specified as a place when the woman make cloth (on loin-looms, etc.); spin yarn, etc. The pillars marking out the Phamen and Naktha are to be set up in such a way that they should maintain specific distances as laid down in the Meitei traditional beliefs. The gap between the right end of the Verandah and the

pillar positioned on the Phamen is much wider than that maintained between the left end of the Verandah and the pillar positioned in the Naktha. The traditional beliefs affirms that the wider gap maintained in the Phamen enhances fertility and thereby increases the number of people living in the house. The narrower gap maintained in the Naktha is said to reduce the number of deaths in the family.

40. There are several customs and practices related to the placing of Hoomdang (lower roof-support) which are based on certain beliefs. When placing the Hoomdang over the Loikhang (lower horizontal support beam), care is taken not to put the former in places which are directly in line with the pillars. It is believed inauspicious if a Hoomdang is placed directly above the pillar. However, this strict code is relaxed to allow a single Hoomdang to be placed above a pillar which stands in the excluded area where the 'Sanamahi' is worshipped. This is referred to as 'Hoomdang Kokthong-Naba' (the literal meaning is to bear the Hoomdang on the head). There might be several opinions on the topic, but the Hoomdang Kokthong Naba' is nonetheless a symbol of sexual copulation; hence incorporating the fertility concept in the architecture.
41. From whichever side the placement of the Hoomdang is begun, the rule or practice is to end the process eventually in the corner of the roof, overlooking the left side of the Verandah. The belief behind this practice is that the 'live souls' are placed first into the house and the 'death souls' are placed last.
42. When placing the Hoomdang in the corner of the roof mentioned above, it is disallowed to put the bamboo with its 'eye' facing downwards. The belief is that on doing so 'the 'dead soul' look down upon the household all the time. This is considered inauspicious for the

family. Hence care is always taken to put the bamboo with its 'eye' facing horizontally either to the right or to the left.

43. Again, when placing U-ra above the Hoomdang the number of U-ra placed to the right side of the roof and those placed on the left side are unequal. It is seen to it that the U-ra placed on the right side should be greater in number from those placed on the left side. The belief behind this is that by doing so, a greater number of 'live souls' and a lesser number of 'dead souls' (represented respectively by the U-ras) are incorporated into the being of the house.

44. It was not customary for the Meiteis to thread with needle completely over a Phanek or other cloths the designs of flowers, animals, fishes etc. The reason was that the needle worker did not consider herself as a perfect worker and an expert. It was because of the belief that there existed the Almighty, the Great Master and doing 'His' work with perfection was considered to be a sign of egoism. It was therefore customary to leave while stitching or weaving a cloth, a part uncompleted when it would be hardly noticed. Again at times, in continuation of the belief, it was not unusual to put up an unnecessary design over a completely perfected design so as to make the impression of an incomplete work. As it was done at the time of needle work, a designer, while designing a patterned clothe leaves his/her design uncompleted as completed design would mean showing disrespect to the Almighty.

45. There used to be a tradition when the person who brought the mulberry leaves for feeding the worms were received by making fire of Khoiju Leikham (*Inula cappa, Sesquipedalus guniothalamus*) and letting smoke out. This was done following the belief that it would ward off evil spirits and thus protect

the worms from death. The same ritual can be observed at the time of Lai Loukhatpa (i.e., invocation of the divine spirit) during the time of Meitei Lai Haraoba. Besides, the same ritual is practised in each and every house at dusk so as to ward off evil spirits from the family members. The same ritual tradition was followed while taking care of the worm because of the belief that it was turned from a royal female (Leima).

46. Since very early times, Meitei women have been doing the work of dyeing threads and cloths by using varieties of plants leaves, flowers and barks. In their own homesteads, the women used to grow such plants (from which dyeing colour could be extracted). Besides, such plants were available in the surrounding hills. Though it was used for domestic purposes, the indigo colour from 'Kumna' (*Strobilanthus flaccidifolius*) plants was found to be on sale till recent times. If one grows 'Kumma' amongst the various plants used for extracting dye one should not let it die; if one should, then it was believed that it would lead to misfortune. Here, it seems, the belief was introduced in view of the economic value of the plant.

47. While preparing the Kum-indigo, some people, after examining the stage of the Kum dye also add juice taken from Heibung (*Garcinia xanthochemus*), sugarcane juice (molases), puffed rice, etc. Such Kum which is being kept in a pitcher for making dye is also regarded as 'Lairemma' (Goddess). As such, whatever fruit or food items added into Kum as mentioned earlier, is believed to be an offering which is offered to the Kum Lairemma, only when she gives indication. Such prepared Kum (indigo) which could now be used for dyeing, was put into small pitchers and these are used to be brought to the Khwairamband Keithel (Khwairamband market the

main market of Manipur) for sale at high price. The ritual treatment of Kum (indigo) kept in the pitcher by offering different items at time intervals may be treated as a way of attaching extreme importance to the final end product which is ready for market.

48. Of all the preparation conducted for making dyeing colours by the Meitei, the preparation of Kum was considered to be the most important and carefully conducted. The pitcher in which Kum is being preserved is not to be touched by women in menstrual period. The principle of social taboo is strictly observed. No one can also see directly into the pitcher by opening its lid. If somebody does see it in this manner it is believed that he or she will be striken with a kind of disease known as 'Kumlai Chuba'.

49. Leirum is used in binding the types of clothes used as bed covers and blankets which are to be carried by the bride to the house of the bridegroom. [Leirum is one of inseparable cloth used by Meitei at the time of marriage from early times till today]. Delivering the clothes in such fashion would, it is believed, ensure a happy married and long life. While making the bundle with Leirum there is a practice known as Oina Namba (i.e. letting the left end of cloth over the right end while tying the knot) or Yetna Namba (i.e. letting the right end over the left end while tying the knot). According to this practice it is believed that the first born child of the married couple would be a girl if it is Oina Namba and a boy if it is Yetna Namba.

50. Circular hook-like motif was found to be widely used not only in the art of weaving but also in the illustrated manuscripts. Not only this, the early Meitei goldsmith and craftpersons engaged in lost wax casting employed hook-life motif in their trades; hook-like motif is therefore considered to be the oldest.

There are also reasons why the above designs have been employed in this land. One reason was the belief that the use of circular hook-like motif in clothes would help in warding off insects.

51. While purchasing a Yangkok (winower made of bamboo, circular in shape), some Meitei use the words Chang/Shee while counting the cane split that bind the rim of the basket. If the counting ends with 'Chang' then the basket (Yangkok) is purchased. It is believed that such circular basket, if used, would bring prosperity and well-being in the family.
52. The belief of this land treats 'Naktha' the left side of Verandah as 'Ashithong' (the passage of death). So leaving the house for a mission on the 'Naktha' side of Verandah is considered inauspicious.
53. In the tradition of this land the house itself is a temple, a secluded place for worshipping. So, every part of a traditional house has its name. 'Houdong Chakthapham' is also one of them. It a reserved place for feeding a cat. A cat cannot be fed at another place of the house. It is located in the 'Chakshang' (kitchen) part of the house. And it is just near a post. It is considered inauspicious if one stands inclining to the post. Further it is believed that the person will become a slave if he or she does incline to the post.
54. The Chakpas of Andro village has a similar belief regarding the flowering and fruits in the early part of the year. It says if there are plenty of flowers and fruits in the beginning of the year it is believed that there will be plenty of rain with hailstorm. Further it is believed that the coming season will be stormy. The observation is done in early fruits particularly in mango. In Manipur mango flowers mostly since January and by March fruits are appeared. By observing the amount of flowers and fruits the prediction is made. However, such beliefs has rooms

to explain in scientific reasons. In some areas the plants and animals are more sensitive than human beings. It is a way of feeling a stormy weather in advance and preparing for it by producing excessive amount of flowers and fruits.

55. If there is an earthquake in the early morning of Saturday it is believed that the people will face a famine in future. Further it is also believed that a flood is also imminent.
56. If someone falls down when he is running during an earthquake it is believed that the person will suffer from epilepsy.
57. If a person bites the earth during an earthquake it is believed that the person will possess a strong teeth.
58. If someone shouts with the words 'Chak, Chak' during an earthquake it is believed that the people will enjoy with plenty of foods.

B. PRACTICES

It is rekarkable that in their daily life Meiteis perform a number of practices which are bound by customs and tradition. This actions or practices are various in number. Many of them are simply the by-products of beliefs and superstitions, the reasons of which are simply obscure. Some of them are found to be based on gender inequality. In the midst of these, however, there are practices which indirectly instills discipline in their daily life. The following discussion may help us in determining how the beliefs, superstitions, customs and tradition shapes these practices among the Meiteis.

1. Plucking of vegetable in the night is prohibited. It simply says that it is not good to pluck vegetable in the night. It may be by the belief that the plant is sleeping in the night. But science will say that

plucking in the night may reduce the nutritious value of food.

2. Felling of the banana stem for food and slicing of Mairen (pumpkin) and Khongdrum (gourd, *Lagenadria vulgaris*, bot.), by women are prohibited for no reason. What is usually done is to make a small cut first by a male and the rest preparing for cooking is done by woman.
3. As a custom one will visit when someone is fallen sick or when death occurs to a family. But restriction is imposed to a pregnant woman in visiting the ailing person and on enquiring the death. She is prohibited from doing so as the belief says that bad fortune may occur in the ailing family or in the death occurring family.
4. A woman is also prohibited from using a plough. It is for no reason and simply says that it is bad in doing so. However, the handling of a plough needs skill, agility and strength. A woman lacks all these. Again a woman wearing a 'phanek' (traditional lower garment which slings from armpit to ankle) may not be suitable in handling a plough. Because of all these factors the restriction might be imposed on them.
5. It is considered unusual to touch the clothings of woman by man. So, much care is taken by both man and woman not to touch their clothes. However, in the time of mating it is a different case. Here, we may examine the reason on two counts; it may be a way of treating woman in subordinate position; the other may be a way of imposing restriction in loose life.
6. A man who returns from a journey or from crematorium is welcomed at the gate of the house with a small bonfire. The person has to step upon

the fire. It may be due to the belief that evil spirits may be accompanying the person from his journey from crematorium to home.

7. Trimming of hair and nails are done only on auspicious days. It is not done on birthdays. Simply it says it is bad to do so on inauspicious days and birthdays.
8. If one sees a shooting star (meteorite) shooting down the sky the person will spit immediately.
9. As a practice the rain water which is collected in a container is used for drinking purposes only when a small piece of earth is dissolved in it. Here, science may give us the reason that rain water lacks mineral salts and hence improper for drinking. The deficient minerals salts may be compensated from the dissolved piece of earth.
10. There is an ailment named 'Erai Khonglai Chuba' which is believed to be the acts of deity 'Erai Khonglai'. The symptom is a severe allergy on skin affecting the whole body. The practice to cure this is to perform a rite to this deity by an Amaiba (priest-cum-medical practitioner).
11. While stepping out from house for a purpose a person will check his breath. The person will step out from the Mangol (Verandah) either by left or right leg depending upon the side of nostril which has a free breath. By doing so the person believe that this will help in the success of his mission.
12. Mat made of 'Kouna' (reed) is still popular in Manipur. When purchasing a mat one will count the number of compartments made by the ropes. One will use the device 'Chang, Shee' and prefers to purchase the mat which ends with 'Chang'.
13. The same practice is followed in purchasing a mattress also. The person will count the compartments with the device 'Chang, Shee' (Chang = live,

Shee = death) and will purchase the mattress which ends with 'Chang'. The belief says that a mat or mattress which ends with 'Chang' will bring good fortune and long life to the family.

14. As a natural process the old teeth are replaced by new teeth in childhood. In the event of such replacement the old tooth or broken tooth is thrown above the house with the following words to 'Pitai-Khomtaibi'; and it says 'Ha-Pitai Khomtaibi', let us exchange my old tooth with your new tooth'.
15. As a custom a male has to enjoy the 'Chakmai'—the uppermost layer of cooked rice. This privilege is not extended to woman. Again, a man is abstained from eating the 'Chaka'—the burnt part of rice in a cooker. Here, again we may refer that this is an act of treating woman to a subordinate position.
16. In the past flower was used in inviting a person for a ceremony. Now this is replaced by invitation card. Here, with the passing of time, we observe a change in the means of invitation, i.e. from flower to invitation card. But what remains unchanged is that the distribution of invitation card is still the monopoly of male. Women are still abstained from this task. This is an act of discrimination against woman thereby keeping her to a subservient position.
17. As a practice in marital life mating is avoided during the mense period. She will not cook during the five days. She will not touch the person too who is cooking during these five days. Utmost care is taken not to touch the cook while handing over something for use in the kitchen. This may be due to the belief that mating during menses is unsafe. Keeping woman at a distance during menses may be by the reason that treating woman with disgust at this time reduce the temptation of mating for the couple during the menses period.

18. Normally in a house sweeping is done one in the early morning and one in the evening. In the day time also one use to sweep if it is necessary. In the case of sweeping in early morning all the dirts are swept out of the house. And opposite is the case in evening where all the dirts are swept inside the house and are kept in a heap at a selected place. In the past it was placed near the 'Funga'—the hearth. The dirts are removed in the next morning. So the language used is also different. In the case of morning one will say 'Wai Shittok-U' meaning sweep out. For evening one used to say 'Wai Shitchillu'—meaning sweep inside. There is a selected place for keeping broom in the house. And the broom is kept only at this place. When keeping, it is kept upside down, i.e. the handle touches the ground and broom stands above the handle. 'Shumchit' (broom) is considered unsacred. So, if the broom touches someone while sweeping the person will step upon the broom at least once. Two kinds of brooms are used in a family. The one used in the kitchen and the other used outside the kitchen. The one used in the kitchen cannot be used beyond the kitchen. And vice-versa is the case for the broom which is used outside the kitchen. The one used in the kitchen is known by the name 'Cha-khum Shumchit' and the other used beyond kitchen is known as 'Emung-Shumchit'. There is difference in size also; the one in the kitchen is shorter in size. Again there is a difference in material also; straw and more conveniently thatch is used for the one used in kitchen and generally the flower of 'Charot' is used to the one used outside kitchen. However, such environment is gradually disappearing in the urban area where modern kitchen and dinning sets are fast appearing.

19. Trimming of nails inside the house is prohibited. Again trimming in the night is also restricted. So, one has to trim the nails in the daytime only and it should be outside the house, otherwise it is believed that acting against this practice will bring bad fortune to the family.
20. While sleeping on the bed the head faces either the east or south. It never faces either north or west. And this is strictly practised for no reason.
21. When measuring rice from 'Chengfu' (pitcher used for storing rice) for a meal's use a few handful of rice is again returned to the 'Chengfu'. This is considered unavoidable. But this practice may be interpreted as a traditional way of small saving in the form of rice.
22. While leaving bed early in the morning one use to come out in the front door. Using backdoor at this time is only at unavoidable circumstances. This practice might have been moulded by age-old tradition of praying sun-god early in the morning.
23. If an outsider enter the house for a purpose, then the person has to leave the house in the door that the person entered. If the person entered from the front door, then he or she cannot leave in the backdoor, but has to leave in the front door. The same is the case for the backdoor and doors at other areas. If this practice is not followed it is considered that misfortune may occur in the family.
24. Sometimes the body of a person may be unable to trace although it is certain that the person is dead. The corpse of a person, according to the tradition and custom of this land, is a necessity for cremation. In such a situation a tree named 'Panggong' is used as substitute of the person in cremation.

25. *'Thawai-Mee Koukhatpa'*—This is usually practised among children, although adults are not the exception. Accident of the kind of falling from a height or drowning in water are frequent among children. When a child is rescued from drowning it is believed that the five souls of the child are already departing the child. In such a situation 'Thawai-Mee Koukhatpa' is held to return the five souls and 'Mee' (shadow). It is believed that 'Mee' (shadow) always accompany the five souls. So the five souls and the sixth with Mee (shadow) are invoked to return to the child by uttering the words 'He Thawai Mangamak, Meega Thana Tarukmak, Ku, Ku Ku' and the child is pretended to drink a handful of water fro thrice from the site.
26. The longing for a male child is on the increase when there are girl children only in a family. This is particularly true in a patriarchal society like the Meiteis. So in order to beget a male child certain rule is adopted with the belief that the one who follows the rule will get a male baby. For this a counting of days beginning from menses day of the mother is observed and it continues to the 16th day after menses. And even number days beginning from 10th and 12th, 14th and 16th are marked for mating days. The odd number days are to be avoided. The days should not be birth days of the husband and wife, whereas for the father it should be strictly observed. The mating should be before 12 p.m. A clean bowel is a necessity. For this, foods which can help in cleaning the bowel must be taken on the night preceding the day of mating. On the appointed day both the husband and wife must clean the bowel along with urine. Before mating both should eat a sweet food; may be sugar or banana, etc. And the practice 'Shor Yengba' is held. In this one will blow

one's nose by closing one of the nostrils. If the right nose is free for both male and female then it is permitted for mating. In tight situation, at least for the male, the right nose should be free in blowing. The mating should be performed in a happy mood. After mating both husband and wife should sleep for about 10 to 15 minutes by placing the body on right side. Any movement is not permitted for the wife during rest after mating.

27. An interesting custom of the Meiteis is the bathing of children, who are recovering from an illness due to venturing out doors, with which leaves of the Utang bamboo have been boiled. This is done on the seventh day after a child's recovery. The custom is still in practice till today.
28. While keeping the *Yangkok* (winnower) the practice is to keep it face down and the bottom up, never the other way around. It is treated as inauspicious to keep two Yangkoks in one house.
29. In a traditional *Yumjao* (main dwelling house), as a practice, the main door is usually placed a little to the left, not in the middle or to the right.
30. As a custom the *'Leima Til'* (silk worm) is looked after by woman of Manipur with utmost care and love. However, woman do not touch these while they are in menstrual period.
31. The Chakpas of Andro Village (in Imphal East District) do not use the goat as food. They do not domesticate it.
32. Pottery is very old craft in Andro. And it is still flourishing. But this craft is reserved for womenfolk of Andro. Men do not take part in pottery. However, it is the duty of menfolk to perform the rituals like "Leipak Leithong Hangba", "Leipak Leiyengba", etc. which are related with the collection of the raw

material—the clay. The above rituals which are performed since fifth day of Phairen (January-February) month formally permit the womenfolk to collect the 'Leitan'—the clay. So, the collection of 'Leitan' (clay) from the designated place (Leitanpekpham), the preparation of mud paste with 'Leichreng' (coarse soil or sand) on a wooden dugout with wooden pestle, the making of pots of different shapes and designs and finally the burning of the raw pots in open ground with straws, etc., all these are done by women themselves. But here in this craft a 'Leishabi'—an unmarried woman is not allowed to take part in pottery. She can do so only after her marriage. But here it implies that a learning-teaching process is naturally involved.

33. The Chakpas of Andro Village has a similar practice in using agricultural tools like plough etc. 'Potpu-Langol' are agricultural tools used in ploughing. Women take part in agriculture in this region. They take part since the transplanting till harvesting. But women are not allowed to touch that 'Potpu-Langol' and again they are not allowed to carry it. They are also not allowed to carry 'Papot'—a device to carry articles by using a pole of bamboo where it is placed on the shoulder and the weights are fixed at the two ends of the pole. If a woman touches a 'Potpu-Langol' by mistake or by intention it is believed that the people will face a drought in the coming season.

34. In purchasing a ' Yangkok' (winnower) the Chakpas of Andro village follow a certain norm which to some extent is similar with that of the Meiteis. The rims of a 'Yangkok' is enforced by strips of cane at several points. When purchasing a 'Yangkok' the enforcing strips of cane is counted with the words 'Chak - Nga'. And one will purchase it which ends with

'Chak' when counted to the end. In short one has to purchase a 'Yangkok' which ends with an odd number. In Manipuri 'Chak' is rice which carries the sense of live. So one who purchases a 'Yangkok' with enforced cane strips which ends with 'Chak' may experience prosperity and long life. The cult of fertility is found entrapped in the very practice of purchasing the winnower. The passion for a long life induces the community to cultivate such a belief and practice.

35. However, the above norm is just the opposite in purchasing a 'Long' (sieve) for catching fish. One has to purchase a 'Long' which ends with 'Nga' when counting the cane strips with the words 'Chak-Nga'. It means one should buy it which ends with an even number when the whole of the strips are counted. In Manipuri 'Nga' is fish. The one which ends with 'Nga' may also carry the sense that it may facilitate in catching more fish.

36. 'Nongmangkha' is a medicinal plant. It has a strong bitter taste. People are advised by custom not to go near the plant early in the morning, at noon and at the dark. If by chance someone faces an evil spirit during the above mentioned time near the 'Nongmangkha' plant it is believed that the person will face death. If someone is forced by circumstance to stand near the plant, then the person is further advised by custom to clap for three times while entering near the plant. Further the collection of leaves of the plant on Sunday is prevented by custom. However, the aura of belief and practice around this plant has its moral values. Being aware of the extreme medicinal values of the plant it is natural to impose such restrictions so as to protect it from unrestricted collection of the leaves.

37. A man do not eat the left out food of a woman. It is also unusual to touch a man by woman while he is taking food.

38. Every year around Nov.-Dec., the barn is repaired or cleaned when all the old stored paddy is removed thereby providing room for the fresh paddy. But while doing so as a practice a small amount of paddy, around two or three handfuls, are left in a corner of the bam. The usual practice is that a small amount of paddy is stored in a small earthern pot and the same is placed in a corner of the barn. While removing the previous years paddy the paddy in the pitcher is spared. And the same is replaced by new paddy only when the fresh paddy is unloaded in the barn. But here the practice can be counted as a means of small saving. The same practice is found in maintaining 'Chengphu'—a container for rice. While measuring rice for cooking the rice is not completely removed *from* the 'Chengphu'—instead a small amount, around one or two handful, is left in the container. The practice is not found to be associated with any household deities, particularly with 'Phouoibee'—the grain God. But the apprehensiveness of the people to deities or to spirits tend them to follow the practice with fear and sincerity without citing any resean behind it.

39. *Phouoibee*—the grain god.

Harvesting is normally executed by active co- operation between men and women. However, women are excluded from the activities like 'Phoubee Haiba' - thrashing of the paddy blundle with hands and subsequently thrashing with 'Cheirong' - the thrashing stick. So naturally the task of women in harvesting is concentrated in milder areas like collecting of paddy into small heaps, sheaving the paddy from the thrashed straws and in winnowing with 'Humai' (the traditional winnower) the thrashed grains. But paradoxically the part of "Phouoibee Shaba"-acting as grain God is performed mostly not by a woman but by a man. This act of "Phouoibee Shaba" is performed only when harvesting come to an end to the particular family. If this ritual is performed, one easily notices that harvesting is accomplished for the particular family on that day. A person may own many 'Shangams' [unit for measuring farming land] three, four or five or more, but he cannot perform the above ritual in harvesting in between the' Shangams', it should be on the last' Shangam'. Normally harvesting a' Shangam' in a day is the order.

So, the ritual is executed in harvesting the last' Shangam'. If a woman acts as 'Phouoibee' she should be the one who has taken bath and should be free from monthly cycle. If the last day of harvesting falls during "Yummangba" (in the polluted days) then the ritual cannot be held on the day but it is held on an auspicious day. The person in 'Phouoibee' goes around the field and collects the left out paddies. It is thrashed on the mat with hands only, not with the harvesting stick. The small amount of straws is bound into a broom (= *Shumjit* in Manipuri). But this is no longer a 'Shumjit' (broom), instead it is referred as 'Hanubi'. This 'Hanubi' is brought from the field along with the fresh paddy, in fact the broom is kept in one of the paddy bag. The 'Hanubi' is kept in the barn near the small earthen pitcher (Chafu) which is filled with paddy. The old paddy in the small pitcher is also replaced by the fresh paddy. This 'Hannubi' (broom) is used in cleaning the barn when the next harvesting season comes,

40. 'Loutaba' is a simple ritual performed in the early morning on the fifth day of 'Phairen' (January - February). The farmer goes to his field along with

a spade and makes a dig on the ground. He will return with the spade but he cannot speak to anybody till he reach his house. As a tradition a farmer does not start his agricultural activities till the 'Loutaba' ritual is performed. The same ritual is performed in Andro (a Chakpa village) also but with a different fashion. It is a simple prayer which includes the offering of a chicken. The offering is done at the corner of the field. The prayer is simple and pray for a good harvest for the coming year.

C. SUPERSTITIONS

The ancient Manipuris were the abode of superstitious beliefs which were widespread in their everyday life. To a certain extent the behaviour of the Meiteis was moulded by this superstitious beliefs. The influence of the beliefs are so firm that modern education cannot loosen its hold among the Meiteis. Rational thinking, a wonderful gift of modern education has little effect on the minds and behaviour of the Meiteis. However, the force of modernisation and urbanisation is gradually shaking the firm foundation of superstitious beliefs. Superstitious beliefs are not found in isolation from the life of the Meiteis but are found in their everyday activities. It may be interesting to examine how the superstitious beliefs influence the mind and behaviour of the people in the following manner.

1. In a traditional Meitei home 'Polangkhok' (poles for hanging clothes) was placed in the left of courtyard (Shumang) just near the 'Awang Shanggoi' (out-house on the left side of courtyard). Crossing below the pole is considered inauspicious. And it has not further explanation.
2. Rats spoiling food and artifacts is not uncommon. But one does not rebuke to the rats. It is believed that rebuking will do more harm to the family.

3. It was considered that the *Amangshang* (lavatory) was infested with evil spirits. So entering the lavatory without a fire in the night time was considered unsafe from evil spirits. What was practised was to clap for three times while entering the Amangshang. It was believed that this would ward off evil spirits from lavatory. But this belief is gradually disappearing at least in the urban areas.
4. Lending of money to somebody could not be executed on everyday. Thursday is considered an inauspicious day for lending and one does not lend money on this day. While lending money the number should not end by zero. Ending by zero is considered inauspicious. So what is usually practised is to lend Rs. 101 in place of Rs. 100.
5. Traditionally the Manipuris practised lunar calendar. Basing on this a married woman cannot enter her original home (Mapam) on first, ninth and twentyninth day of a month. Even if she likes to communicate with her mother or some other person of her original home she would talk with them near the fencing or at the gate. The above days are believed as inauspicious for entering their home. However, this is left aside in case of emergency or tight situation.
6. In a traditional home the barn was kept outside the house somewhere near the Makha Shanggoi (the outhouse on the right side of the courtyard). One cannot withdraw paddy from the barn on any day of the week and on any month of the year. Thursday is the restricted day of a week. One can withdraw paddy only on auspicious days of a month. Usually the newly reaped paddy is stored in the barn in November and December. This newly reaped paddy cannot be withdrawn from the barn till the month 'Wakching' (January). And one can withdraw the

paddy from 'Fairen' (February) after performing the ritual 'Kotlai' Thaba.' This simple ritual is mostly performed in the month of "Fairen".

However, one can perform it in the coming months, i.e. March, April, etc. according to one's convenience. So what is usually done is to preserve sufficient amount of paddy from the previous harvest for use till the ritual *'Kotlai Thaba'* is performed. However, maintaining auspicious and inauspicious days in withdrawing paddy from the barn may be a way of indirectly imposing a discipline in using the grains.

A scene of 'Kotlai Thaba' in front of 'Kot'.

Kotlai Thaba—Meiteis believe that 'Fou-oibi' the goddess of grain resides at the barn (Kot). Once in a year this goddess is worshipped beginning from the month of 'Fairen' (February), and the ceremony is known as 'Kotlai Thaba'. A small offering is made near the barn by cleaning the floor with water. Some fruits, Kwa and Mana (betal nuts and leaves), seven handful of puffed rice, seven grains of rice, etc. are offered to the goddess by placing on a banana leaf. A light is also lit. A herb known as 'Khoiju Leikham' is burned in the offering. The ceremony is simple and ends by praying to the goddess for wealth and prosperity. At the end of the ceremony the puffed rice is thrown inside the barn. The belief behind the burning of 'Khoiju Leikham' is that it help in warding off an insect known as '*Foujum*'.

7. In the past every household maintained a small bamboo grove in their homestead. However, this bamboo could not be felled on any desirable day. Bamboos were felled only on auspicious days. [As an instance bamboo could not be felled on Saturdays]. It also seems maintaining a discipline in utilizing bamboo.
8. Restrictions are imposed on male persons on the use of creeper vegetables as foods as it is believed that this will lead to weakening one's intellect, wit and agility. However, this bears another sense as regard to 'incest taboo'. It says that sexual relationship with close relatives is harmful to society and the involving persons.
9. Facing a broom while coming out of the house for a venture is considered inauspicious. It is considered as a bad omen. In order to avoid such a situation what is usually done is to hide the broom by the sweeper if a person comes out of home while sweeping.
10. Meeting a cat while coming out of house or on the way of a journey for a venture is also considered as a bad omen.
11. Again meeting a brushing person (who is brushing his teeth) while leaving the house is believed as bad omen.

12. Marriages are not performed during the days of 'Hari Soyon'. Marriages are also not performed in the month of Wakching (January) for no reason.
13. A person who has stepped out of house for a venture will not re-enter the house even if the person forgets something to carry for the trip. In such a situation the person will ask someone to hand over the left out article.
14. Constructing a house during pregnancy of the woman of the family is considered inauspicious. Following this she is not permitted to purchase ornaments for her during her pregnancy.
15. A ritual named 'Sharoi Khangba' is performed on the first and second Saturdays of 'Lamta' (March) month of Meitei Calendar. Tradition says that evil spirits stalks in the lanes on these days. So, children are advised not to go outside the house on 'Lamta Thangjas', first and second Saturday of Lamta (March).
16. There are particular days in some months which are considered inauspicious. These are termed as 'Tatnaba Numit'. As these days are considered inauspicious no important venture or job is executed on 'Tatnaba Numits'. The following is a chart for Tatnaba Numits' (inauspicious days):-

    Shajibu (April), Thawan (August), Poinu (December)—Nongmaiching (Sunday) and Ningthoukaba (Monday)

    Kalen (May), Langban (September), Wakching (January)—Erai (Friday),

    Yumshakeisha (Wednesday).

    Enga (June), Mera (October), Fairen (February) – Leibakpokpa (Tuesday),

    Engen (July), Hiyangei (November), Lamta (March) —Shagolshel (Thursday), Thangja (Saturday).

17. In the past a homestead was generally as big as 3 to 4 Paris land. And the traditional house stood somewhere in the western side of the garden leaving more space in the eastern side. A number of fruits, vegetables, trees and bamboos were planted in the garden. So there was an environment for the bees to make its hive. And bee-hives were frequently available in the garden or in the house or in the out houses. A good variety of bees, wasp, etc. were available. By observing the location of the bee-hive some conclusions were made which was based on traditional beliefs. Still these superstitious beliefs has its place in the society. The following is the conclusion derived by observing the direction of bee-hive.

    Nongpok (East)—One will get riding a horse, an elephant, meaning he will be successful in his work.

    Meiram (South-east)—One will fall sick.

    Khada (South)—One will get sorrow and suffering.

    Moiranglaiji (South-west)—One will fall sick.

    Nongchup (West)—Death of wife and child may occur.

    Koubrulaiji (North-west)—He will get a long life for his wife and children.

    Awang (North)—He will get a good harvest.

    Chingkhei (North-east)—He will get a higher post.

18. A traditional house is not relatively clean as compared to modern house. So there were every chances the house to be infested by flies, mosquitoes and insects. In such an atmosphere lizards must be planty in the house which lives on insects. Lizards, in frantic scramble for its preys sometimes falls on one's body. But the falling of lizard on the body is considered as a message that something bad or good will happen to the person in the near future.

Such a prediction is made by observing the part of the body which the lizard falls. And the following is the chart of the predictions by observing the part of the body which the lizards falls.

i) on the head – one will get wealth.

ii) on the ear – one will get ornament.

iii) on the eye – one will get friend.

iv) on the nose – one will get sweet smell.

v) on the mouth – one will get sweetmeats.

vi) on the neck – one will get one's desire.

vii) on the breast – one will get a good luck.

viii) on the chest – one will quarrel with another person.

ix) on the back – one will get land.

x) on the loin – one will get garments.

xi) on the anus – one will meet death.

xii) on the thigh – one will get a high post or promotion.

xiii) on the arm – one will loose his wealth.

xiv) on the leg – one will travel from place to place.

19. Sometimes, by circumstances, two members of a family use to venture out in different directions. Such a situation is traditionally known as "Shamji Khainaba". And such a situation is not desired by anyone and is considered inauspicious. It is widely believed that something bad will happen to the family. A person leaving his or her house from the backdoor is also treated as "Shamji Khainaba". A girl leaving her house from the backdoor while eloping to her boyfriend may face death of her child.

20. T.C. Hodson, the British anthropologist who traveled and visited Manipur during the colonial period, categorically mentioned in his book *"The Meitheis"*

on the superstitious mind of the Manipuris regarding day, date and direction to travel a place. According to him; the Meiteis are also extremely superstitious with regard to days and dates for setting out on journeys in different directions, although on emergencies these ideas are put to one side. The following are unlucky days and dates, as mentioned in his book, for travelling in different directions:-

Monday – East

Tuesday – North and East

Wednesday – North and East

Thursday – South and East

Friday – West

Saturday – North and East

Sunday – West and South.

The date upon which it is unlucky to travel on as follows:

To the North – 2nd, 10th

To the South – 3rd, 4th, 11th and 13th

To the East – 1st and 9th

To the North-East – 8th, 15th, 30th

To the North-West – 7th, 15th

To the South – 4th, 12th.

CONCLUSION

From the above short discussion we are enlightened that there is hardly any area in the life of the Meiteis where beliefs and superstitions have not penetrated. It seems these beliefs and superstitions have, to a certain extent, regulated their daily life. Still in this scientific age these superstitious beliefs have acted as a brake to their free actions and thinking. Their minds are not still free from fear of the fallout when someone acted against the custom imposed by superstitious beliefs. And here such unfounded beliefs poses a question mark on the present education which aims at cultivating scientific temper to the population. In fact, this chapter may have its value if one succeeds in classifying the daily actions as one of beliefs, superstitions and plain practices. However, treating these beliefs and practices as rubbish would be an imbalance treatment of the topic. In the midst of such vast beliefs and practices there are few which has their value in society mainly in the form of maintaining a discipline in utilizing their home products. Some has their value in maintaining personal discipline.

In the past bamboo constituted the main plank of material culture of the Meiteis. So it is natural to encircle the bamboo by an aura of beliefs. There is no wrong in imposing some kind of discipline in the form of belief in using bamboo in view of its extreme importance in their everyday life. Prohibition of felling bamboo at least a day in a weak (Saturday) may be a means to prevent unscrupulous felling of bamboo by greedy users. Imposing such discipline in the form of belief is more pronounced in storing and withdrawing paddy from a 'Kot' (barn). At least a day in a week is restricted in withdrawing paddy from barn. The restriction has got its moral standard when the 'Kot' (barn) has been placed under the care of the goddess 'Fou-oibi'. Now the restriction has become a firm custom which no one can disobey. Under the command of the goddess no one can withdraw the new reaped paddy from the barn till the ritual 'Kotlai Thaba' is performed more conveniently in the month of Fairen (February). Similar is the case in using Yangkok (winnower) which, in view of its extreme utility in their daily life, has treated as soul. A house cannot remain separated from Yangkok—its soul, for even a night—meaning it should be treated carefully and one should not keep throwing it outside the house after use. The practice of returning a few handful of rice in the 'Chengfu' (pot for storing rice) after measuring for a meal's use cultivate a sense of small saving in the form of rice, though traditional in nature. The ritual treatment in preparing Kum (Indigo) and further treating the prepared Kum in the 'Chafu' (pitcher) as 'Lairemma' (goddess) enhances the virtues of Kum. But it may be counted as labelling extreme importance to the end product which is ready for market.

Among the beliefs and practices the nature and characters of patriarchal society is found hidden in one form or the other. As this being a male dominated society due importance is given to male of the family in the time of decision-making in the family and society. A long with this certain privileges are also reserved for male in their usages of goods and articles. The reserving of 'Chakmai' —the uppermost layer of cooked rice in a pot for male and again obstruction of male from eating 'Chaka' the burnt rice in a cooker is tantamount to treating women in subordinate position while extending priority of everything to male. A rare psychological treatment is also found among the practices in the form of treating victim of drowning, falling from a height, etc. particularly in children. The practice of 'Thawai Mee Koukhatpa' is not other than but a psychological treatment to the victim to return to normalcy.

REFERENCES

1. Oral interview with K. Apabi Singh, Uripok, Imphal.
2. Oral interview with N. Manijao, Palace Compound, Imphal.
3. Oral interview with M. Bahadur, Keishampat, Imphal.
4. Oral interview with M. Noren Singh, Khongman, Imphal.
5. Oral interview with Ksh. Boro Singh, Top Khongnangmakhong, Imphal.
6. Emoinu Ahongbigi Tungnapham, Yumnamcha Budhichandra, Pishumthong Ningom Leirak, Imphal.
7. Bahadur, Mutua, *Cane and Bamboo Crafts of Manipur*.
8. Bahadur, Mutua, *Traditional Textiles of Manipur*.
9. Hodson, T.C., *The Meitheis*.

7

Rites of Passage

A number of rituals and ceremonies are performed from birth to death in the life cycle of the Meiteis. There is a strong belief among the Meiteis that the cycle follows even after death, and death itself is treated as a part of the cycle. This belief in transmigration of soul strongly influences their life and as a consequence of this influence some of the rituals and ceremonies are held as an observance of this belief. As we find in the present setup the ritual begins immediately after birth known as 'Epan' (birth ceremony). The more essential part of this is held in the morning and the remaining part is held in the evening. The morning part is basically a prayer to 'Pitai Khomtaibi' deity asking for good health and long life of the baby. This goddess, according to tradition is considered as the one who accompanies the baby from the womb of mother till birth. She looks after the baby even after birth till 'Chak-Umba' (rice feeding ceremony). As Meitei society is a plural society the evening part of 'Epan' is held in two ways; one traditionally for traditional believers and the other in the style of Hinduism for Meitei Hindus. For traditional believers the same goddess 'Pitai Khomtaibi' is again prayed with the inclusion of 'Eratphu' and begged good health and long life. The Meitei Hindus continues the evening part as '*Swathi Puja*'.

On the birth of the baby it is considered that the house involved is desecrated. So a simple ritual is held on the twelfth day after birth in which the house involved is made sacred again. As a part of this ritual—'Yumshengba', the baby and the mother are also thoroughly bathed. When the baby girl reaches three, four or five months and six and seven months in case of baby boy, the rice-feeding ceremony, traditionally known as 'Chak-Umba' is held in the morning at the Mangol (Verandah), not at kitchen. The ear of a baby is pierced when the baby (either girl or boy) reaches, three, five or seven years of age. This is meant for putting ear-ring. But this is held in a pompous form including fire worship. This ceremony is not held if the baby is less than three years of age. Puberty rite as is found in the other societies is conspicuously lacking in Meitei society. This is found to be expressed more strikingly functionally, involving the young boy and girl in the traditional social institutions. But nowadays with the demise of such social institutions, such a tradition is no more in Meitei society. When the boy and girl reaches their marriageable age they are married. Since marriage, especially for the Meiteis, is a long process involving different stages till the final ceremony 'Luhongba' is performed, it is discussed separately as a chapter namely. 'Marriage and Rituals'.

A discussion on rituals and ceremonies relating to death is the major part of this chapter. Cremation is the only way of disposing death in this age which according to the chronicle *'Cheitharol Kumbaba'* it was officially adopted since 1724 A.D. during the reign of Maharaja Garibniwaz (1709-1748 A.D.). Although it was found to be practised since ancient past, as early as during the reign of king Nongda Lairen Pakhangba (34 A.D.-154 A.D.) among the Chakpas of Andro, a village in the foothill of Nongmaiching hill in eastern side of Imphal. Otherwise also, four forms of disposal of death were prevalent in Manipur, e.g. in air, water, fire and in the ground. Immediately before the introduction of cremation, disposal of death by secondary burial is found to be practised everywhere in Manipur. And literature dealing on secondary burial is not lacking. What is more interesting is that the findings of recent excavations is corroborating the accounts of various literatures.

The account of secondary burial is mostly available from literatures like *Thawanthaba Hiran*, *Cheitharol Kumbaba*, *Puroi Mashin* and *Loyyamba Shinyen*, though the account seems to be mostly on royal families. Cremation involves a long and meticulous process which even begins before the death of the person. Traditionally an Amaiba (priest-cum-medical practitioner) is always involved in the care of the dying person. The moving out of the dying person from inside the house to Khangenpham, to the coffin and finally to crematorium, all these are executed with strict adherence to traditional belief in life after death. The Lanna Thouram'-the death ceremony is held either on thirteenth or fourteenth day after death and accordingly 'Lamboiba' was performed to the dying person or not. But there are post-cremation performances till *Lanna Thouram*. Beginning from cremation day 'Lairik Taba' is held in the evening in which mainly elderly persons attended it. And it continues till the day before *Lanna Thouram*. On the fifth or sixth day after death, a ritual known as 'Mangani Leihun' or *ashthi* is held. The ritual is held only in morning at Mang (crematorium) in which the ashes or bone collected in the cremation is ritualistically purified and brought to home. The *Lanna Thouram*—death ceremony consists of morning part and evening part. The morning part is mostly ritual in nature whereas the afternoon part is often treated as a festival. 'Firoi', the death anniversary, is held after a year of death of the person. Again in this context also the ritual adheres to the belief in transmigration of soul. The soul is considered timely to transmigrate to a new living being after spending twelve months in the care of Almighty.

A. BIRTH CEREMONY: *EPAN THABA*

In the ceremony *Epan Thaba* the goddess 'Pitai Khomtaibi' is worshipped. It is believed that this goddess looks after the baby since the pregnancy period. The goddess accompanies the baby on its birth. And she continues to take care of the baby even after death. On this day of 'Epan' a ritual is performed to this goddess asking the long life of the baby.

For the ritual a *Foudang Fou* is included. It is a basket full of paddy reaching its brim. A pair of salts (Meitei Thum), a pair of coins are placed above the paddy. Two payas (thin bamboo strips) are inserted by both ends to the paddy believing it as handle of the paddy basket. A garland of seven Ngaris (fermented fish) known as 'Ngari Pareng Achumba' is also placed above the paddy. One 'Pannao' and one 'Shingnao' (Ginger) are included. Cotton and tobacco leaf are placed above the paddy. This two items are especially offered to the deity 'Loklao Leima' for immunity of the baby from cold and cough.

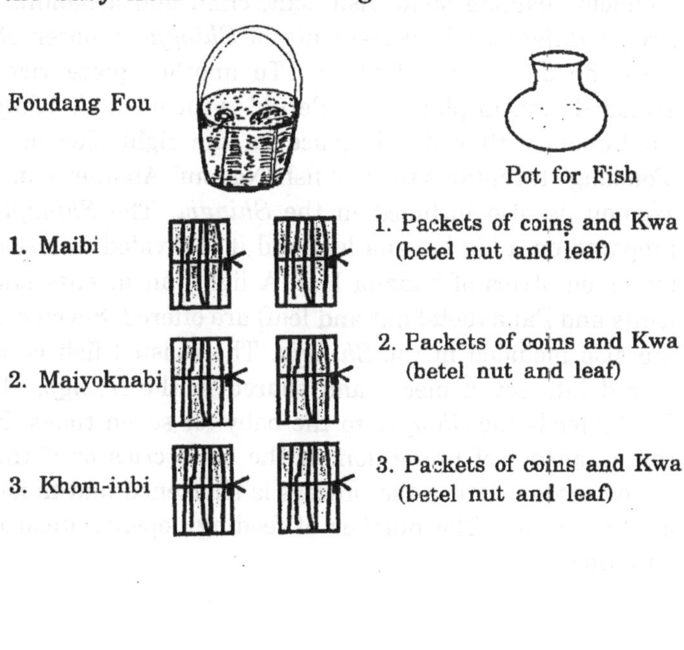

Three packets of banana leaf containing a coin each are made for the *Maibi*, Maiyoknabi and Khom-inbi. In the like manner three packets of banana leaf containing 'Kwa' (betel nut) are also made for the above three persons. They are placed in a row after the Foudang one after another beginning by the packet of *Maibi* then followed by those of Maiyoknabi and Khom-inbi.

[*Maibi* here performs the duty of midwife, otherwise she is also treated as priestess. Maiyoknabi is the assistant of *Maibi*. Khom-inbi is the one who will offer breast milk to the baby till the mother is fit to offer her milk. Postnatal milk of the mother is considered unfit for the baby. So the mother takes the help of Khom-inbi which later on included in the ceremony. Nowadays the role of Maiyoknabi and Khom-inbi is gradually vanishing and mothers are increasingly feeding their postnatal milk to their babies.]

After these arrangement and placement a *Shingju* (raw vegetable palao) is prepared containing *Heibi Mana*, 'Yendem', banana stem, fish, salt, chilli and a handful of rice. A difference in ingredients of *Shingju* is observable with the difference of places. To another place rice is excluded, and in place of it 'Peruk' is included. A 'Khujai' (container) with water is place on the right side of the 'Foudang'. It contains the live fish 'Ngamu'. Another roasted 'Ngamu' is also included in the *Shingju*. The *Shingju* is prepared on a big banana leaf and it is divided into seven pieces on strips of banana leaf. A light, an incense stick, fruits and Pana (betel nut and leaf) are offered. Seven coins are also included in the *Shingju*. The roasted fish is also teared into seven pieces and shared in the *Shingju*. The 'Maibi' feeds the *Shingju* to the baby for seven times. But this is an act of pretention. If the child cries or if there is any inconvenience the process is shortened and finishes at three times. The number of feeding depends upon the situation.

Fig. 7.1: A Scene of Feeding *Shingju* in 'Epan'.

BEGGING AT THE POINT OF FEEDING *SHINGJU*

The *Maibi* (priestess) with the *Shingju* in her palm is begging the long life of the baby from Mangang, Luwang and Khuman deity. While holding the rice, Shingju and fish the palm should be placed upward. The prayer goes in the following manner—'He', the five souls, has become six with 'Mi' (shadow), from to-day you have started taking food. 'Se-Se'—in the event of your illness your father is

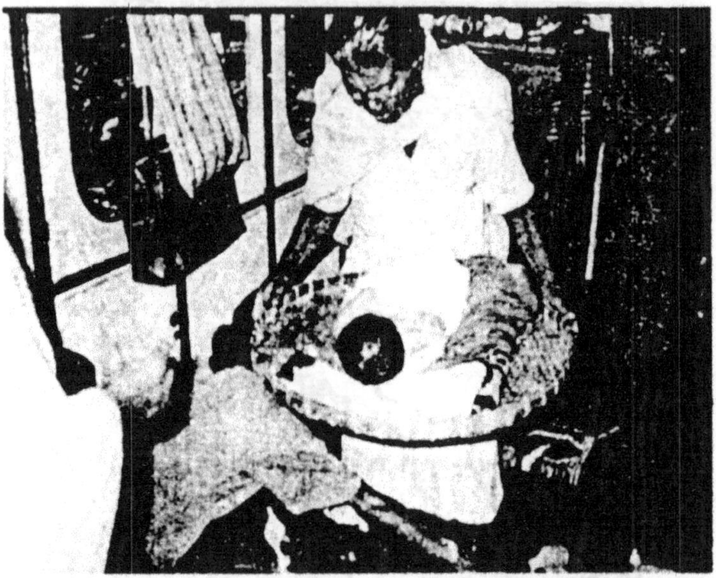

Fig. 7.2: A scene of 'Mei-Okpa' in 'Epan'; birth ceremony

feeding the fish (Ngamu) sitting on your right side and mother on left side with the uttering—'Tinkoklashi', 'Laikoklashi', 'Tinhallashi', 'Laihallasi'. You spent three months in your father's body and the rest months in your mother's body.

Whatever offered to the baby—*Shingju*, rice, water and fish, all are placed on the Yangkok (winnower) and carried out at the gate. These are again offered to 'Pitai Khomtaibi'. At this point the *Maibi* prays to hand over the good health, strength and intelligence to the baby. You please carry away the ill health, weakness and ignorance from the baby. Now your diet is offered.

A different version is found from other respondents. It says—'Se, Se'—Hanu Kokchao, Hanu Laikham', your food is offered. You should not come back again. When you go back you carry away all the evil residues from the house which may affect the baby.

After offering to 'Pitai Khomtaibi' at the gate the Maibi' come to the house carrying the 'Yangkok' by her right hand. Now the 'Yangkok' is placed near the raging 'Fungga' (fire place, the hearth). A Khudei (a loin cloth) is placed above the Yangkok, and above the cloth the baby is placed.

Mei-Okpa

For male baby—The 'Yangkok' containing the baby is carried around the fire for three times. In the first instance the Yangkok is moved around the fire in the clockwise direction and utters—'Do you want gold or silver or Yangkok or baby?' The grandmother replies—'I want the baby'. In the second instance the Yangkok is moved around the fire from anti-clockwise direction and utters—'Do you want silver or gold or Yangkok or baby?' The grandmother replies—'I want the baby'. In the last instance it begins from clockwise direction and utters- 'Do you want gold or silver or Yangkok or baby?' The grandmother replies – 'I want the baby'.

For girl baby—In the case of girl baby the Yangkok is moved around the raging fire in anti-clockwise direction and utters the above words in the same order. And the process is repeated thrice in the like manner. In the same manner the grandmother replies, "I want the baby". Some coins are offered at the Yangkok. Now the 'Maibi' wraps the baby with the same Khudei (loin cloth) placed above the Yangkok and the baby is now handed over to any woman relative of the baby. When receiving the baby the face of the receiver is faced either east or north. While offering money to the *Maibi* one should not stand facing south. Standing facing south is considered inauspicious. Finally the baby is laid rest on the bed of the father.

A mark difference is visible with the difference of place at the ending part of the ritual. To some place, a few paddy grains are taken out from the *Foudang Fou* and thrown above the air offering to 'Pitai Khomtaibi'. In the process the long life of the baby is begged from her. The paddy is thrown from 'Manggol (Verandah) down the ground at the place where eaves-drops fall (Churitapham). At the conclusion all the three women—the *Maibi* (priestess), 'Maiyoknabi' and 'Khom-inbi' will leave the house carrying their respective packets of coin and 'kwa'. At their home they will offer it to 'Sananmahi' deity at their respective home.

To some other place the paddy in the *Foudang Fou*, salt pair, coin pair, the garland of Ngari (fermented fish) are offered to the *Maibi*. If the *Maibi* do not accept the paddy, then money is offered in place of it. The left over paddy, left by the *Maibi* is ready for storing in the 'Kot' by a male of the family. If a male is not available a woman can do it.

While storing in the 'Kot' it is prayed that this paddy is the share of my baby and it is meant for its lifelong use. If the storing is done by someone in the absence of the father, then the father when he comes back will stand near the Kot and will repeat the above prayer to his mind.

Belief behind the offering of baby to the raging fire—In the stage 'Mei-okpa' in the ritual 'Epan' the Yangkok containing the baby is moved around the raging fire. And the *Maibi* says, 'Do you want gold or silver or Yangkok or the baby. The grandmother replies, 'I want the baby'. The belief of this reply is that- in this world the true wealth of a person is one's child. If the child is not there it is considered that the linkage between this world and the heaven is discontinued. So, in order to continue the link a person needs a child. At one time the child when grown up will perform the necessary rite to their parents residing at heaven by offering at least a flower or a fruit. Why the baby is placed above the Yangkok? – The Meiteis consider that the shape of this earth is like that of a 'Yangkok'. Though the child is given birth by the mother the place to grow up by the child is the earth. The child will be brought up by the mother earth not by the parents. So, as a mark of respect to the mother earth the baby is placed above the 'Yangkok'.

Evening Part of Epan

Another ritual is also performed in the evening of 'Epan'. In this also the long life and good health of the baby is begged from 'Pitai Khomtaibi'. The difference is that in the evening the ritual is held with the offering of 'Eratphu'. As it would be mentioned later in 'Lanna thouram', here also the Almighty is first summoned to the 'Eratphu'. And ritualistically moved out of 'Eratphu' to the 'Phamɔal' – an altar. In this way the long life of the baby is begged from 'Pitai Khomtaibi' and thus ends the birth rite, the 'Epan'.

The Goddess 'Pitai Khomtaibi'

The goddess 'Pitai Khomtaibi' looks after the baby till rice feeding ceremony (Chak-umba) of the baby. But after this ceremony the goddess leaves the baby and returns to heaven. The day the baby starts taking worldly food the goddess cannot stay with the child. She goes back to heaven by answering that She will come back again to lead the soul of the person to heaven when the person is about to leave the earth after completing life's journey. But when she comes back to lead the soul of the person to heaven her name is changed to another one. Her name is changed to 'Khamnung Kikoi Lou-onbi'. At the dying moment a person experiences extreme suffering. The person faces emotional and bodily suffering when the soul is about to leave the body, and the soul cannot easily leave the person.

In such a situation the goddess relieves the suffering of soul and leads to heaven happily. At this juncture the goddess will appear in the eye of the person as his/her mother, father or his/her closest friend. She courts the person's soul with sweet words and lead out of house, and carried away to heaven. So, from her ability to charm a person's soul as well as courting, her name has been transformed to "Khamnung Kiko lou-onbi.'

B. YUMSHENGBA

After the birth rite, 'Epan', another ceremony named 'Yumshengba' is held on the twelfth day of birth of the baby. Both the baby and the mother are taken bath on this day. In a sense this is a day of cleaning. The house is desecrated at the birth of the baby. This ceremony sacreded the house again. For this an 'Eratphu' is prepared. A 'Khujai', a container is essential. With this Kwa (betel nut), Kwa Mana (betel leaf), banana and coins are included. At the neck of 'Khujai' three leaves of mango tree are tied with paya (bamboo strips for binding). A 'tanga' is prepared with banana leaf and over it a few paddy grains are scattered. Finally above this the 'Eratphu' is placed. A small offering including fruits, Kwa and coins is also prepared. Milk, banana, chuhi, rice, thoiding, tingthou (a grass) are offered to Almighty asking the long life of the baby. The mixture is poured at the hand of the baby to let it fall at 'Churitafam' —the point where the rain drop fall from eaves. For good health of the baby the fallen banana is put on the head of the baby. In this way the simple ceremony 'Yumshengba' is performed. After this the baby, mother and the house is treated as sacred.

C. CUSTOMS IN BETWEEN 'TARUKNI CHAKOUBA' AND TILL CHILD BIRTH

After marriage the woman would visit her mother at least once in a month. In return the mother also use to visit her daughter in the like manner. During this exchange of visits the advancement of pregnancy of her daughter is easily known to the mother.

With the advancement of pregnancy the mother prepares some items which are necessary by her daughter after delivery period. But the presentation of the items is executed either on seventh, ninth or tenth month of pregnancy. The items include 'Chafu' (an earthen pot) for boiling water, another 'Chafu' for cooking rice. Pieces of pine, fish (dry), rice and Meitei thum (local salt), etc. are the essential items to be presented to her daughter. The presentation of these items is known as 'Chafu Uyan Thinba'. But the lid of the earthen pitchers and Uyan (another earthen pitcher for cooking curry) are presented on the day of 'Epan'. Now a mark change is that these earthen pots are replaced by metal pots. But pieces of pine and Meitei thum (local salt) are enduring the change and still the custom continues. The pine is used in cooking rice as spoon. Till to-day, in almost all the families, 'Meitei thum' (local salt) is used by women for many days after delivery period.

In the past, present medical facilities were rare and almost non-existent in most areas of Manipur. Still there are many areas which are lacking these facilities. So, in those days, if the mother is found suffering from 'Hingchabi Changba' (affected by evil spirits) or from other complicacies in child birth, an offering known as "Chaban Thaba" was performed. For an easy delivery, free from doubts, a knot known as 'khongji' of the 'Kangkhal' (mosquito net) is let loose on its 'Khuya' (leg) side. The lid of 'Chengfu' (pot for storing rice) is also opened. The Almirah (cupboard) is also kept open. The goddess 'Pitai Khomtaibi' is prayed at 'Lukhum' (headside) of her bed. Coins are also offered to the goddess and prayed to her for an easy delivery. In the olden days the mud wall of the house is opened from Mangol (verandah) to inside the house by making a hole with a knife. Now this is replaced by the opening of window and doors. A coin is offered by placing on a piece of banana leaf nearby the hole. In the similar manner coins are also offered to 'Sanamahi' and 'Leimarel' deity. After delivery

Fig. 7.3: A scene of 'Chak-Umba'; rice-feeding ceremony.

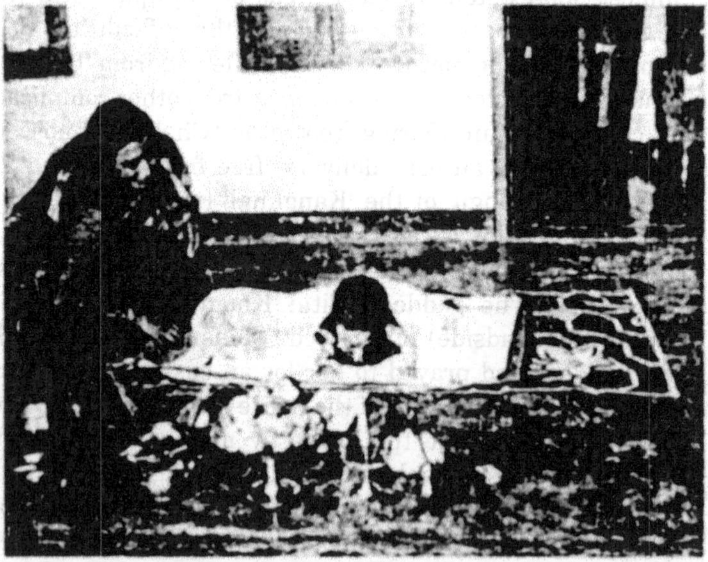

Fig. 7.4: Allowing the child to touch any one of the items plac before the child in 'Chak-Umba'.

the baby is thoroughly bathed by the *Maibi* (midwife) with warm water. While bathing the *Maibi* lift up and down the baby by singing—

"Epa Machup Taro, Epu Machum Taro, Chaoro Shanglo . . ."

The umbilical cord of the baby is cut by 'Wakthou' (fine bamboo strip) made from Wak, a kind of bamboo. The *Maibi* will spit to ground and mud paste is made out of it. This mud paste is rubbed to the cut off umbilical cord. However, the cord is tied by a thread before cutting.

D. CHAK-UMBA

Chak Umba; rice-feeding ceremony is performed when the baby (girl) reaches three, four or five months. For baby (boy) it is performed on sixth or seventh month of their age. The ceremony is held in the morning. For this the baby is thoroughly bathed and new clothes are put on. An 'Athenpot' is offered to 'Sanamahi' deity begging long life of the baby. Then the food is cooked in a new 'Chafu' (earthen pot). Now 'Chafu' is no longer in use and in place of it metal utensils are used. The utensils are thoroughly cleaned and the food is cooked in it. What is found from literature is that seven different fishes, seven different animals and seven different vegetables are cooked for the ceremony. But what is practised at present is to cook a fish item. Even vegetable item is hardly included. The well-cooked food is offered to 'Apokpa' deity begging long life of the baby. Fruits and flowers are also offered to 'Phunga Lairu' and prayed to "Emoinu Ahongbi". Now all these are shortened and nobody follows it as 'Fungga Lairu' is missing in a modern house. Rice feeding ceremony is held at Mangol (Verandah) not in kitchen. The baby is placed on the lap of clean dressed mother who is sitting on a mat. According to literature the feeding is done by the father by holding the food by his five fingers. The baby is given food for five times by chanting the name of five souls. But nowadays the opposite is the practice. The baby is placed on the lap of the mother and the feeding is done by herself. But the feeding here is mere act of pretending because a baby of this age cannot eat properly. After the termination of feeding the baby a few grains of paddy, gold, coin, book, pen, a piece of earth, etc. are displayed in front of the baby on banana leaf. Now the baby is let loose and allowed to touch any one of them. From this one tries to acertain the future of the baby e.g. if the baby touches book, he or she will be intelligent, etc. And here ends the ceremony.

E. 'NA-HUTPA' (EAR-PIERCING CEREMONY)

Fig. 7.5: Fire worship is in progress in 'Na-Hutpa' ceremony.

Ear-piercing ceremony is held when the child reaches three, five or seven years of age. The year is the same for both the sexes. And it cannot be held before completing three years of age.

For this ceremony an 'Eratphu' (earthen pitcher) and 'Mei Eratpa' are essential. The 'Eratphu' – the ritual pitcher is placed above the 'Kangla Men Pafan'. The drawing of the Pafan is made on the ground by flour. The preparation of 'Eratphu' is the same as is done in *Lanna Thouram*. Near the 'Eratphu' a 'Phambal', an altar for the Almighty is placed.

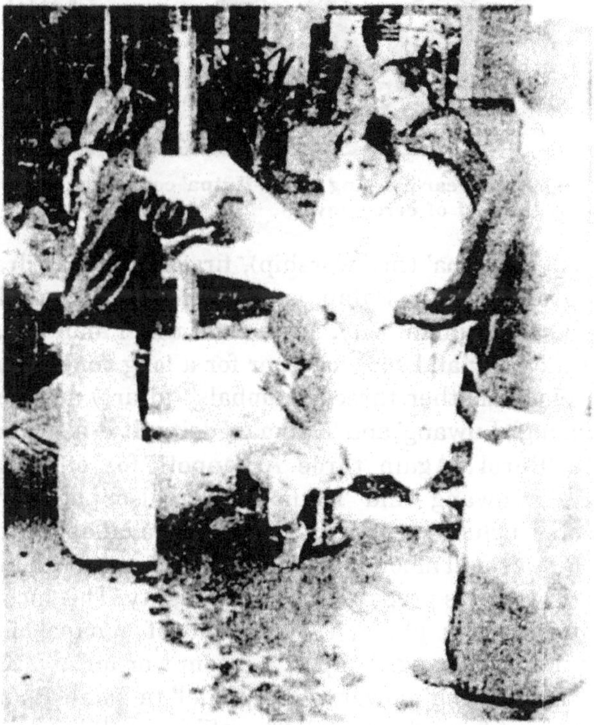

Fig. 7.6: Showering sacred water on the clean shaved child as a part of 'Na-Hutpa' ceremony.

Fig. 7.7: A scene of ear-piercing in 'Na-Hutpa' ceremony performed at the end of ceremony.

For 'Mei Eratpa' (fire worship), first a Pafan is drawn on the ground. This Pafan is 'Pallandabi Pafan'. This represents the human body. The use of this Pafan aims at keeping the body and soul together for a long time. Nearby the fire place another three 'Phambals' (altars) are placed for 'Mangang', Luwang' and 'Khuman' deity. It is also known as three 'Purol'. Again three Athenpots for offering to 'Mangang', Luwang' and 'Khuman' are also placed. The 'Athenpots' includes a varied vegetables available in the season. But a small amount of rice is a must in the Athenpot. Again a 'Kubipot' is prepared for the Almighty. This includes a "Kambi (earthen plate), rice, a hand of banana of odd number (Laphoi chang thokpa), a coconut or an Awathabi, a petal of 'Leishang' flower, a 'Laiphidol' (a small Phanek, lower garment for girl), a small 'Ennafi' (a small long cloth), a scented fruit (this scented fruit is essential, if the fruit is not available a leaf can replace it), a coin, a Kwa (betal nut) and leaf. Any available fruit of the season like apple and orange, etc. are also included.

In preparing the fire place, four banana stems are erected in the four corners. Along with this four young bamboos and four sugarcanes are also erected in the same corners. A small 'Thak-Khan' (canopy) is placed above the fire place standing on the banana stem, bamboo and cane sugar. This banana stems, bamboos and cane sugars are surrounded seven times by 'Lang Ahingba' (a sacred thread). In the centre of such prepared fire place the elements to be burned are placed. They are:

(1) Heibong,

(2) Shai,

(3) Boroi,

(4) Heikru,

(5) Khongnang (Banyan),

(6) Heinou (Mango), and

(7) Nongleishang.

All these are in small amount. The ritual commences with the summoning of Almighty in the 'Eratphu'. And it remains the same as is done in *Lanna Thouram*.

On the other side the child or children to be involved in the ear-piercing are cleanly shaved and bathed. Meanwhile the fire worship begins by igniting the fire woods. When the fire started raging flower, rice, Mekruk, Thoiding, Ghi are offered occasionally. The seven elements mentioned above are also offered occasionally to the fire. Now the shaved child or children are allowed to sit nearby the ritual site. And above the child or children the sacred water collected by three girls from a nearby pond in three 'Chafus' (earthen pitcher) is poured passing through a white cloth hanging above the child by other two girls. This pouring of water is repeated for three times alternately. The three girls involved in collecting sacred water from the pond are the ones who have taken bath thoroughly. And they are also dressed with new clothes. While collecting sacred water from the pond flowers are offered first and the deity in water is invoked by chanting the words—'Erai Leima Etheirel Namungba Namungbi, kindly bless us. Get away all the 'Akhaba 'Ayakpa' and 'Afakpa'—Emu Mayoltabu Loujarage—let me collect only the prime water. Only then the water is collected in three small earthen pitchers. These 'Chafus' (earthen pitchers) are new ones purchased recently for the purpose.

After pouring the sacred water above the child or children they are dressed with new clothes, specially prepared for the ritual. Then they are allowed to sit along with their parents near the fire place. They are allowed to offer flower to the raging ritual fire. While offering they pray to god begging good health, long life and to dispel evil spirits when encountering. The 'Piba' also praise the fire by chanting its different names. And finally bowed to fire begging a brilliant life like fire for the child. Now the ear is pierced by an experienced person and ear ring or the like is inserted in the hole. Thus ends the Na-Hutpa ceremony.

F. DEATH CEREMONY

I. Disposal of Death: Secondary Burial

Cremation is the only form of funeral service now practised among the Meiteis. This seems to be a relatively new practice which according to '*Cheitharol Kumbaba*' came into force since A.D. 1724 during the reign of Maharaja Garibniwaj (A.D. 1709-1748). Before this, according to the literature 'Shakok Lamlen', four forms of disposal of death were in practice among the Meiteis. The four forms were: (a) Nungshitki Potloi (keeping the dead in open air), (b) Eshing Potloi (throwing into water, most probably in river),

(c) Leipak Potloi (burying in ground), and Meigi Potloi (burning the dead into ashes). Since the reign of Maharaja Garibniwaj disposal of dead by burning was encouraged and all other forms were abolished. A similar tradition was found among the people of Funan society in fifth and sixth century A.D. There the dead are disposed of in four ways; by throwing the corpse into the current of a river, by burning it to ashes, by burial in a trench, and by exposure to the birds. However, according to the literature *'Poireiton Khunthokpa'*, cremation was in practice among the 'Chakpas' of Andro (a village in the foothill of Nongmaiching range, around 25 kms. from Imphal). Poireiton – the leader of a band of wanderers who wandered during the reign of Nongda Leiren Pakhangba (34 A.D.-154 A.D.) in search of better habitable place; came across the Andro village and saw a raging fire. And he enquired about the fire in the following manner:

> *"Chakpa kaitong Pakhangpa-O, Meipi Tangkoi Pai, Meikhu Nonglol Kapa Ashipu Kari Meino Paohangpapu Hempa Puchet Mei, Chekai Kakup Mei, Charu Tangshoi Mei, Laimom Poktok Mei, Futit nonglol Meira Haina Paohangpapu Hoita Yiyuwa Chingkhong Poireiton—O Aiyum Hemcheng Fuyikmei, Charu Tangshoi Meishung Nate. Chakpa Khampok Mei, Leima Fal-lao Ngambi Mapari Shangfuraipapu Khara Khutyon Thina Nongmal-le. A-em Chakpa Meeyeek Mei, Hemcheng Meerou Meine Haina Paokhumkhiye".*
>
> It goes in this way:
>
> "He enquired about the fire to a male person. What is that raging fire with tall smoke? Is the fire meant for slash and burn, or for igniting earthen pots, or for burning 'Charukhok (cut out straw in the field), or for preparing puffed rice, or for burning straws? No, the fire is not related with non of the above—the person replied. The fire is meant for cremation, for burning dead into ashes, he said".

From the above discussion what is observed is that all the four ways of disposal of dead might be in practice in different areas of Manipur simultaneously. Disposal by burning seems to be a tradition of the Chakpas. According to literatures like Puroi Mashin, Thawanthaba Hiran, *Loiyamba Shinyen* and *Cheitharol Kumbaba*, the majority of the Meiteis adopted the way of disposal by burial. These literatures deal at length on the practice of secondary burial.

Secondary Burial

For the moment a definite time period cannot be mentioned when the secondary burial began to practice in Manipur. However, according to literature 'Mashin' a vivid account is available on the duties allocated to certain lineages to carry out secondary burial since the reign of King Naothingkhong (A.D. 663-763). Regarding secondary burial, which is found practice in many parts of the world, a mention may be made on this kind of disposal of dead from E.B. Taylor's book *Dictionary of Anthropology*. It says,

> "A final burying of a person's bones, after the first temporary burial during which the flesh had decomposed. Secondary burial has been found in many parts of the world. The bones are usually concentrated in packages."

The tradition of secondary burial might be in existence since the early days. However, the performance of funeral service with the allocation of certain fixed duties to some selected lineage came into operation since the reign of King Naothingkhong (A.D. 663-763). In this a reference can be made from the literature 'Mashin' on how the secondary burial was executed by the persons of these selected lineages in the burial of a member of royal family including the king.

Beginning from mourning, making of coffin, etc. till the secondary burial, all these were done by persons from the selected lineages who were assigned for their respected duties. In this way the mourning was the duty of the two lineages viz., Nahakpam and Pamkhaicham. The coffin was prepared by Thongbam. The burial site was dug by Thokchom. The duty of Ayam was to offer rice at the crematorium. He was also to perform the rite 'Mangthong Thingba'. It is a rite performed at the primary burial. The person engaged must be an Amaiba (a priest cum medical practitioner). The banana leaves required in offering rice at the burial site was supplied by Thaudeicham. Chinggangbam was responsible for collecting the necessary amount fire wood for use in royal kitchen. A rite known as 'Mangthong Hangba' was performed by Ayam after completing a year of burial. This was the rite used in extracting the corpse from ground. The items included in the rite were viz, a spade, *Nahei Thang* (a knife for ritual use), *Khunet yot* (piece of iron meant to be stepped upon), *Khunet sel* (coins meant to be stepped upon), two broad cloths, rice, flowers, egg, gold and silver etc.

After performing the rite 'Mangthong Hangba' the burial site was dug by Tokpam. Sathokpam was responsible for removing skeleton from the burial. The cleaning and removing of dirts was done by Siyatpam. The hair was combed by Akham. He was also responsible for removing maggots from the corpse. Sharotkhaibam was to extract the skeleton from the corpse. Washing of the skeleton was duty of Khoirom. However, most part of the skeleton was washed by the five lineages, viz., Loitongbam, Thoitingcham, Longcham, Ahalthem and Akoicham. But the finishing touch was given by Amakcham. Washing was done by using 'Long' (a traditional sieve made of fine bamboo chips). This 'Long' was supplied by a tribe known as 'Tingshang'. The collection of decomposed flesh and dirts was the duty of Soukulakpam, Khoipam and Sampanturam. The dirts were collected in an earthen pitcher and buried in the ground. The above two lineages were also responsible for making the pitcher.

The cloth required for wrapping the thoroughly washed bones was made by Yimlenpam. Hanglem and Kolom performed 'Porom Thopthilba'. The thoroughly washed bones were dried in the sun for five days and buried on an auspicious day. However, the burial is not done without much fanfare. In the event of burial of the dried bones a ceremony known as "Sharu Leitengba" is performed. In this the dried bones are well decorated with flowers. The ceremony ends when so decorated bones were put inside a big 'Kharung' (earthen Jar) and once again buried in the ground. In the course of the ceremony 'Yurangba' was also performed. It is the festivity after burial which includes local liquor.

The account of secondary burial may remain incomplete if the information on the relics as mentioned in the literatures are not taken into consideration. There are evidences from literatures like *Thawanthaba Hiran*, *Cheitharol Kumbaba*, *Puroi Mashin* and *Loyyamba Shinyen*, that the skull was masked with gold and silver. And a detail account is available from the literature 'Thawanthaba Hiran' (adventures of Meitei King Thawanthabam 1195-1231 A.D., against Khuman principality by using boats) in the event of funeral service of Khuman Chanu Meiteileima Chakpa Shamphabi and Tampha Wangngamlon, daughter of Thawanthaba. And the reference runs in this way:

> *"Nongyai Khuman Ningthou Adon Punshiba Mammom Khayoironbu Wakyei Meinaida Tongcheng Lunaida, Khamnou Yaisi Lomna Hida Tongjeng Kuyai Chal-le . . . Mapalna Sasang Maril Fatna Tongjeng Kumai Hangna Yaithong Sahulla Wanglel Punghoula Khunung Paotakla Thang-e Leiron Chan Yamchang Leikup Sirabada Korou Tharaochina Kasa Paotakle, Hayeng Loidam Kumollaba Madairem Sinai . . . Sankheire . . . . Adon Punsibasu Mammon Chakpa . . . Sumna Puroi Leikoira Haoshi Mangchalle, . . . Meidingu Thawanthaba Mamom Tampha Wangamlonbu . . . Tangjalutenglaga,*

Madairem Sinaiyaihanbagi. . . . Khajai Naklou sit, Laibak Khellai Thongbu Choinou Pumna Yumna Yoichainare, Khunungpaotakle, Yaithong Sahulla Wanglen Punghonla Haoshi Mangthille".

In brief it says that the

corpse is placed inside a boat-shaped coffin and buried in the ground after performing funeral service. After a year the burial is excavated and the skull is separated from the skeleton by a skilled person. Such a separated skull is first wrapped by silver and finally by gold. While wrapping so by silver and gold the place for the eyes and lip are clearly slit open. The impression for nose and cheeks are also well marked. Finally such a skull masked by gold is buried in the ground.

In order to buttress what is mentioned in the literature 'Thawanthaba Hiran' a cross reference can be made from the royal chronicle "*Cheitharol Kumbaba*". The text is :

Meidingu Paikhombagi Hakthak, Keisham Lanhangna Cheithaba Kum Sok 1606/Ing 1684 /Langban Thada Erom Loinai Ngashingbaga Lukram Monshambaga Ani Manachingduna Leipak Pumnamagi Lu Tou – e. Sana Lupadi Ningthemda Katle. Senchao Pukhamdi Kori Tanduna Shang Angangbana Toman Pungjao Shai-e.

It says that

in the year 1684 A.D. all the burial sites were excavated under the leadership of Erom Loinai Ngashingba and Lukram Monshaba when Paikhomba was the reigning King (1666-1697 A.D.) of Manipur. The acquired treasure of gold and silver was deposited to royal custody. And a royal drum, Tomal Pungjao, was also casted out of the collected bronze dish plates. So, a study of these literatures reveal us that secondary burial was extensively practised in Manipur by majority of the population.

The accounts of secondary burial as found from the above discussed literatures are corroborated by the findings of recent excavations conducted by State Archaeology department in the year 1994 at Sekta which is located at a distance of 18 km north-east of Imphal on the left bank of Eril river in Imphal East district of Manipur. A report of 1994 excavation of Sekta, Manipur, says that there are eight layers in the burial site. Both masked and unmasked skulls are found in the site. In one case the face and part of the skull upto the sagittal suture is covered by a very thin copper mask. Again in one of the burials, four jars in the sequence of the smaller ones being kept inside bigger ones are interned inside a big jar. The skulls and other fractured bones (mostly limb bones) and teeth are also found buried separately in different jars. In layer No. 2 of the jars that contain the skulls are covered by a lid and the skulls face generally south-west. In layer No. 3 also the skull and limb bones are buried separately along with grave goods. The skulls are kept inside the jars facing either southwest or north but the mask skulls faces either north, west or south. Burial of two skulls, one masked another unmasked, putting in separate jars is the significant character of this layer. In layer No. 5 in two of the burial (6 & 9), the jars contain only sandy soil. This suggest that the primary burial was done near the river bank and when the bones became decomposed, only the soil was collected in a jar and buried into the common burial mound.

The interning of the skulls and bone fragments into jars suggest the practice of secondary burial. In some of the burials no bone is found, except some grave goods and sandy soil. This suggest that even though the practice of secondary burial in a common place was a social dictum, there was no definite socially prescribed period for the collection of the bones from the primary burials. Perhaps the secondary burial was performed according to the convenience of the deceased family.

II. Disposal of Death (Cremation).

As mentioned earlier cremation is the only form of funeral service now practising among the Meiteis. And this practice came into force since A.D. 1724 during the reign of Maharaja Garibniwaz (A.D. 1709-1748). In the context of adoption of cremation as state funeral service a reference can be made from 'Cheitharol Kumbaba', the royal Chronicle. The reference is:

> *Haobam Kiyambagi Kum Sak 1641Shajibu Thada Haobamcha Pukhrambagi, Lunachingna Leipak Pumnamaki ; Lu Tou-a . . . Moirang Khoidonggi Kum Sak 1646 (A.D. 1724) Chahi Ahumgi Matungta Lamda Thagi 20 Ni Nongmaijing Numitta Ningthemna (Garibaniwaj) Mabudhou Khibikpu Meida Ek-a. Engthida Tumge Chatle. Leipak Pumnama Meida Ekpasung Adungei Hou-a. Ningthembu Maharaj Koubasung Adungei Hou-a. Erai Numitta Ningthou Engthi Chatpa Thunglei-a.*
>
> It says:
>
> In the year A.D. 1719 under the leadership of one Haobamcha Pukhramba all the burial sites of the country was excavated. Again in the year A.D. 1724 after lapse of five years, all the bones of His forefathers were cremated. And went a pilgrimage to immerse the ashes in Ningthi river (Chindwin river in Kabow valley). Since then cremation became the funeral service of the country. All other forms of funeral services were stopped and cremation became the popular funeral service.

The procedure of cremation is relatively long. And in many stages the practices are greatly influenced by beliefs of the society. In the event of death of a person an Amaiba (a priest cum medical practitioner) will sit by side of the dying person. At the point of death the dying person is shifted out of the house to Mangol (verandah—the front porch of the traditional Meitei house). This is done by the influence of the belief that if the person dies inside the house then the house is desecrated. The Amaiba will take care of the person at Phammen—the right side of the Mangol. The duty of the Amaiba at this juncture is known as 'Famshennaba'. Here the Amaiba will take care of the dying person. He will observe the pulse of the person. In view of changing pulse rate he will advise the people around to prepare coffin, Shangkhanba (preparing a small hut), etc. In preparing the Ku (coffin) it should not be broader and longer than the body of the dying person. If it happens it is believed that the misfortune may repeat in the family. A small 'Shang' (hut) is prepared at 'Khangenpham'—the area of the courtyard in south-eastern side of Tulshipung/ Tairenpung; a small mound at the centre of the courtyard where the herb/ tree named Tulshi/ Tairen is planted. The Ku (coffin) is to be placed at the 'Khangenpham' when the corpse is finally shifted out from the house.

Before placing the coffin at 'Khangenpham' a coin is placed at 'Khangenpham' and in return a small amount of earth is collected, and placed inside the coffin. The belief behind this act is that the soul of the person has got a small place to stay and for this he is not depending on others. At this moment a small fire is lit in a 'Meihouchafu' (a small earthen pitcher filled with paddy husk and burn with some sticks). At this juncture the drummer, singer and musicians are made available who are required for funeral service. All the relatives are well informed to attend the funeral service. In the past a practice known as 'Lamboiba' was performed as a part of funeral service. At about 5/6 days before the death of the person 'Lamboiba' is performed to the dying person at 'Phammen'. The person is clean shaven. A staff is placed nearby the person. A small Yempak (a traditional umbrella), a Juli (a small bag), a hat, a Yubi Khujai (a container made from coconout shell) are also kept by side of the person. At this juncture a priest will chant *Gopal Sasranam*. And the singer will sing 'Mon

Sikha'. When the person is dead the hat is worn. Finally the dead body is carried out from the Mangol (verandah) through Naktha (northern or left side of varandah); which is believed as the passage of death. The Ku (coffin) is kept ready inside Khangenpham. Before placing the corpse inside the coffin it is carried around the coffin thrice in clockwise direction. While placing the corpse inside the coffin the head is placed facing north. A few coins are tied into two knots by pieces of cloth and they are fixed one each at the headside and legside of the coffin. The one tied at the 'Lukhum' (head side) is known as 'Lukhumsen' and the other tied at the 'Khuya' (leg side) is known as 'Khuyasel'. These coins are accompanied upto crematorium. They are removed only at the crematorium. The act of purchasing a piece of earth from 'Khangenpham' and placing inside coffin, and the act of attaching some coins in the coffin clearly expresses the belief that there is life after death among the Meiteis. It is widely believed that the person is dead but the soul is not. So a piece of earth is purchased for the soul as his plot of land and for this the soul is not depending to others. The act of attaching some coins in the coffin implies that the coins are for use by the corpse for his/her trip from home to crematorium. This is done by the influence of the belief that till now the soul is not departing the body and still accompanying the corpse.

The news of death reaches to all the houses in the locality. At this juncture a small bonfire made by paddy husks (wai) is lit along with 'Khoijum Leikham' (a small medicinal herb) at the gate of every house on the way to crematorium. The belief in this practice is to prevent the intrusion in the house by evil spirits that are accompanying the corpse.

Women also accompany the corpse to the crematorium. Two 'Payas' (thin bamboo chips which are used for binding) are tied into a knot and the same is tied above the Phanek (the lower garment of Meitei woman which reaches the ankle) at the belly as a belt. Now this is replaced by cloth which is known as 'Khwangchet Lakpa'. The coffin is carried to crematorium accompanied by a death procession which consists of drum, cymbal, singer and mourners. The procession also carries the 'Meihou Chafu'. A practice in the past is to shed pieces of 'Lang Ahingba' on the way to crematorium. This practice is not totally death and is still a continuing tradition in isolated cases.

Lang Ahingba

It is raw thread extracted from cotton before conditioning in water and starch. The row cotton is dried in the sun, The cotton is separated from the seeds by Kaptreng- ginning machine. Then the carding is done by a Huitri. Cotton rolling is done with a Lang-gom stick and the process is known as Moithap Taba. Finally spinning is done with the right hand against the thigh. Such an indigeneously prepared thread is known as 'Lang Ahingba'.

Before proceeding the death procession an advance party is sent to crematorium to clear and clean the spot. A few coins are thrown on the ground and a small plot of land is purchased. But this is an act of imagination. Then follows the cleaning and clearing of crematorium. Here also the belief goes in this way that the soul of the person is not taking shelter in somebody's house but living in his plot of land purchased with coins. While making preparation at the 'Mang' (crematorium) a small ditch is dug at lengthwise. Again at the northern end of the lengthwise ditch another round ditch is made. The purpose of this small round ditch is to collect the fluids and brain from the head when the body is consigned to flame. Placing of firewood is made across the longer ditch, and water is sprinkled in the round ditch before assembling the funeral pyre.

The funeral pyre is prepared across the longer ditch by placing firewood one above the other which are separated

Fig. 7.8: A scene of cremation in modern crematorium. The *thak-khan* (canopy) is hanging above the pyre. The small fire made near the *mang* (crematorium) is also seen.

by 'Shingkhan' (firewood which are placed as separator). These 'Shingkhans' are seven in number; it cannot be less and more. Such arranged firewood with seven 'Shingkhans' are enclosed by the frame of six posts, one each at the four corners of the frame and the rest two; one each at the middle of eastern side and western side of the pyre. All the six posts have their names and they are christened as (1) Atenba, (2) Ashangba, (3) Awangba, (4) Anemba, (5) Akuppa, and (6) Apouba. Again around the funeral pyre four bamboo posts are erected at the four corners at a distance which cannot reach by fire easily. The 'Thak-khan' (canopy) is held by these four posts well above the pyre at a height which cannot be reached by fire.

Now all the six posts are well tightened by 'Utang Paya' (bamboo chip from Utang bamboo meant for binding). The next step is to lift the coffin above the pyre. But before this the coffin is carried once or thrice or five or seven times around the pyre in clockwise direction. Lifting of the coffin is done in three stages. The coffin is put to rest for a while first above the first two posts, second at the middle posts and finally at the last two posts. Now the coffin is ready for cremation. Already a small bonfire is made some where near the pyre.

As a part of the ceremony, 'Mei Koiba' is performed. In this 'Mei Koiba' a burning firewood is held by the nearest member of the deceased person by his right hand where a 'Pun' (earthen jar) full of water is held by left hand at his shoulder. The march begins from head-side of the corpse in the clockwise direction. He will go around the pyre for one or three or five or seven times. In the process he will lit the fire first at the posts standing at the four corners of the pyre. At the same time when the fire start raging at the pyre he will pour small amount of water from his back at the posts at the four corners of the pyre. In the past the fire meant for lighting the pyre was lighted from the 'Mei Chafu', but now this is shortened and the fire is lighted from the bonfire made nearby the pyre. Now pouring of water continues and it is poured a little to the round ditch. But the present trend is that the water is poured to all the six posts. The reason is to arrest the burning of Shingkhans'. If it burns early the pyre may be fallen and scattered. Now the belief behind the act of pouring water at the round ditch is that the soul will depart from the body with calm and peace. Human head is considered as the repository of knowledge and wisdom. And the occasional sprinkling of water will relieve the head and will pass away the soul peacefully.

[At the point of lighting the firewood from Mei Chafu *'a ritual is performed by offering Kwa (betel nut and leaf), fruits, fire (candle or pine chip), and dhup (insense stick). It includes* cheng *(rice) and* thoiding, *etc. The ritual culminate with the chanting of nine or 12 names of fire.]*

With the progress of cremation the corpse is engulfed by fire and it reaches such a stage that the limbs begins falling apart. At such a time the 'Thak-khan' along with the four bamboo poles which carries the 'Thak-khan' are pulled down and burn to ashes. It is believed that Almighty in the sky sees and observes what is going on at the crematorium. So, in order to hide the corpse and as well as a respect to heavenly god the 'Thak-khan' is used.

In the course of cremation a piece of bone is collected from forehead. The piece of bone is roasted till the fluids are dried. The piece of bone is collected and put inside a small bamboo pipe, and buried in the ground at a safe place in the Mang (crematorium) so that it is not carried away by dog and others. The present trend is to collect ashes and put in a small bottle. This small bottle is buried in the ground in the previous manner. Now the pyre is perfectly burned down and everything present there is also burnt to ashes. The burning charcoal is doused by water. The extinguished charcoal is buried in the ground at the leg side of the 'Mang'. Again the crematorium is buried by the earth deposited around the ditch which was dug before setting up the pyre. The small ditch shaped mound is plastered by mud and a small offering consisting of fruits, *kwa* (betel nut and leaf), a fire (piece of pine) is made on it. On this mound a small amount of fried peas and mustard seeds are scattered. After some days the mustard seeds will grow into tiny shoots. They are treated as medicinal plants. If by chance the mustard flowers and produces seeds, then oil from such seeds is believed to be more useful medicinally.

What is signified by the fried peas is that the soul is asked to come back again to the family when the fried peas germinate, flowers and finally produces peas. But the fried peas will not germinate again, meaning that the soul of the deceased is asked not to come back again. What follows after this is that a small earthen pitcher with water is

Fig. 7.9: The ritual of *asthi lokhatpa* is in progress

hanged above the plastered (with mud) crematorium by the support of two bamboo poles. A small hole is made at the bottom of the pitcher and drops of water are let loose above the crematorium at a place which is considered the areas of chest. By doing so it is believed that the soul may rest in peace. It may help in lessening the heat faced during cremation. Here ends the rite of cremation and all those who take part returns to their respective home. Women take part generally up to "Mei Koiba" but sometimes they will stay till the pulling down of 'Thak-Khan'. They will make a holy dip or ablution in a nearby pond or in river. Men follow the same and returns home. At home they are welcomed by a small bonfire made at the gate.

III. AFTER CREMATION PERFORMANCES

In the afternoon 'Lairik Taba' is performed at the house of deceased family. In this the text from *Bhagabat Geeta* is read out for Hindu Meiteis. For the traditional Meiteis the genelogy of the Salai (clan) that the deceased belongs is narrated. It is held for five or ten minutes only. The listeners are mostly old men and women. Children are also allowed to participate it. But generally it is the business of old persons. This 'Lairik Taba' continues upto the day before *Lanna Thouram*, the ultimate death ceremony.

In between cremation and *Lanna Thouram* (death ceremony) a ceremony known as 'Mangani Leihun' is performed on the fifth day after the death of the person. For Meitei Hindus the ceremony is performed as *Ashthi Loukhatpa*. If 'Lamboiba' is performed to the death then 'Asthi' is held on the sixth day from the expiry day of the person. If not, then it is held on the fifth day. For the death who performed 'Lamboiba', the *Lanna Thouram* or 'Shradha' is held on the fourteeth day after death. If not, it is held on the thirteenth day after death. As a consequence 'Lairik Taba' is also held for thirteen days or twelve days accordingly.

'Mangani Leihun' or *ashthi*

'Mangani Leihun' or *ashthi* is, in one sense, a ceremony to inform everyone that the person is dead. In the past, as a custom, nobody will enquire the death of the deceased family till *ashthi* is held. Those who attend the ceremony of Mangani Leihun will be invited for the final death ceremony *Lanna Thouram*. If anybody fails to attend this ceremony or if anybody fails to enquire the death even after this ceremony, then the person will not be invited for ***Lanna Thouram*** —the final or main part of death ceremony. But now the change is such that if anybody fails to attend *ashthi* or fails to enquire the death after *ashthi* he will be invited for *Lanna Thouram*. There is a mark difference in the way of invitation also. In the past flower was distributed to the house of the person invited. Nowadays, this is replaced by invitation card.

This *Ashthi Loukhatpa* is performed on the sixth day after death if the deceased performed 'Lamboiba'— by this ritual it is considered that the person become a monk at the point of death. It (Ashthi) is performed on the fifth day after death if the deceased performed 'Kirat Thangba'. The collected ashes from crematorium or the piece of bone from forehead is kept outside the house till *ashthi* is performed. The ashes or the piece of bone is kept carefully to a safe area of the crematorium. In the past it was kept inside a bamboo pipe, but nowadays it is put inside a small bottle. Then it is buried in the ground in the 'Mang' (crematorium). This *Ashthi Loukhatpa* or 'Mangani Leihun' is the ceremony of ritualistic purification of the ashes or the bone and finally letting it to be carried home. Chuhi, Milk, water of Tulsi leaves, water of cowdung, gold piece and silver piece, are kept displayed in the ritual at crematorium. The ashes or bone touches all these one after another, and then it is considered that the ashes or bone is purified. After this the ashes or the bone is tight by a piece of brand new white cloth. The white cloth containing the purified ashes or bone is kept somewhere in the Mangol (Verandah) or in the secluded place of main household deity—Sanamahi. Meitei Hindus immerse the *ashthi* to Ganga river either at Brindavan, Nabadwip or Jagnath Kshetra, etc. Those who cannot afford to go to Ganga the same is immersed to a river in Manipur. In the early stage of Hinduism in Manipur, the Meitei Hindus used to immerse the same in Ningthi river (Chindwin river in Kabow valley). But later on, the face turned to west and Ganga river became the destination.

The traditional Meiteis also perform 'Mangani Leihun' in an almost similar manner with the Ashthi Loukhatpa of Meitei Hindus. But it is held on the fifth day after death as there is no, traditionally, the practice of 'Lamboiba' or 'Kirat Thangba' to a dying person. In the similar manner with Meitei Hindus, the ashes or bone is purifed in the 'Mongpham' (crematorium). The difference is only in the ingradients in the ritualistic purification. *Tairen* leaves, *pungphai* (a grass), *wakok* (a small plant), *ukok* (Uhal), *napi* (a grass) and *shingbi* (a grass) are used in purifying the ashes or bone. The purified ashes or bone is tied by a white cloth. Then, in the like manner with Meitei Hindus, it is kept either at 'Mangol 'or at the secluded place of supreme household deity—Sanamahi. The immersion is held in a river or in a big water. The immersion is to be executed only after 'Lanna Thouram' on an auspicius day. A point to be noted is that both the 'Mangngani Leihun' or *Ashthi Loukhatpa* is held only in the morning time.

IV. *LANNA THOURAM* (SHRADHA)

The main or essential part of *Lanna Thouram* is held in the morning time before noon. The festival part of death ceremony is held in the afternoon in a pompous form. For the morning part or essential part of *Lanna Thouram*, first, a preparation is made to summon the Almighty in the secluded place of the ceremony. First of all a 'Pafan' (believed to be related with the creation of Universe) is drawn with flour on the thoroughly cleaned ground. This 'Pafan' represents the 'Paring Langshang Hunba'—it is the procedure in finding out a point of reference in laying the foundation—of a traditional Meitei house. The 'Eratphu'—the ritualistic earthen pitcher is placed above the drawn Pafan. Four 'Chuks' ('posts) are erected on the four corners of the Eratphu. These four 'Chuks' are made of bamboo strips in the form of arrows. Again, the four 'chuks' represents the deities—Koubru, Wangbren, Chingkhei and Thangjing. The 'Chuks' are surrounded by 'Langja Taret'—a thread having seven pieces. This 'Langja Taret' represents the 'Shingli Pafan'. The world is created by the fusion Mei (fire), Eshing (water), Nungshit (air), Leipak (the earth) and Atiya (the sky). These five elements are summoned to a secluded place and they have transformed into a 'Langbum'—meaning that it has transformed into a definite

Fig. 7.10: *Lanna Thouram* (*Shradha*), death ceremony is in progress (morning part)

shape. But the summoning of the five elements are ritualistically done into the 'Eratphu' one after another. First, the fire, then water, air, earth and finally the sky. The earth crust is created by the fusion of fire, water and air. The resting place of 'Malem Leisha'—the earth crust is in the sky.

['Paring Langshang Hunba'—is the model of the vast universe. In this universe the 'world' emerges out of fusion

of five elements—fire, water, air, earth and sky. The ritualistic earthen pitcher 'Eratphu' is the embodiment of the world—which again rest in the Universe i.e. on the Paring Langshang—again represented by a Pafan. The " Eratphu' which is resting on the Pafan is providing a place for the Almighty.]

On the eastern side of the 'Eratphu' an altar (Phambal) is prepared. For this a wooden seat is placed on the ground. This 'Phal'—wooden seat is covered by a white cloth. The 'Thak - khan', canopy is placed above the 'Phambal'. A Kokyet (turban), Feijom (dhoti), Enafi (laifi)—a long cloth for wearing round the body are placed on the 'Phambal'. It is believed that the Almighty is wearing the above cloths while resting on the 'Phambal'.

Now after summoning all the five elements into the 'Eratphu' one after another, a definite shape has taken place. And it has taken the shape of Almighty. In the next step this Almighty is again ritualistically called out of 'Eratphu' and has given His resting place on the 'Phambal' (altar).

The clothes once used by the deceased person, fruits, flowers, sweetmeats, etc. all are sacrificed along with souls of the deceased to Almighty. The offering consists of a 'Luklen' a well prepared meal. The Almighly is prayed by offering 'Meira'—a light of pine or candle, and flowers. In the process it is prayed to the Almighty for the well being of the family as well as for the departed soul for its easy blending to Almightly. And here ends the essential or morning part of 'Lanna Thouram'.

Afternoon part of *Lanna Thouram*

For the afternoon part of *Lanna Thouram*, a stage known as "Shonnabunggi Shanglen' or 'Mandop' is installed in the courtyard. The architecture of this stage is imitated from the structure of human body, though in an indirect manner.

Fig. 7.11: *Lanna Thouram* (*Shradha*) death ceremony is in progress (agternoon part)

Fig. 7.12: A conch is in action in death ceremony: to his right is the *amaiba* (with glass) who took care of the dying person. His place is reserved in the area.

The nine pillars of the stage is in representation of the nine 'Laibungthou'. The architechure of Meitei Yumjao (traditional house) is derived from the structure of human body. In the architecture of 'Meitei' Yumjao' a number of secluded places are associated or reserved for a number of household deities, including the supreme household deity—'Sanamahi'. In the like manner, in the architecture of 'Shanglen' the stage, all the household deities are moved out of house and their definite places are reserved in the stage. As the ceremony cannot be held inside the house, so the deities are moved out of house and are placed at the stage in the courtyard. The main pulse at the belly is personified by the 'Pung Yeiba'—the drummer. Again 'Sentreng-Kuptreng' is personified by the singer and his associate, i.e. 'Sheishakpa' and 'Sheikhumba'. In a sense the two singers are the personification of the two deities—'Sanamahi' and 'Pakhangba'.

In the meantime everyone coming to attend the ceremony will bow down first praying the 'Chingkhei Guru' where a secluded place is reserved at the gate of the deceased person's house. In the traditional mode of settlement the gate is opened at the north-eastern side of the homestead, and hence the name 'Chingkhei Guru'—where Chingkhei is the north-eastern direction. A few simple items including Heiruk-Pana (fruit, and betel nut and leaf), Meira (a light of candle or pine), etc. are offered to 'Chingkhei Guru'. Nearby it a chair is placed. Formerly, an earthen pitcher full of water was also included in the offering. Now it is replaced by other container. Here, a transformation is observed. Formerly this chair was the seat of 'Mandapmapu'—someone like the chairman or president of a functioon. He would come early and would sit there on the chair. Everyone coming to attend the ceremony will bow down to the 'Mandapmapu' and then he or she will proceed to the stage at the courtyard. In due course of time the 'Mandapmapu' stopped sitting at the gate but his chair still continues standing at the gate. Now this chair is considered as the place of 'Chingkhei Guru' and the practice of praying to him carry on in this way.

In continuation of the ceremony the ritual song is sung for the five souls. The owner or responsible person of the house hand over the souls of the deceased to the Maiba, thinking that the Maiba (priest) is the personification of the deity 'Wangbren'. [He is considered as the god of death]. Again the Maiba hand over the five souls in the form of five 'Khudeis' (long loin clothes) to the five male singers for the emancipation of the souls. The singer in turn will hand over the souls to the 'Mandapmapu' who is sitting at the 'Santhong Apanba' (All these are to be imagined). The place of Santhong Apanba' is at the south-western side of 'Shanglen' (the stage). 'Shanthong Apanba' is nobody but 'Sanamahi'.

The song is broadly divided into two parts—(a) Sheihou Eshei (opening song) and (b) Sheiroi Eshei (closing song). Now the closing song begins. At this juncture a 'Paya' (binding material made of bamboo chips) is loosened which is located above the 'Shanthong Apanba'. The meaning of this act is that the human soul departs the body at the head. And here ends the 'Lanna Thouram'.

G. *FIROI* (DEATH ANNIVERSARY)

Firoi, the death anniversary is performed after a year. The popular belief among the Meiteis is that when a child is born the course begins from father. The child spends two months in the body of father, and then another ten months in the womb of mother. Thus a child is born after a year after completing its full course beginnig from father and finally to mother. In the like manner, the belief says, a soul needs a year for its new birth. So, the ceremony is held by offering 'Firoi Fingam' believing that the soul is ready for its new birth. For the male; a Feijom (dhoti), a Furit (shirt) and an Ennafi (a long cloth) are offered in the 'Firoi Fingam'. And for female, a Fanek (lower garment for woman), an Ennafi and a Furit are offered. The soul is finally released after a period of twelve months for its new birth by wearing the above offered cloths.For the last twelve months the soul is believed to be by the side of Almighty, the Sun. After twelve months the time is ripe for the soul for its new birth. So, 'Firoi' is performed for the formal release of the soul, and for its new birth the above clothes are offered. At the end of the ceremony a feast is held where elder persons take part. A well-prepared meal (Luklen) is also offered to Almighty.

H. CHUP SHABA

Generally we may divide the deaths into natural and unnatural deaths. Death by drowning, hanging, poisoning, lightning and death occurred away from home, etc. are categorised as unnatural death. A miscarried child is also termed as unnatural death. For natural deaths, death ceremony known as *Lanna Thouram* or 'Shradha' is performed either on 14th day or 13th day after death accordingly as 'Lamboiba' was held or not. But for unnatural deaths, over and above this normal death ceremony, another additional ceremony known as 'Chup Shaba' or 'Chupsha-moithemba' is performed. This 'Chup Shaba' is performed to a miscarried child also. In the past this was performed to a child of seven years of age. For the current this is performed to a child of three years of age. The tradition of 'Chup Shaba' is found to be very old. This seems to be a well-established tradition even before the reign of king Taothingmang (264-364 A.D.) as it is found mentioned in the literature 'Tutenglon'. As mentioned in this literature this 'Chup Shaba' was performed not only to a dead person but also to a living person who had encountered an accident. Yoymongba, the elder brother of Taothingmang was once carried by the giant mythical bird named 'Kakyel Mingamba'. In order not to re-occur such an accident Yoymongba urged Taothingmang to perform 'Chup Shaba'. The literature also mentions a detailed account of the items to be included in the ritual including its procedure. 'Chup Shaba' is held after cremation is over. It is performed in the morning either on the day of 'Mangani Leihun' or on *Lanna Thouram*. It is favourably performed on 'Tatnaba Numit' i.e. on an inauspicious day. It may also be performed after a month, after three months or after three years. But the earliest performance is considered to be the best. For the belief says that if Chup Shaba' is not performed the soul of such unnatural death may transmigrate to a pregnant woman of the deceased family. Such soul of unwanted unnatural death may enter the family and the same incident may re-occur in any member of the family. This is the belief behind the earliest performance of 'Chup Shaba'. Again a delayed performance of 'Chup Shaba' may result in the appearance of the deceased person in the dream of the family members; and may also occur frightening sounds in the nights around the house.

In the course of ritual it is prayed to Almighty not to re-occur the unnatural death to the particular family. And an inedible leaf is included in the ritual. The leaf is scapegoat of the family and it will carry away anything unwanted occurrence that may happen in the family. If any edible item is included then that particular plant is forbidden to use as food for the particular lineage. It is believed that such taboo food, if used, will bring harm to body. If such an incident takes place that particular plant will be maked known to the whole population of that particular lineage. And it is declared that the particular plant is 'Yelhan'—meaning it is forbidden to use as food for the particular lineage.

I. DISPOSAL OF (DEAD) BABIES

A child whose ear-piercing ceremony is performed is entitled to dispose by cremation. Such a child (dead) is termed as 'Mei Changba', i.e. the child can be disposed by cremation. A child who has not attained this age and without 'Na-Hutpa' (ear-piercing) ceremony, then the child cannot be disposed by cremation. The child is to be buried in the ground. But a baby who has not attained the age of cremation, the *Lanna Thouram*, the death ceremony for the baby is performed. And it is held on seventh day after death. An infant died at birth, died after a few days after birth or died within three months after birth are categorised as "Shoiren" i.e. miscarried child. They are also buried in the ground. They are buried according to the wishes of the family, either in the homestead, at Mang (crematorium) or at the bank of river.

Procedure of Burial

First a ditch is dug out in the ground. After attaining the necessary depth, seven Shingkhan (separators), made of small bamboo strips, are placed one after another beneath the ditch. The baby is wrapped by a cloth, and further it is wrapped by the flesh of banana stem. The baby is now placed beneath the ditch. Again above the baby another seven 'Shingkhans', made of the same material is above, are placed one after the other. The baby as now buried. Several bamboo pieces are strucked on the ground (burial). Finally a pointed bamboo strip is fixed at the centre of the burial. The fixing of bamboo pieces is a sign to let the people know that the burial is meant for a "Shoiren". Further it is also a protection from animals. While burying the responsibility of the baby is handed over to mother Earth and father Sky. It is believed that the baby is placed on the chest of mother Earth and father Sky has covered it as a lid. And it is prayed to Almighty not to re-occur the incident in the family.

The necessary ritual of burial and handing over of responsibility of the dead baby is done before witnesses. The witnesses are the number of days counting from the birth day of the baby till the last day of the week; again the counting begins from the last day till the seventh day, and the process continues till the birth day comes out the end. As an instance the birth day of the baby is Sunday and the counting goes in the following manner:

Sunday, Monday, Tuesday, Wednesday, Thursday, Friday, Saturday—1.

Saturday, Sunday, Monday, Tuesday, Wednesday, Thursday, Friday—2.

Friday, Saturday, Sunday, Monday, Tuesday, Wednesday, Thursday—3.

Thursday, Friday, Saturday, Sunday, Monday, Tuesday, Wednesday—4.

Wednesday, Thursday, Friday, Saturday, Sunday, Monday, Tuesday—5.

Tuesday, Wednesday, Thursday, Friday, Saturday, Sunday, Monday—6.

Monday, Tuesday, Wednesday, Thursday, Friday, Saturday, Sunday—7.

In this way the seven days of the week are counted for seven times and finally Sunday, the supposed birth day of the baby comes at the end. And hence there are in total 49 days. The total number of days involved may be different depending upon the birthday. The witnesses are these 49 days involved. The necessary rite is performed and so the soul of the baby is warned not to come back again to the family.

J. 'KAIREN KAIJAO'

'Kairen Kaijao' is the well decorated coffin for use by the royal family and noblemen. It is offered by the king— as an honour to the person. It was for the exclusive use of the royal family and noblemen. But the women of the royal family were not entitled to use this kind of coffin. The Kings were cremated at 'Manglen" which is located inside the Kangla fort in Imphal. This 'Kairen Kajao' is placed above the 'Ku' (coffin). It has three storeys and a 'Kai' is also attached at each side of it. Small flags are fixed in all the three storeys. And the storeys are made of white cloth. The 'Kai' (Chirong) is fixed at both ends of the top storey. This 'Kairen Kaijao' stands with four legs on the ground. Two long bamboo proles are fixed on both the sides (lengthwise) of the 'Ku'(coffin). With these poles the 'Kairen-Kajao' can be carried by four men easily.

Fig. 7.13: *Kairen Kaijao* is the well decorated coffin for use by the royal family and noblemen.

Some Customs

(1) For a missing person or in the event of non-availability of the corpse, the tree 'Panggong U' is cremated as a substitute of the body.

(2) Death by hanging was disposed at 'Mangarak Kanbi'—a place on the hill top of 'Langol range' on the western side of Imphal. For other areas it was disposed at places which are not frequently visited. But it is a thing of past and nowadays they are cremated at the community crematorium.

CONCLUSION

The Meiteis perform a number of rites and ceremonies from birth till death. From different ancient literatures there are references that these rites and ceremonies were part and parcel of Meitei life. However, in due course of time a change is observed in the rite and ceremonies. Epan—the birth ceremony is basically a prayer to deity 'Pitai Khomtaibi' for health, wealth and long life of the baby. This ritual is held only in the morning. The evening part of Epan is held in two ways, one traditionally for traditional believers and the other in Hindu fashion. The morning part, which is also the essential part is performed both by traditional believers and Meitei Hindus. The Meitei Hindus do not discard it, rather, it is held with reverence and all sincerity. The addition of evening part seems to be a development after adoption of Hindu religion by Meiteis.

The Maibi, Mayoknabi and Khominbi are the persons who play vital role in delivery. Their role is crucial for the survival of the baby and mother. Any negligence on their part may cost the life of the mother and baby. Soon after delivery it is the Khom-inbi who feeds the baby and this continues for some days till the mother is fit to feed the baby by her proper milk. No doubt this has been done by the blind belief that postnatal milk is injurious to health. In view of the role of the three women which is crucial for the survival of the baby and mother, there is nothing wrong in extending ritual treatment to the offerings for the three women in Epan. In fact they are next to goddess 'Pitai Khomtaibi' as their action has delivered safely the baby to the mother. Again the repeated queries of the Maibi, 'Do you want gold, silver or Yangkok ?, and single reply of the grandmother— 'I want the baby'—affirm that the real wealth in this world is one's child. Neither gold nor silver nor Yangkok can continue the generation. It is the child only who will and can carry on the generation.

As discussed in the text the rites and ceremonies were held under direct or indirect influence of certain belief system. Under the influence of such beliefs the complicacies developed in delivery was considered, as the act of evil spirits. In order to free from such troubles an offering known as 'Chaban Thaba' was performed. In addition to this a knot known as 'Khongji' of the Kangkhal (mosquito net) is let loose. The lid of 'Chengphu' (a pot for storing rice) is opened. The Almirah (cupboard) is also kept open. All these are done with the belief that this will help in let loosing the evil spirit from the body of the mother. And consequently this will help in free and easy delivery of the mother. But with the contact of modern education, especially that of medical science, people are now freed from such beliefs and practices at least in urban areas. And the resultant is the disappearance of such practices in the society.

The forms of disposal of death is a matter of controversy. Although cremation is the only prevailing form among the Meiteis in the present society. Before this, four forms, i.e. in the air, water, ground and in fire were prevalent in Manipur. Among this, secondary burial seems to be the most popular one. Now question can be raised, whether they (all the four forms) existed side by side at the same time or prevalent in specified areas at different stages of history? And here arises the need for further research.

The use of coffin in transporting the corpse either to burial site or to crematorium is common to both the forms of disposal of death. Again death anniversary is also performed at the completion of one year in different forms; secondary burial in the case of disposal by burying and 'Firoi' in the case of cremation.

The procedure in cremation is strictly carried out within the purview of a belief system. The crux of the belief is that soul is immortal, only the body is mortal. And the soul do not immediately depart the body when the body is dead, but only after completion of death ceremony, i.e. *Lanna Thouram*. Letting loose of a 'Paya' (bamboo strip for binding) at the post near 'Shanthong Apanba' deity at the last stage of death ceremony is symbolic of freeing the soul from this earthly world to heavenly abode. As a component of cremation procedure there are practices like making small bonfire at the gate of every house on the way to crematorium and the welcome of the person who attended the cremation by another small bonfire at the gate. These are outside the purview of the main belief system but a simple act of warding evil spirits. For the traditional society the fear of evil spirit is insurmountable and is believed that evil spirits follow a person as shadow follows the person. And death is considered as an act of evil spirits. So warding off evil spirits by employing a form of ritual or practice became inseparable to their life. Again the concept of heaven is also found crept in the procedure of cremation. The hanging of Thak-khan (canopy) above the funeral pyre is an act of hiding the corpse from Almighty who is considered looking down the earth observing the occasion taking place on earth. This is a clear indication that heaven, the abode of Almighty, is in the sky.

Ashthi or *Mangani Leihul*—the act of ritualistic purification of the collected bone or ashes (collected on the day of cremation) may be treated as death ceremony as it completes the formalities to be executed to a dead body. But another grand ceremony namely *Lanna Thouram* or 'Shrada' is held after some days of Mangani Leihun". This seems to be an addition after the introduction of Hinduism in Manipur. Again the observance of 'Firoi'—the death anniversary is an additional testimony of the belief that soul is immortal, only the body is dead. In fact the observance of 'Firoi' is an act of freeing the soul after spending twelve months under the care of Almighty to lead a new life to a new living body.

REFERENCES

1. Oral interview with Kangabam Apabi—Uripok, Imphal.
2. Oral interview with Mayanglambam Thabal—Kakching.
3. Oral interview with Athokpam Thoiba—Nongmeibung, Imphal.
4. Oral interview with Mutua Bahadur—Keishampat
5. Oral interview with Moirangthem Norendra, Khongman, Imphal.
6. Oral interwiew with Nongthonbam Ningol Ngangom ongbi Fatombi (Tombi) -Maibi—62 years,—Oinam Awang Leikai.
7. Oral interview with Hidam Ningol Laishram ongbi Ngambi—Maibi—87years, Wangkhei Ashangbam Leikai, Imphal.
8. Oral interview with N. Manijao, Palace Compound, Imphal.
9. Cheitharol Kumbaba—MS
10. Poireiton Khunthokpa—MS
11. Shakok Lamlen—MS
12. Thawanthaba Hiran—MS
13. PuroiMashin- MS
14. Loyyamba Shinyen—MS
15. Naothingkhong Phambal Kaba—MS
16. Thaloi Nongkhailon—MS

17. Mashin—MS
18. Tutenglon—MS
19. A report on the 1994 excavation of Sekta, Manipur, Ed. O. Kumar Singh, Pb. State Archaeology, Deptt. of Art and Culture, Imphal.
20. Khelchandra, N. and Madhav, *Khunung Lichat Shajat*.
21. Hall, D.G.E., *A History of South-East Asia*.
22. Tylor, E.B., *Dictionary of Anthropology*.

8

Conclusion

The emergence of Meitei family is inseparably linked with the evolution of Meitei identity. The Meiteis are the product of a long historical process of unification and integration of different nine major clans along with some minor clans. The seed of Meitei identity which was sown early during the reign of King Nongda Lairen Pakhangba (A.D. 33-153) was germinated much later during the reign of King Sameirang (A.D. 1518-1568). But it took centuries to mature this identity and the same happened during the reign of King Charairongba (A.D. 1697-1709) when he annexed the Agnom principality to his kingdom.

Traditionally the lineages are 432 in number. And it was the king who offered the lineages to different Pukoks (progenitors) considering their respective background. Within its dynamics this community accommodated the migrants from the west and east who are historically treated as 'Nongchup Haram' and 'Nongpok Haram'. And consequently at present the lineages are much more than this i.e. 432. During kingship the families were very close to state administration. In fact, it was part and parcel of the administration. However, such closeness disappeared with the eelips of kingship coupled by the introduction of money economy in Manipur by the Britishers.

Though land was abundant in the past still the society was a stratified one which is evident by the existence of three main types of houses viz., four or five-roomed house for the common man, seven-roomed house for the nobleman and nine-roomed house for the king.

Still there is a 'Khangpok' (hut) for the poor. Traditionally Meitei house is a temple with many household deities including the principal deity 'Sanamahi' at their designated secluded places. Even marriage ceremony is culminated with the offering and prayer at the principal household deities. A traditional family works to impart some kind of moral and social education which are traditional in its form and content. Wits test is one among them which works to sharpen the intellect of the child. Funga, the hearth, occupies the most important place for teaching children with its warm environment. And the time is suitably in the evening when all the children are gathered in the house.

The beliefs in this community has powerful influence on their daily life even regulating their actions and behaviours. Still in this scientific age these superstitious beliefs have acted as a brake to their free actions and thinking. Their minds are not still free from fear of the fallout when someone acted against the custom imposed by such superstitious beliefs. And here such unfounded beliefs poses a question mark on the present education which aim at cultivating scientific temper to the populace. In the midst of such vast traditional beliefs and practices there are few which has their value in society mainly in the form of maintaining a discipline in utilising their home products. Some has their value in maintaining personal discipline. Again among the beliefs and practices the nature and character of patriarchal society is found hidden in one form or the other. As this being a male dominated society due importance is given to male of the family in the time of decision-making in the family and society. Along with this certain privileges are also reserved for male in the usages of goods and articles.

Cremation, the only prevailing form of disposal of death, is strictly carried out within the purview of a belief system. The crux of the belief is that soul is immortal, only the body is mortal. Again there is the concept of heaven in the sky. 'Lanna-Thouram', the death ceremony is nothing but a ritual to send the soul to the place of Almighty in the sky. Again the belief continues that the soul take shelter in the heaven for twelve months only. After this the soul is free to migrate to another living being with a new birth. Now a profound change is visible in the family establishments because of modernisation, even altering its attitude to the household deities. But such modernisation has little impact on the belief in the immortality and transmigration of soul.

Index